complete guide to

pilates yoga meditation & stress relief

p

This is a Parragon Publishing Book
This edition published in 2004

Parragon Publishing
Queen Street House
4 Queen Street
Bath BA1 1HE, UK

ISBN: 1-40542-216-5

Printed in China.

Designed and created with the Bridgewater Book Company Ltd.

NOTE
Any information given in this book is not intended to be taken as a replacement for medical advice. Any person with a condition requiring medical attention should consult a qualified medical practitioner or therapist before beginning any of the exercise programs described in this book.

contents

Introduction

Modern living imposes stresses and strains on all of us—physical, mental, emotional, and spiritual. This book offers four approaches to help you to unwind and to enjoy life to the full. Learn how to break free from the confines of a potentially damaging lifestyle, and discover how, with a little effort and by focusing on ways of looking after yourself better, you can increase your vitality, find serenity, and get the best out of every day.

The four sections of this book can be read as stand-alone modules, but they are complementary. Together they offer comprehensive and practical advice to help you to overcome the pressures of modern life the natural way, to maintain health, regain vitality, and achieve peace of mind.

Read them all and take elements from each to develop your own personalized approach to taking care of yourself that suits your circumstances and your lifestyle.

Pilates is a physical therapy that works on different muscles to tone and condition the body, while developing correct breathing, good posture, and mental concentration and focus. It improves balance, coordination, and flexibility, and streamlines the body. It is a great way of changing your body shape for the better without creating muscle "bulk."

As well as improving your physical health, yoga enables you to become more balanced, centered, and calm.

Yoga can help you to improve your physical health, tone your muscles and internal organs, relieve inner tension, reduce weight, and strengthen your bones. But it not only works on your body, it also guides you toward relaxation and shows you how to become more balanced, centered, and calm.

It is whole-life philosophy which teaches that attaining control over the body is the key to controlling the mind. Mastering the art of relaxation and learning how to breathe "properly" are two of the most important aspects of yoga. Once you have mastered these skills, you will experience a positive, healthy outlook on life.

Meditation is for everyone, whatever their lifestyle.

Meditation is an important element of yoga, too, but it is of course also a therapy in its own right, and there is more to it than just relaxation. This book shows how, with practice, meditation can be used to restrain the wanderings or "chatter" of the mind, so that you can bring yourself back to full awareness and experience things as they really are. Meditation can improve your concentration, increase your self-awareness, and combat stress in your everyday life by helping you to relax and cope. Meditation can improve physical and mental well-being and can be a route to inner harmony.

The final section of this book shows you how to relieve stress in your life. It reinforces many of the messages of the earlier sections, but also offers other options that can leave you refreshed and rejuvenated.

No matter what your age or level of fitness, your life can be made better. This book shows you how to find the time to take better care of yourself and guides you slowly toward an improved sense of well-being in all areas of your life—physical, emotional, and spiritual.

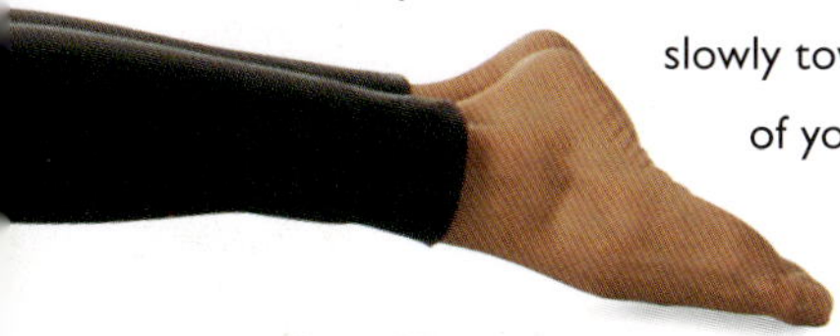

pilates

Introduction

Throughout history, people have looked for new and innovative ways to exercise. We can trace yoga to the Indian sub-continent as far back as 4,000 years, and t'ai chi ch'uan, a flowing form of movement, to the China of 2,000 years ago. Developed in the 20th century, Pilates combines ancient wisdom with contemporary knowledge.

The Olympic Games, which started in Greece around the 8th century BCE, attracted athletes from all over the world. Although the games were stopped in 393 CE, their revival in 1896 once again put them in the spotlight. They continue to attract top athletes today and the Games held every four years are a world event. Like the Games, many ancient forms of exercise are still widely appreciated today, but all over the globe people have continued to find new and fascinating ways to keep their bodies in top condition, from competitive sports such as football, basketball, and ice hockey, to the new body-conditioning systems, including weight-training and aerobics.

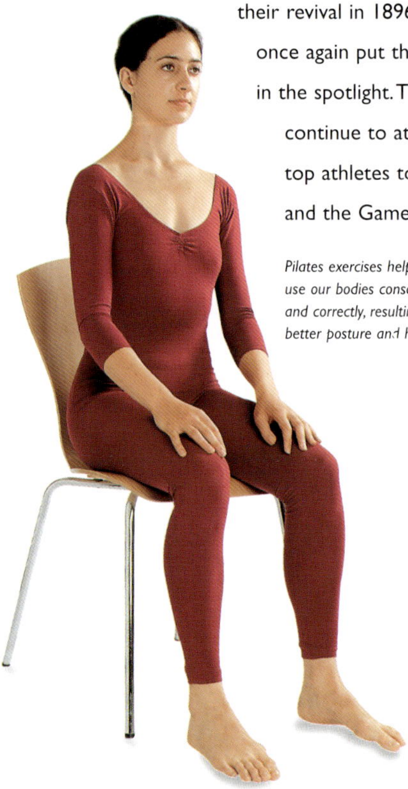

Pilates exercises help us to use our bodies consciously and correctly, resulting in better posture and health.

The aim of Pilates

The Pilates system of exercise was developed in the 20th century. Practiced regularly, it helps to keep the mind and body working in harmony because it requires a focused mind as well as flowing physical movements. The aim of Pilates is to work different muscles to tone and condition the body, while developing correct breathing, good posture, and mental concentration and focus. It improves overall balance and coordination while it streamlines the body and also helps to improve flexibility in all the muscles and joints.

Pilates for everyone

Since it began, this mind-body system of exercise has attracted many rich and famous people from around the world, and it is popular among many Hollywood celebrities. Since the actor Gregory Peck first embraced the teachings of Pilates, many others have followed suit. Today, stars such as tennis player Pat Cash and pop singer Madonna have adopted Pilates as their favored system of exercise. Top models, dancers, and sportspeople have all reaped the benefits of practicing Pilates. Yet the good thing about Pilates is that you do not have to be an athlete to do it. The exercises are gentle and are designed to put as little strain on the body as possible. This means that almost anyone of any age and level of fitness can do it. Whether you are young or elderly, a fitness fanatic or someone who hasn't exercised for years, you can reap the benefits of Pilates. You do not need any equipment either—you can do Pilates in your own home.

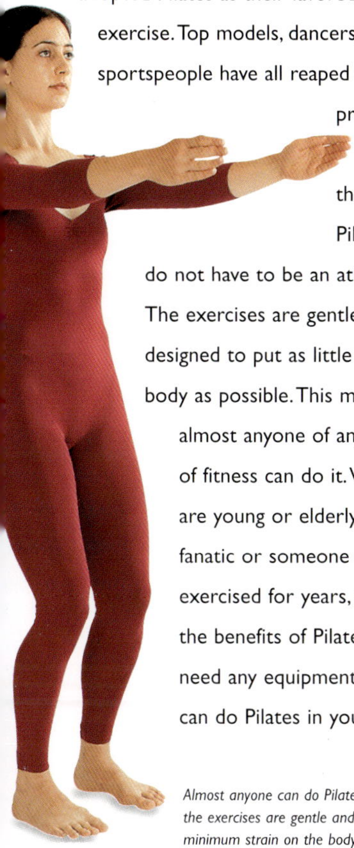

Almost anyone can do Pilates; the exercises are gentle and put minimum strain on the body.

Stress and exhaustion are facts of modern life, but Pilates can help you to counteract them and enhance well-being.

Health benefits

Pilates can really improve your health. The carefully designed exercises are very effective for helping you to tone your body and achieve a longer, leaner look and great shape, without creating muscle "bulk." They will help you to reduce stress and beat fatigue, as well as build up your self-confidence and heighten your sense of well-being. You will start to look and feel superb, and move with a new grace that comes from improved coordination and greater muscle flexibility. There is no better time to start reshaping your body—all you need is a little time and the desire to succeed.

PART 1: BACKGROUND

What is Pilates?

Pilates is a system of exercise that allows you to take control of your mind and your body. It uses smooth, flowing movements that tone and stretch your body and increase strength and flexibility in your muscles and joints. It also utilizes the power of the mind to help with the exercises and to increase the harmony between body and mind.

Pilates has been referred to as "a yoga-like system that uses machines." Although Joseph Pilates, the founder of this system, did take some of his inspiration from yoga, the exercises are different. If you have a Pilates studio near you which has special apparatus, such as pulleys and springs, these can be helpful but are not essential. Through performing the exercises in this book you will see that the only equipment needed to reach optimum fitness and health is the body itself.

Minimum time, maximum results

Pilates exercises have been designed to work the muscles of the body as efficiently as possible in the minimum time. These low-impact exercises treat the body as a whole and are very effective. There is therefore no need to spend hours each day in the gym: you need to practice only two or three times a week, and can start with 10-minute sessions and build up to longer ones slowly.

The Pilates exercises work the body as a whole rather than overemphasizing individual areas or particular muscle groups.

Reshaping the body

The capacity of the Pilates exercises to reshape the body has attracted many people from all walks of life over the years. While it is certainly true that this form of exercise can alter your physical appearance, it should be remembered that each person has his or her own individual body shape. It is important to work with what you have already and to recognize that you cannot totally change your shape. The chart below shows how the human body can be classified into three basic shapes, which are known as the ectomorph, the mesomorph, and the endomorph.

These shapes help to define how we look, but some people believe that a person's body shape can also be linked to certain personality traits. Some of these are listed below.

Body shapes

Body type	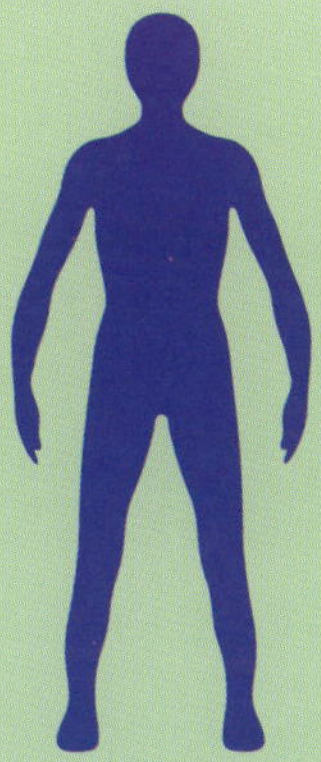 Ectomorph	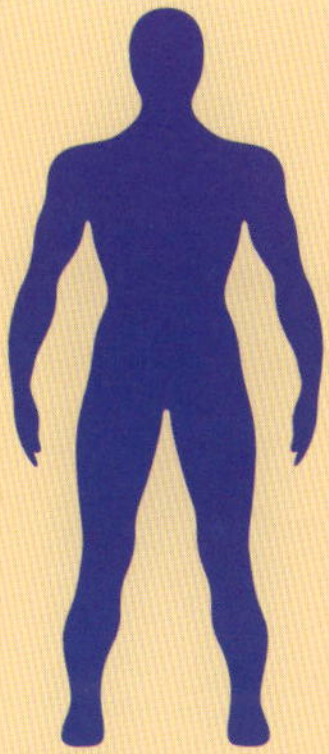 Mesomorph	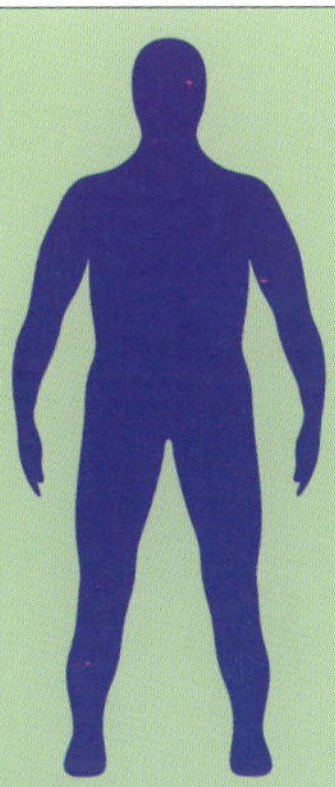 Endomorph
Build	Light and delicate; often tall and thin, with long limbs	Athletic or muscular; large chest, limbs, and muscles	Heavy or rounded; may have trouble keeping body weight down
Other characteristics	Sometimes linked to alertness and an inhibited and intellectual personality	Sometimes associated with an aggressive tendency; mesomorphs are often athletic and can excel at many different sports	Quite often linked to placidity, as well as a relaxed attitude and hedonism

History and development of Pilates

The Pilates system was developed by a German called Joseph H. Pilates. He suffered from rickets and other illnesses as a child and grew up determined to strengthen his weak body. His interest in fitness was fueled during the World War I, when he served as an orderly and became involved in the treatment of patients who were immobile.

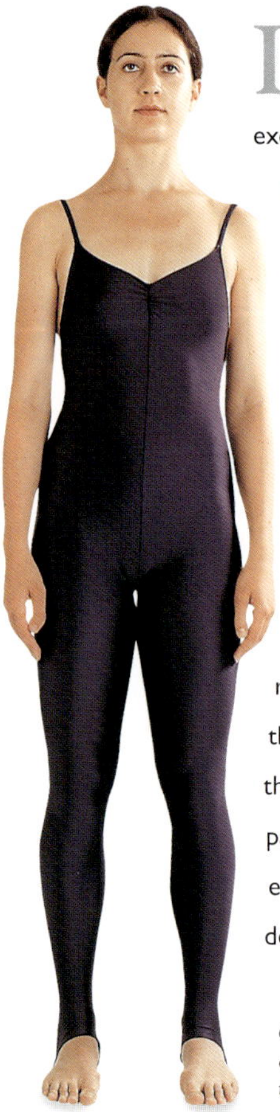

During the 1920s, Pilates developed a series of exercises that used various pieces of apparatus to increase efficiency. For example, he devised exercises that patients could perform in bed and he attached springs to their beds in order to increase the efficiency of the exercises. He quickly noticed that patients recovered more quickly when the springs were used. In fact, those springs became the first part of his extensive exercise equipment and he went on to develop many more.

Good balance is an integral part of Pilates, and the system includes standing exercises that can be practiced anywhere, at any time.

After the War

When World War I came to an end, Pilates moved to America and opened a fitness studio in New York. His techniques soon attracted the interest of famous, wealthy, and influential people. He went on to develop and perfect his methods, and continued doing so for the rest of his life. Although he often used pieces of apparatus in his exercises, his original system was based on matwork and was every bit as efficient as his later equipment-based exercises. Pilates' core principles concentrate on rhythmic breathing, a centered posture, flowing, smooth movements, and a focused mind.

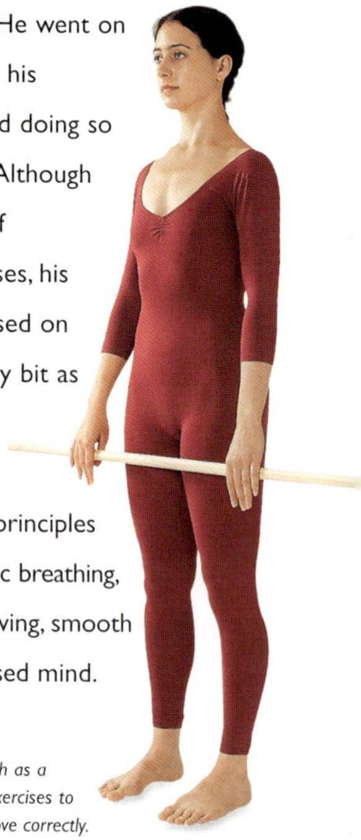

A simple piece of equipment, such as a broom handle, is used in some exercises to help you to train your body to move correctly.

Harnessing the power of the mind is an important component in all the Pilates exercises and brings great benefits.

Pilates today

Originally there were 34 Pilates movements, but over the years different practitioners and teachers have brought in their own modifications to these very powerful techniques. As a result, there is no one true system anymore: people have introduced their own ideas and innovations over the decades, so that the whole practice of Pilates has evolved and brought with it other exercises and modifications to earlier ones. However, they still conform to the basic principles behind the original system.

One of the best things about Pilates, however, is its flexibility. Once you know how the system works, you can translate its movements for use into other systems, and many people use it to enhance their work in other disciplines. The exercises can help people to achieve better balance, muscle coordination, and graceful movement, as well as increased stamina and flexibility. No wonder it is popular with so many sportspeople today. Many of them have adapted Pilates techniques for their own use and there is no doubt that more and more ingenious ideas, based on Pilates' original principles, continue to flourish.

In all Pilates exercises, you should go only as far as your body can comfortably take you.

Why do Pilates?

The Pilates system offers a complete work-out for the body that exercises not just the main muscle groups, but weaker, less-used muscles too. It therefore enables you to achieve a perfectly toned body and realize your true fitness potential. It is also an exercise system that is open to all, because anyone of any age can do Pilates.

Benefits

There are enormous rewards to be gained from doing Pilates regularly. In addition to greater self-confidence and an increased sense of well-being, practicing Pilates can offer the following advantages:

- **Improved balance:** The exercises give you a greater understanding of your body and muscular systems. You will become more aware of the symmetry of your body and how every movement has its own balances and checks.
- **Less stress:** Pilates enables you to relax, and also to work off the chemical effects of stress, such as excess adrenaline in the body.
- **More efficient digestion:** Pilates can help to tone and strengthen the muscles of the stomach. Since it also helps to reduce stress, this will help to ease the digestive process, which shuts down during times of severe stress and tension.
- **Increased oxygen intake:** This helps the body's systems to function efficiently, resulting in clearer thinking, greater energy levels, and muscular health.
- **Better circulation:** Pilates helps to improve blood flow, which means more efficient circulation of nutrients and oxygen, and easier removal of toxins.
- **Improved skin:** Improved cardiovascular function means more efficient removal of waste products and a clearer skin.
- **Enhanced immune system:** Pilates exercises the muscles, which helps lymph to circulate around the body. Lymph carries white blood cells, which fight disease.
- **Sculpted body:** The exercises help you achieve a longer, leaner look.
- **Greater strength and coordination:** As you practice, your coordination, strength, and balance will increase. You will move with greater ease and grace.

In order to get the most from Pilates exercise, you need to make sure that your body is correctly aligned when you start.

Tip

The best physical fitness programs are those that improve flexibility, build strength, and increase stamina. Pilates helps you to build your strength and flexibility, and improves your muscular coordination, but to get the maximum results you should combine your Pilates program with a form of cardiovascular exercise, such as aerobics, in order to build up stamina.

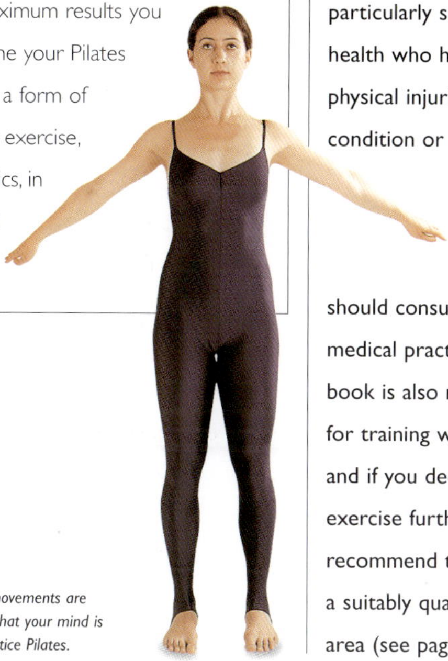

Make sure that your movements are slow and smooth and that your mind is focused when you practice Pilates.

Learning to practice Pilates

This section provides a basic introduction to Pilates, and will be useful to anyone who wants to find out more about Pilates and learn how to do some of the basic exercises. It is particularly suitable for people in reasonable health who have no medical conditions or physical injuries. If you do have a medical condition or injury, however, or you are in any doubt whatsoever about your level of fitness or the suitability of Pilates exercises for you, you should consult your doctor or other qualified medical practitioner before you begin. This book is also not intended to be a substitute for training with a qualified Pilates teacher, and if you decide to explore this system of exercise further, we would strongly recommend that you seek out classes with a suitably qualified instructor in your local area (see page 67).

How Pilates works

Pilates exercises work on the body in a very effective way. Rather than isolating particular muscle groups, they work on the body as a whole, equipping you to perform everyday tasks more efficiently, such as carrying shopping, gardening, and moving furniture. Practicing Pilates will also enable you to become more supple and flexible.

Emotions

Practicing Pilates can contribute to good health on an emotional level as well as a physical one. It can increase your self-confidence and enhance your sense of well-being. It can also reduce your stress levels and help you to be more relaxed.

In a life-threatening situation, or in other circumstances that cause a lot of stress, the stress response, or "fight-or-flight mechanism" as it is known, is activated in your body. As your body gears up to meet the immediate threat, adrenaline is released, the heartbeat, metabolism, and breathing become more rapid, and cortisol and other hormones are circulated around the system. Any function that is not essential to immediate survival—including the immune system and digestion—is automatically shut down.

This fight-or-flight response helped our ancestors to run away from predators, preparing the body for physical effort. The physical exertion involved in running away

Pilates and the body

Pilates is an excellent body-toning and conditioning system of exercise and works on the body on many different levels:

- Emotions
- Nerves
- Tissue
- Muscles
- Bones

Pilates exercises help you to breathe using the muscles of your diaphragm.

or fighting released the stress. Once the immediate danger was over and the effort had passed, the body would return to normal.

Nowadays, we cannot always use physical exertion to counter the stress response. So the stress chemicals stay in the body, draining energy and hampering the digestion and the immune system. Pilates helps to reduce the stress response, enabling our bodies to function normally. Breathing is more relaxed, the heartbeat is slower and steadier, and the metabolic process is more regular. We digest our food more easily, and are less susceptible to colds. As we begin to feel more relaxed, our mood improves and we feel happier.

Tissue

Pilates exercises can help to tone the connective tissue that surrounds, protects and supports vital body parts, including bones, tendons, and muscles. Regular practice of Pilates over a period of time can strengthen this tissue, which will enhance coordination of movement and reduce the risk of injury.

Nerves

At the center of the nervous system are the brain and spinal cord, but the nervous system is in fact a vast network of cells that carry information between all the parts of the body in order to control the body's activities. It is responsible for movement and coordination. Nerve impulses are sent to and from the brain and tell us how we feel. They also coordinate our movements. Pilates helps us to find a balance between relaxation and tension, and to develop awareness of the nervous system.

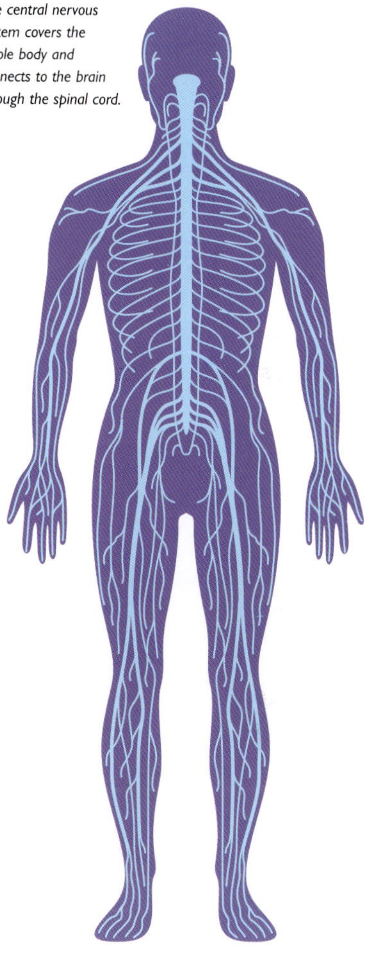

The central nervous system covers the whole body and connects to the brain through the spinal cord.

Muscles

There are over 650 muscles in the body and they do a huge amount of work. They enable the body to move, they allow us to sit and stand, and they control key body functions. The heart, for example, is a large muscle that pumps blood around the body. The stomach and intestines are also muscles that are responsible for the digestive process. Pilates helps to tone and strengthen these muscles so that they work more effectively.

Isolating one muscle or set of muscles in physical exercise is contrary to the principles of Pilates, however. Pilates concentrates on working the whole body, and in this way prepares it more thoroughly for performing everyday tasks. Muscles often work in pairs or groups anyway, and so concentrating on one muscle will only work to the detriment of another. However, it is a good idea to know where different muscles are situated in the body, so here is a quick reference guide.

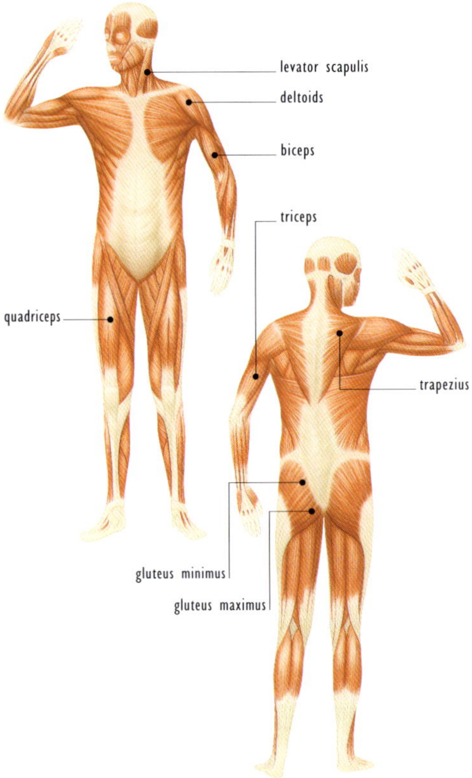

Muscles in the body

Muscle	Area of body
Biceps	At the front of the upper arms
Deltoid	On top of the shoulders
Gluteus maximus	A pair of muscles in the fleshy part of the buttocks
Gluteus minimus	Paired muscles in the buttocks just above the fleshy part
Levator scapulis	At the sides and back of the neck
Quadriceps	Situated in the thighs
Trapezius	Flat triangular muscle covering the back of the neck and the shoulder
Triceps	Muscle at the back of the upper arms

Bones

Pilates exercises work to bring the bones of the body back into their natural and correct alignment. With regular practice, this helps to improve posture and coordination of movement. The exercises also increase stability, which in turn enables you to perform physical movements and exercises more efficiently. Regular practice of Pilates can also mobilize joints and keep the whole body working smoothly. This can be especially valuable as you get older, because you will be able to increase your mobility and stay more active well into your later years.

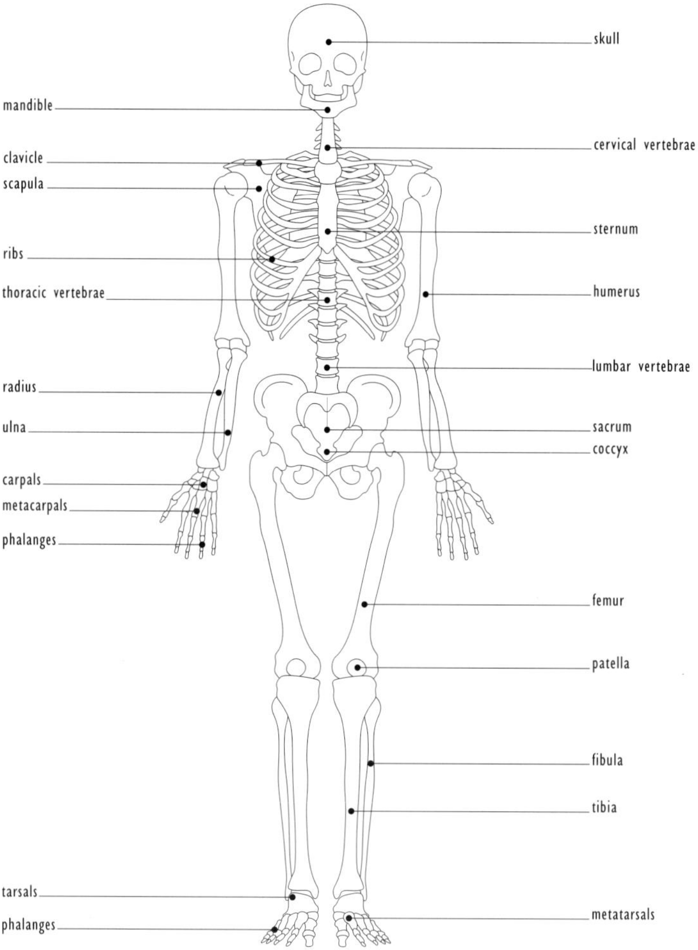

PART 2: PREPARATION

Equipment, environment, and safety

Although Joseph Pilates devised many ingenious pieces of equipment to enhance his exercises, and there is no doubt that the apparatus can produce very beneficial results when used in a specific training program, there is no need to purchase any special equipment in order to practice this system of body-conditioning.

Where to practice

If you have a Pilates studio near where you live, this is helpful but not essential. Anyone can practice Pilates in the comfort of their own home. You do not need any special apparatus to do the exercises, but you should ensure that your working area is both comfortable and safe. For the floor exercises, a thick carpet or rug that helps to protect your spine is important. As you progress onto the more challenging routines, you may decide that it is worth investing in a thick sports mat, but again this is not essential.

Your working space should be warm enough to keep your muscles relaxed. However, avoid working in very sunny spaces or near sources of artificial heat because your body will become too warm. Ensure that there is a good air supply and that there is no clutter around you or any other obstructions.

A mat protects your spine and helps to keep you warm when exercising on the floor, while a folded towel can be used to aid alignment.

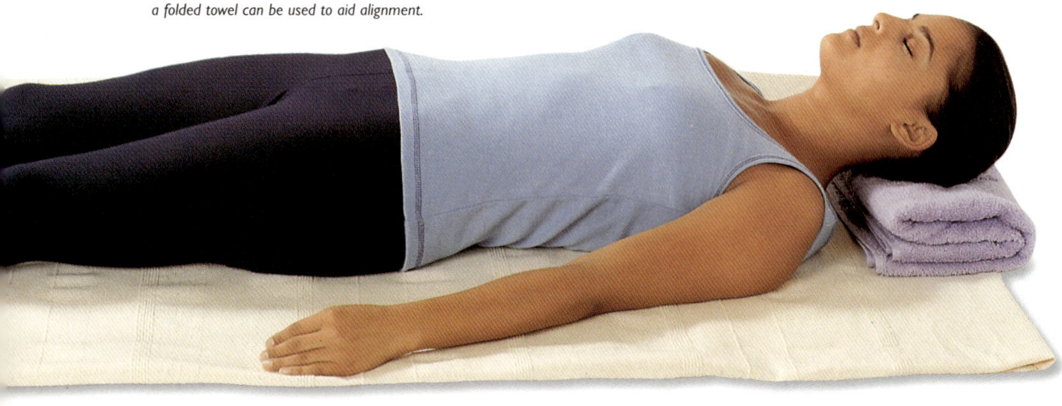

What to wear

Leotards, training shorts, and vests are ideal because you can see your muscles as you work them. These are not vital, however, and if you haven't got any working-out gear, you can use any comfortable, loose-fitting clothes instead. Avoid any clothing that is tight around the waist. It is preferable to choose something in cotton because it will help to keep you cool. With regard to footwear, you can practice either barefoot or in trainers. Remember to remove your watch and any jewelry before you start.

Timing

You can practice Pilates whenever you feel like it, at any time of day. Some people feel more like exercising first thing in the morning, while others prefer to exercise during the day or in the evening. The choice is yours. However, you should avoid doing Pilates directly after a meal, or if you are tired or feeling unwell.

Exercise sessions can be as short as five minutes or as long as an hour. Some people like to do one daily session of, say, 15–30 minutes, while others prefer to do several shorter sessions in a day. Whatever you decide, the most important thing is to do it regularly, and not to rush. If you only have five or ten minutes to spare, it is better to go for quality rather than quantity, so aim to do a few exercises slowly but well. Never be tempted to rush the movements in order to fit in more repetitions.

If you want to see steady results in a reasonably short time, you should aim to do a 15-minute Pilates session at least four times a week. However, any time you spend doing Pilates will not be wasted. Short sessions during work breaks can be particularly valuable for reducing stress and increasing relaxation.

One of the best things about the Pilates system is its flexibility—you can practice at the time and in the place that suits you best.

Safety

Whether you are going to do a five-minute session or one hour of Pilates, you must always warm up first to avoid injury. If your muscles are cold they will naturally tense up and this is when injuries are most likely to occur. Walking briskly on the spot or outside for a few minutes will help the body to warm up. There are also warm-up exercises you can do before your workout, and I have given a selection of these later in the book.

If you have an injury or any medical condition, or if you are pregnant or in doubt as to your suitability for exercise, you should seek qualified medical advice before beginning any of the exercises in this book. It is possible to do Pilates while pregnant, but it should only be done after consulting your doctor and under the guidance of a qualified Pilates instructor.

A few of the Pilates exercises can occasionally aggravate some symptoms of menstruation, so if you are in any doubt it is best to avoid it at this time. Also, if you have recently suffered from a minor illness, such as a cold or a throat infection, avoid doing any exercises for at least two weeks after the symptoms have subsided.

It is essential to warm up before a Pilates session to avoid injury; if your muscles are cold and tense, you risk hurting yourself.

Other safety tips

You should always make sure that you drink plenty of water during the day—between 3 and 4¼ pints (1.5 and 2 liters) per day is usually recommended. Never allow yourself to become dehydrated during exercise sessions. When your body is dehydrated, you may suffer from a variety of symptoms including nausea, headache, and exhaustion. An adequate intake of water will help to flush toxins and other waste products from your body, and leave you feeling refreshed and energetic for your exercise session.

Drinking plenty of water is essential for good health and boosts your energy.

Water helps you to flush toxins from your system; a lack of it can cause headaches, nausea, and tiredness.

Some of the exercises may feel very gentle on the body at first, but this can be deceptive because their effects may not be felt until the next day. So take it easy, and do not push yourself to the point of discomfort. Never strain, and if you feel any sharp or sudden pain you have overdone it and should ease off at once. There is no hurry and no pressure, so do the exercises in your own time and do not try to do too much too soon.

Finally, after you have finished exercising, try not to stop moving straight away. Keep active for a few minutes, even if it is just tidying up round the home or walking from room to room. This will allow your body time to settle back into its normal rhythm.

Mind and body

One of the key differences between Pilates and many other forms of exercise is that it uses the power of the mind to help with the physical exercises. This mind-body approach has opened up a new realm of possibilities in the world of physical fitness, enabling the body and the mind to work together to create a framework for exercise that is harmonious, balanced, and focused.

Define your goals

Before you begin your new exercise program, it helps to have an idea of just what you hope to achieve. If you want to sculpt your body to make the most of its natural shape, you can do so with Pilates exercises. You can also look taller, and be leaner and more supple. You can also improve your posture, increase your muscular strength, and achieve a greater degree of physical flexibility. If you want to be slimmer, Pilates will help you to tone and shape your body, but it won't make you lose weight on its own—you will need to adjust your diet too, and take up some kind of fat-burning exercise to achieve the maximum effects.

So before you start, take some time to decide exactly what you want to achieve from your Pilates workouts, and keep that goal in mind as you practice. Being aware of your goals will help you to achieve them more quickly.

Take a little time to focus your mind and think about what you want to achieve from a Pilates program.

You can create a longer, leaner shape with Pilates, but to achieve consistent weight loss you will have to adjust your diet too.

The power of visualization

The mind has enormous power to bring about changes in the physical body. This is because our bodies do not actually distinguish between things we visualize and reality itself. So if we visualize a stressful situation, for example, and do it so that it feels very real, it will trigger the body's "fight-or-flight" mechanism (see page 16), which will release adrenaline and anti-inflammatory agents into the system, and halt body processes such as digestion. Likewise, if we visualize ourselves experiencing a really joyous occasion, the body will respond accordingly by releasing "happy" chemicals such as endorphins into the system.

You can learn to use the power of visualization to help you while you exercise. For a start, simply visualizing yourself how you want to be will help you to manifest that wish on a physical level. It will also help to keep your motivation up. Practicing visualization can also help you get into the right positions and to do the exercises correctly. For example, if you imagine that your lower back is anchored to the floor, or that you are pulling in your navel toward your spine, it will help you to work the right muscles and to perform the required movement correctly.

Visualization can therefore be a great ally in any fitness regime—and it costs nothing to incorporate it. You should use it as much as possible to get the quickest and best results.

Visualizing a positive reality can help it to come true, so remember to focus your thoughts before, during and after exercise.

Imagining that you are pulling your navel toward your spine will help you to isolate and work the correct muscles.

Learning to breathe correctly

Correct breathing is vital to ensure a good flow of oxygen into the lungs: life-giving oxygen cleanses the bloodstream and energizes the whole body. Although as babies, we naturally breathe correctly, many people develop poor or incorrect breathing habits throughout their lives. The correct technique can be mastered with a little patience.

Benefits of correct breathing

The breath is the very stuff of life and there are many benefits to be gained by learning to breathe correctly. It can:

- Cleanse the bloodstream
- Increase your energy levels
- Carry valuable nutrients to the vital tissues in your body
- Energize your organs and muscles
- Help you to exercise more efficiently
- Aid smooth movement
- Help you to think more clearly
- Enhance muscle control

The importance of rhythmic breathing

When you inhale, you take oxygen into the lungs. The act of breathing also circulates blood around the body. When you exhale, you expel stale air and gases, such as carbon dioxide, from the lungs. If you hold your breath during physical effort, carbon dioxide stays in your lungs. In this way, it accumulates in the body and weakens your muscles. Holding the breath can also increase blood pressure, make you tense, and waste energy. This is why it is vital to breathe in a rhythmic and continuous way during exercise.

Regular breathing helps to invigorate and refresh you.

Shallow breathing

Many people do not breathe deeply enough. They breathe into the upper chest only and don't get enough life-giving oxygen into the depths of their lungs. It is important to breathe deeply in order to fill the lungs and ensure that enough oxygen is available to energize and purify the body.

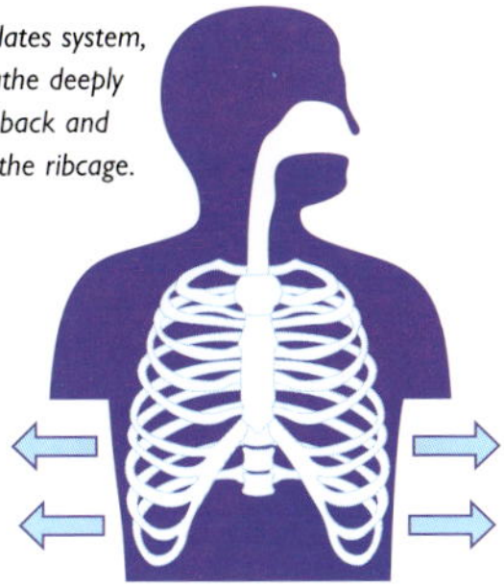

In the Pilates system, you breathe deeply into the back and sides of the ribcage.

Abdominal breathing

Many people have been taught to breathe using the abdomen, which rises and falls with each breath. This ensures a good intake and expulsion of air, but is not suitable for Pilates.

Thoracic breathing enables you to use your lungs fully, while keeping the muscles of the abdominal region tight.

Correct breathing—the Pilates way

Joseph Pilates believed that a strong, tight abdomen was a crucial part of his exercise regime, because it gave the whole body the firm stability necessary to perform his workouts. To strengthen the abdomen, however, it is necessary to contract and tighten the abdominal muscles. For this reason, he decided that the abdominal breathing method was not appropriate for practicing his system of exercise. Instead, he decided to use a method called "thoracic breathing," which is also sometimes known as "lateral breathing." This method involves breathing into the back and lower ribs: as the air goes into the lungs, the back and sides of the rib cage expand, then they contract as the air is exhaled. In this way, the abdomen can stay contracted and tight and yet not interfere with the full intake of breath.

Thoracic breathing

Here is an exercise to help you breathe the Pilates way. It is not difficult to do, but if you have been accustomed to a different method of breathing, it may take a little time for you to get used to it. At first, you will need a long piece of cloth, or a dish towel or scarf, to hold around the bottom of your chest in order to help you perform the movement correctly. When the technique becomes natural to you, you can dispense with the cloth.

1

Kneel on the floor. Keep your toes together but let your heels fall naturally apart, then sit back on your heels so that your buttocks are resting on them. Alternatively, sit upright on a chair. Do not let your body rest on the back of the chair—sit up straight.

2

Place the cloth horizontally around your back and bring the ends round to the front. It should be around your middle, so that you are holding it around the bottom of your chest and ribcage. Keep your shoulders down and let your elbows move out a little from the sides of your body.

Tip

Remember you should exhale on the point of exertion. If you are unsure, just breathe rhythmically—do not hold your breath.

3

Pull your hands together, pulling the cloth tighter around you as you do so. If necessary, allow your hands to cross over in front of you to ensure that you have a firm hold. However, do not pull the cloth so tightly that it starts to become restrictive or feels uncomfortable.

Caution

If you feel unwell or dizzy while you are performing this exercise, stop immediately, loosen the cloth, and breathe normally.

4

Take a slow, deep breath, and feel the back and sides of your ribcage push against the cloth. Let the cloth loosen, keeping some resistance. As you exhale, feel your back and the sides of the ribcage contract. Tighten the cloth a little to help empty the lungs. Repeat 8–10 times, then relax.

Centering the body

Joseph Pilates believed that the area from our abdominal muscles to our buttocks is the center of our body. Imagine the area as a band, stretching round the body at the back and the front. He called it the "powerhouse," and devised his exercises so that all energy and effort travel outward from the center of the body.

Pilates was not alone in believing that the abdominal area is the source of bodily strength. In many Oriental disciplines, for example, the source of good health, energy, and strength is believed to be located here. Some Chinese systems, such as Traditional Chinese Medicine, t'ai chi ch'uan, and kung fu, teach that the storehouse of ch'i (life energy) is situated at the t'an tien, or abdominal area. For physical movements, such as punches, energy is generated from the abdomen and carried to the arms to give the power needed to make the movement. Likewise, the powerful kicks that are a well-known part of kung fu are generated from the abdomen and the hips.

Like Joseph Pilates, practitioners of t'ai chi ch'uan believe that the abdominal area is the center for movement and energy.

What the powerhouse of your body can do

Think of the powerhouse as the center of your body, from where all your energy and movement flows. When the powerhouse is strengthened, the effects can be very beneficial. The powerhouse can:

- Support the spine
- Bring stability to the center of the body
- Improve balance
- Aid coordination and help you make smooth, flowing movements
- Protect the lower back
- Tone the abdominal muscles and the pelvic floor muscles
- Increase physical strength

Strengthening the powerhouse

To strengthen your own powerhouse, try the following exercise. You can perform it while standing, sitting, or lying down.

Note

Once you have mastered this exercise, you will be able to perform thoracic breathing (see page 28) while keeping a strong center.

1

Make sure that your clothing is loose or unrestrictive, especially around your waist area, and that you feel comfortable.

2

Focus on your navel. Using your abdominals, pull it in toward your spine and hold. Do not hold your breath: You should be able to breathe rhythmically while you are pulling in your navel. If you cannot take in enough air, you are using the wrong muscles. Relax and try again.

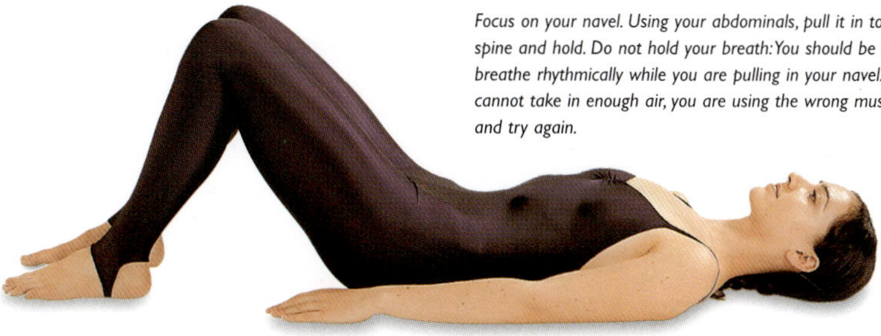

3

When you have found the right muscles to use, you can start toning your pelvic floor at the same time. You can do this as follows: while you are pulling in your navel, gently pull up your pelvic floor. Hold them both for as long as possible, then release them at the same time. Remember to keep breathing regularly throughout.

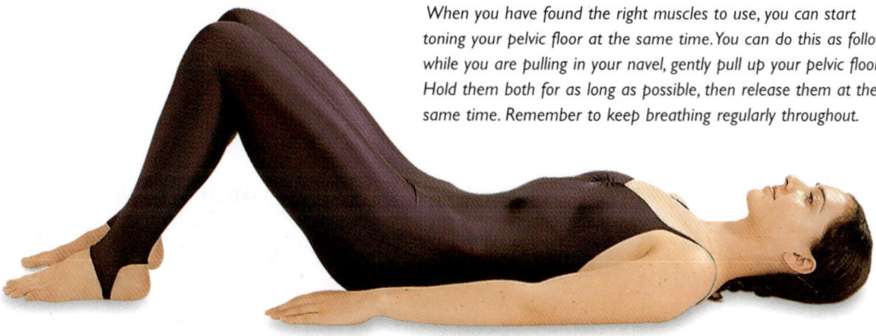

4

When you have got used to these movements, you should hold them for as long as you can. You will need to loosen the tension a little, but not completely, so that you can keep it up for longer periods, breathing comfortably. As a guide, when you are pulling in your navel, pull it in only one quarter of the way. Similarly, pull up the pelvic floor part of the way so you can hold the position longer.

The importance of good posture

Good posture is absolutely vital in our daily lives. It can affect our health and the way we function, and it can also have an influence on our bearing, our balance, the way we move, and how we appear to others. It can even affect our moods and emotions.

Many people pay little attention to their postural habits until they get back pain or develop some other health problem. Yet with a little perseverance most postural problems can be avoided. Here are just a few of the problems that bad posture can cause:

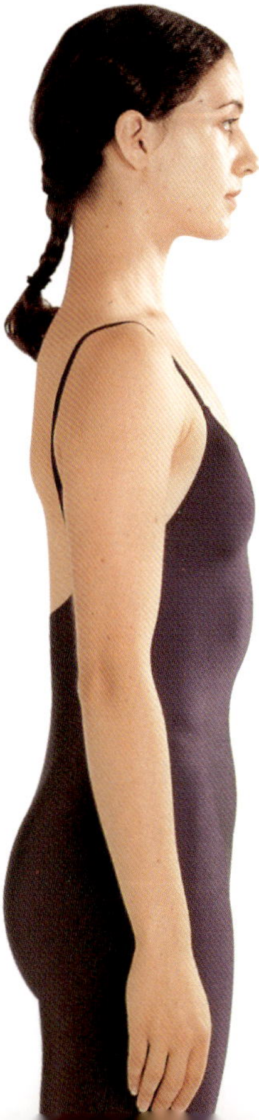

- Poor circulation
- Neck and back pain
- Muscular strains
- Tension and stress
- Headaches
- Fatigue
- Digestive problems
- Poor muscular movements
- Impaired balance and coordination
- Weakness
- Aching joints

Our postural habits and the body

Over the years, our daily activities and lifestyles cause us to adopt some postures more than others. If we do not know that a particular posture is bad, we will continue to use it until it becomes a habit. Over time, our body shapes "mold" themselves into whatever postures we are adopting, so if we regularly sit slumped or stand incorrectly, our bodies will start to take on that "shape," or compensate for the stress on certain parts of the body by placing exaggerated emphasis on others. The shoulders may become rounded, or the stomach may protrude. By this time, any attempt to sit or stand correctly will be uncomfortable, because the body has begun to mold itself to the incorrect posture.

By the time we reach adulthood, many of us will have started to develop postural problems, especially those relating to the spine. If they continue uncorrected, they can cause a lot of pain in later years.

A healthy spine gently curves inward in the lower back, outward in the upper back and inward again at the neck.

In this lumbar lordosis, you can see that the lower back is pushing too far inward, with a corresponding distortion at the upper back and neck.

Here, a kyphosis of the spine is pushing the body forward, causing compression of the chest and the stomach.

Spinal postural problems

One of the main spinal postural problems is lumbar lordosis. Poor posture weakens the abdominals, pulling the stomach forward and creating an unnatural inward curve in the lower back. This causes weakness and pain. The stomach and head drop forward and there is strain on the upper back and neck. The circulation and digestive process are impaired.

In cervical lordosis, the muscles at the back of the neck contract while those at the front expand and the chin protrudes. Over time this condition causes joint inflammation, including arthritis. Another spinal problem, thoracic kyphosis, causes excessive outward curvature of the spine and hunching of the back. This condition can affect the heart, hamper breathing, and put strain on the stomach and intestines, resulting in problems with the digestion.

Other spinal problems include thoracic straight spine, caused by contracted muscles; swayback, where the thoracic spine is distorted and muscles are weakened; and visceroptosis, which causes a weak, bloated abdomen and impaired circulation.

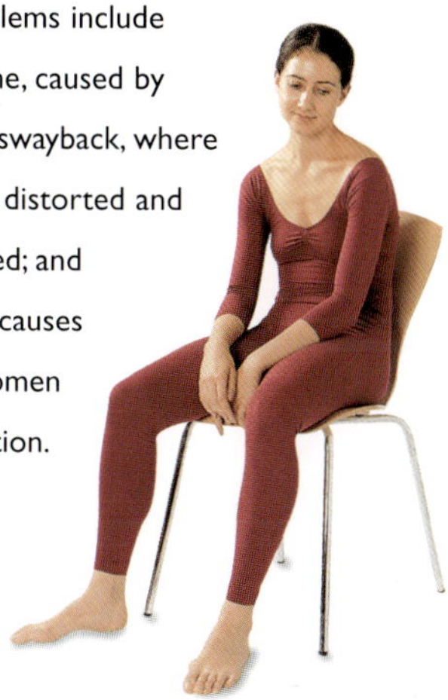

Over time, poor posture and bad sitting habits can cause distortions of the spine.

Correcting bad posture

All is not lost, however. Correcting bad posture is perfectly possible, but it takes patience and time for it to become comfortable and natural. Some incorrect postural habits can be sorted out fairly quickly, but of course in some cases the problem will have developed over many years and will need a longer time and more perseverance to put right. The rewards of good posture far outweigh the effort involved, however. Here are just some of the benefits to be gained from correcting your posture:

- Stronger muscles
- Improved functioning of the heart and stomach
- Improved balance and coordination
- Smoother movements
- More efficient circulation, which means nutrients are carried more efficiently to all body systems, resulting in better health, more energy, and enhanced appearance
- Strengthened immune system to fight off disease

How to check your posture

It can be quite difficult to know if you are standing or sitting incorrectly. One useful way of checking your posture is to ask someone to take two photographs of you: a side view when you are standing up and a side view of you sitting down. Try not to alter your posture for the camera: just adopt a position that you normally use—one that feels comfortable and natural to you. When you get the photographs, examine them for any "tell-tale" signs of bad postural habits. Here are a few of the most obvious signs you should look out for:

Standing
Rounded upper back
Protruding stomach
Head or chin jutting forward
Slumping

Sitting
Slouching
Rounded shoulders
Compressed chest
Lower back curved outward and compressed abdomen

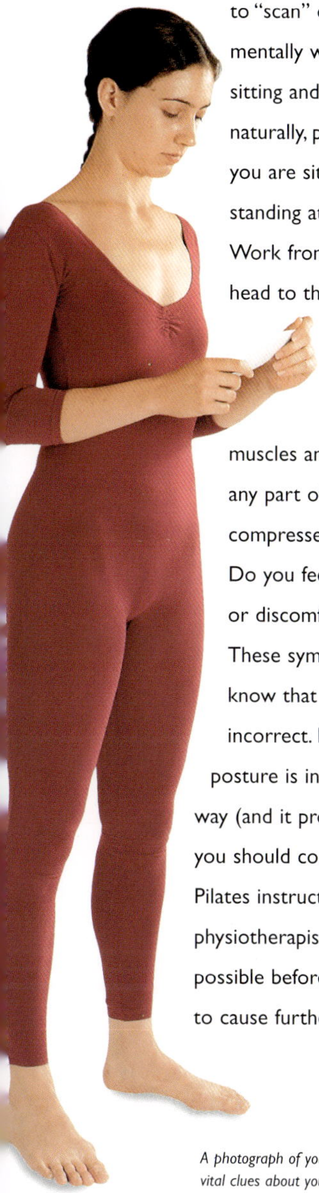

It is also a good idea to "scan" over your body mentally when you are sitting and standing naturally, perhaps while you are sitting at a desk or standing at the kitchen sink. Work from the top of your head to the bottom of your feet, and try to feel your way through all the muscles and joints. Does any part of your body feel compressed or stretched? Do you feel pain, stiffness, or discomfort anywhere? These symptoms let you know that your posture is incorrect. If you think your posture is incorrect in any way (and it probably will be), you should consult a qualified Pilates instructor or physiotherapist as soon as possible before it has a chance to cause further problems.

A photograph of yourself can give vital clues about your posture.

What Pilates can do

Pilates can help you to find your most efficient and comfortable postures when you are sitting, standing, or lying down. Correct postures will also enable you to do the exercises more efficiently and to feel less tired, because there will be less strain on the muscles and body systems. You will be able to breathe more easily, and will feel invigorated and refreshed. The exercises we will be looking at involve standing, sitting, and lying down. Before you start each set of exercises, there will be clear guidelines for you to follow to help you find the right posture.

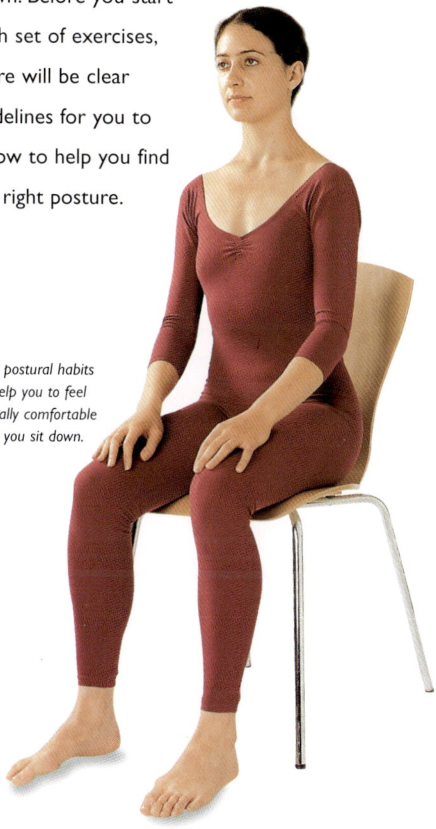

Good postural habits will help you to feel naturally comfortable when you sit down.

Body and movement

Learning to move correctly and at the right pace is an important part of any Pilates physical fitness program. Correct movement and coordination will help you to get the maximum benefit out of the exercises and lessen the risk of injury.

The need to relax

Human beings tend to use short, sharp movements, which appear very jerky when compared with the movements of more graceful mammals, such as cats. This is because humans tend to be tense while they are moving, whereas cats are naturally relaxed.

Too much tension restricts movement and exposes the body to injury. When we are tense, we need to use more energy to get into motion, and expending too much energy over a period of time can lead to fatigue and place an unnecessary strain on the body's systems. We need to be economical with our energy, and not squander it unnecessarily.

So try to cultivate the habit of relaxing when you move. Regularly scan your body both before, during, and after movement so that you can keep tension at bay.

Pilates movements

Unlike many forms of exercise, with Pilates you do not pause after each repetition. The movement is continuous, so that one repetition naturally and smoothly flows into the next. The only time that you stop in Pilates is when you come to the end of an exercise.

Slowing the movements down makes the exercises harder to do and more effective. To demonstrate this, try the following exercise.

Pilates exercises help you to develop good body coordination and get into the habit of making smooth, flowing movements.

Head lift

Make sure you stay as relaxed as possible while you are performing this exercise. Use a thick carpet or rug to help protect your head and spine. Avoid practicing this exercise if you have a neck problem or neck pain.

If you have done this exercise properly, your neck muscles will feel more tired after step 3 than after step 2, because lifting and lowering your head slowly requires more effort. This is how Pilates exercises work, using slower movements to get the maximum benefit.

1

Lie on the floor, with your legs together, knees bent and your arms by your sides. Ensure that your head and neck are straight and in alignment. You may find it helpful to placea folded towel under the back of your head.

2

Lift your head 2–2½ inches (5–6 cm) off the floor, then lower it gently back down. Repeat four times, so that you have done about five raises in 5–8 seconds. Do not hold your breath or use jerking movements. Now, how do the muscles in your neck feel? Rest for a minute.

3

Repeat the exercise five more times, slowing the movement right down. Let your head come up really slowly, to the count of five seconds, then count another five seconds as you lower it. Exhale as you lift and inhale as you come down. Now, how do your neck muscles feel?

PART 3: PILATES IN ACTION

Getting into motion

Pilates exercises are many and varied—in fact too many to include here—so the following pages contain a selection of some basic ones to get you started. If you want to explore this system of exercise further, you should find a qualified Pilates teacher who can give you an exercise program suited to your own body and flexibility.

Warming up the body

Before you do any form of physical exercise, you should always warm up your body first. Whether you are going to do a very short ten-minute workout or a longer program, you need to warm up before you begin. This is because when muscles are cold, they are inclined to tense up, which can cause injury.

How to warm up

There are different methods you can use to warm up. For example, you could try walking briskly on the spot or outside for a few minutes to help the body to warm up. Moving around briskly will always get the circulation going and prepare the body for exercise. Never be tempted to warm up the body artificially using a fire or other heat source, however, because the body will get too warm.

You can also do some warm-up exercises to get your circulation going. Here are a few easy ones to get you started.

Arm swings

Do this exercise gently, and use slow, controlled movements.

1

Stand up straight, with your feet level and shoulder-width apart and your arms by your sides. Do not lock your knees.

Tip

Remember that you should be drinking plenty of water during the day to avoid dehydrating when you are exercising.

2

Slowly raise your arms until they are stretched out above your head. At the same time, pull in your abdominal muscles and inhale using thoracic breathing *(see page 28).*

3

Keeping your abdominal muscles tucked in, exhale and swing your arms down past your knees, curling up your body as you do so. Do not let your arms drop: your movement should be slow, controlled, and flowing.

4

Inhale and swing your arms back up above your head, uncurling your body as you do so, until your body and arms are straight. Keep your abdominal muscles pulled in throughout the movement. Do not pause between repetitions: remember that each movement should flow smoothly into the next one. Repeat this exercise 10 times.

Small hoops

This one is good for increasing your heart rate and blood flow. Do not drop your arms as they come down; control the movement.

1

Stand up straight, with your feet shoulder-width apart and your arms by your sides. Your legs should be straight but your knees should not be locked. Pull in your abdominal muscles.

2

Move your arms out from the sides of your body to about 45 degrees. As you exhale, slowly move your arms forward and up in a circle until they are at their highest point.

3

Inhale as you move them backward and down to complete the circle about 45 degrees out from your sides. Use smooth movements. Keep your head and spine aligned and do not lean forward or backward. Your abdominals should be pulled in at all times and you should use thoracic breathing (see page 28). Repeat 10 times, keeping the circles the same size.

Large hoops

This exercise is very similar to the previous exercise, but the movements are wider, although still slow and smooth throughout.

1

Stand up straight, with your feet shoulder-width apart and your arms by your sides. Again, make sure that your legs are straight but that your knees are not locked. Pull in your abdominals throughout the exercise.

2

Exhale and move your arms forward and up in a wide circle to high above your head. Let your hands touch as you inhale, then move your arms backward and down by your sides to complete the circle. Keep the movements controlled and your head and spine aligned. Do not lean forward or backward. You should use thoracic breathing (see page 28). Repeat this exercise 10 times, keeping the circles the same size.

Progressive hoops

This exercise is similar to the previous hoops exercises, but the movements are in the opposite direction and start off small and get progressively wider. Once again, keep your movements slow and smooth.

1

Stand up straight, feet shoulder-width apart and arms by your sides. Keep your legs straight but do not lock your knees. Pull in your abdominal muscles throughout the exercise.

2

Move your arms out from the sides of your body to about 45 degrees. As you exhale, slowly move your arms backward and up in a circle until they are at their highest point, then inhale as you move them forward and down to complete the circle about 45 degrees out from the sides of your body. Keep your head and spine aligned and do not lean forward or backward. Use thoracic breathing (see page 28).

3

Make more circles with your arms, but each time your arms come down to their lowest point, let them come nearer to the sides of your body. Continue making circles until your arms are almost touching the sides of your body at their lowest point.

4

You will find as you do this that the circles are getting wider each time. Remember to keep your movements smooth and controlled: do not let your arms drop as you bring them down. Also, keep your head and spine in alignment and try not to lean forward or backward with your body. Your abdominal muscles should be pulled in throughout the exercise and you should use thoracic breathing (see page 28). Repeat this exercise until you have made 20 circles, keeping them the same size.

Standing exercises

The following pages focus on exercises you can do while you are standing. In order to do them properly, however, you need to learn how to stand correctly. A good standing posture will help you to perform the exercises more efficiently and improve how your body looks, too. You can appear taller and leaner just by making a few small adjustments to the way you stand.

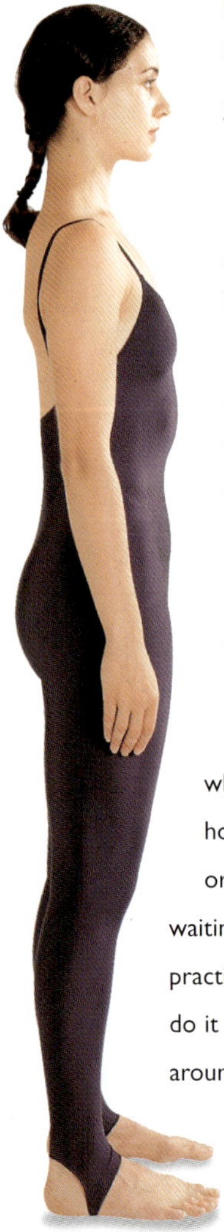

Getting into good habits

The most effective and quickest way of making good posture become natural to you is to practice it whenever you can. Whenever you are standing or walking, you can practice adopting the right position until it becomes second nature to you.

So wherever you are, whether you are cleaning the home, walking to or from work or around the stores, or even waiting for a bus or train, keep practicing. If you keep forgetting to do it at first, try putting reminders around your home or place of work to help you remember. You could put a sticker next to the bathroom mirror or near the kitchen sink or refrigerator, or you could stick a note on the main door of your home at eye level to remind you to stand correctly whenever you leave your home.

Standing correctly the Pilates way

Finding your correct standing position is a relatively simple procedure, but it may take a little time and practice to sort out any bad postural habits that may have crept in.

1

Stand up straight, feet shoulder-width apart. Your weight should be evenly distributed over your feet: do not rock onto your toes, backward onto your heels, or onto the sides of your feet.

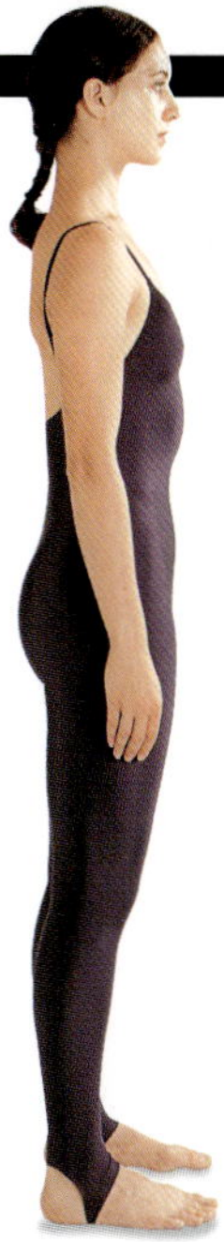

2

Make sure that your legs are straight, and ensure your knees are not locked. Consciously relax the muscles in your lower legs and your thighs.

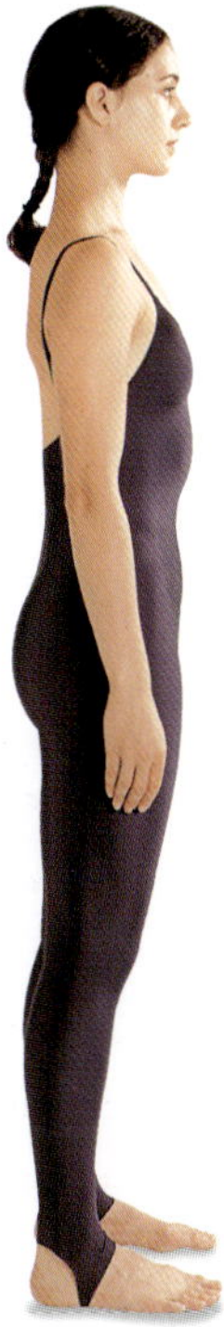

3

Make sure that your powerhouse is strong; pull in your navel and pull up your pelvic floor to about 25 percent of the tension (see page 31). Keep it at this level for all the exercises in this section.

4

Let the base of your spine fall toward the floor, without moving your pelvis forward. Keep doing the thoracic breathing (see page 28).

5

Contract and relax your upper back muscles to release tension. Let your shoulders and arms hang naturally.

6

Let your head and neck rest naturally in a central position. You might like to move your head around a little to find this point.

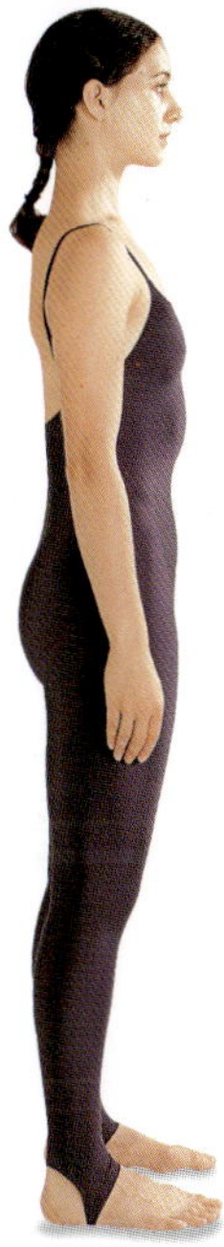

7

Shift your focus to the backs of your ears. Imagine magnets there, pulling upward. Keep doing the thoracic breathing (see page 28) and hold the position for as long as possible.

Arm lifts

This exercise helps you to improve your standing posture by encouraging you to find the right position for your shoulder blades. It also works the muscles in the upper arms. It may seem a very slow and gentle exercise at first, but as with all Pilates exercises, it is very effective. Keep the movements smooth and controlled.

1

Stand tall, feet shoulder-width apart. Make sure your weight is evenly distributed over your feet, and your knees are not locked. Pull in your navel toward your spine and pull up on your pelvic floor, holding at 25 percent tension. Let the base of your spine fall toward the floor, without moving your pelvis forward. Your neck and spine should be aligned, and your hands resting on the outsides of your thighs.

Caution

Avoid this exercise if you have weak or injured shoulders. If you are in doubt, seek professional medical advice first.

2

Exhale and lift your right arm upward and across your middle until your right palm is resting on the top of your left shoulder. Your left palm at this point should still be resting on the outside of your left thigh. Make sure that you keep breathing in and out rhythmically using the thoracic breathing technique (see page 28) and are maintaining a strong powerhouse, through navel and pelvic floor tension (see page 31).

3

Inhale. As you exhale, lift your left arm out to the side until it is in line with the shoulder, palm facing upward. Keep the arm straight but relaxed and do not lock your elbow. Make sure your shoulder blades are down.

4

When your left arm is in line with your left shoulder, do not hold this position but inhale and slowly lower your arm again until your left palm is touching the outside of your left thigh. The movement should be slow, gentle, and controlled throughout. Repeat this exercise, raising and lowering the left arm 10 times, making sure that you do not pause between each repetition. The whole exercise should form one continuous movement.

Tip

Always breathe out on the point of exertion, and breathe in when relaxing.

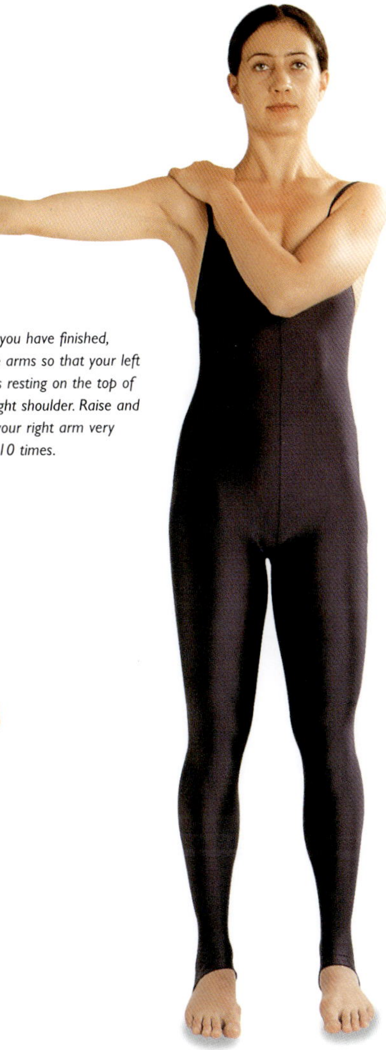

5

When you have finished, change arms so that your left palm is resting on the top of your right shoulder. Raise and lower your right arm very slowly 10 times.

Knee bends and arm lifts

This exercise is relaxing yet invigorating because it helps to get the circulation going. It also helps you to improve your balance and overall stability, while at the same time building on your physical coordination.

Caution

Do not do this exercise if you have weak or injured knees or shoulders. If you are in doubt about its suitability for you, seek professional medical advice first.

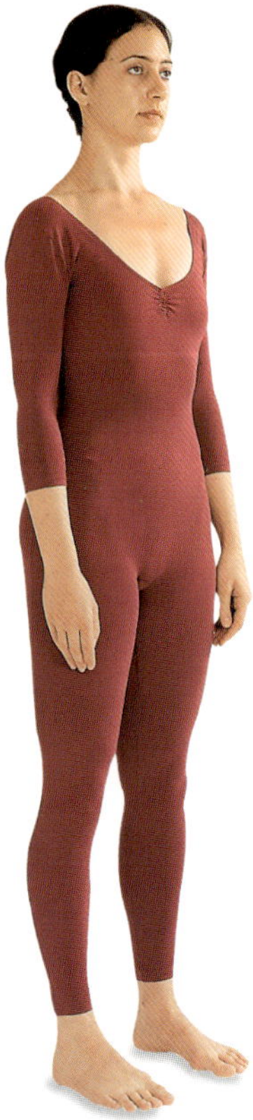

1

Stand up straight, feet shoulder-width apart, weight evenly distributed over your feet. Keep the legs straight but don't lock your knees. Pull in your navel toward your spine and pull up your pelvic floor muscles, to about 25 percent tension; let the base of your spine fall toward the floor, without moving the pelvis forward. Keep neck and spine aligned. Rest your hands on the outsides of your thighs.

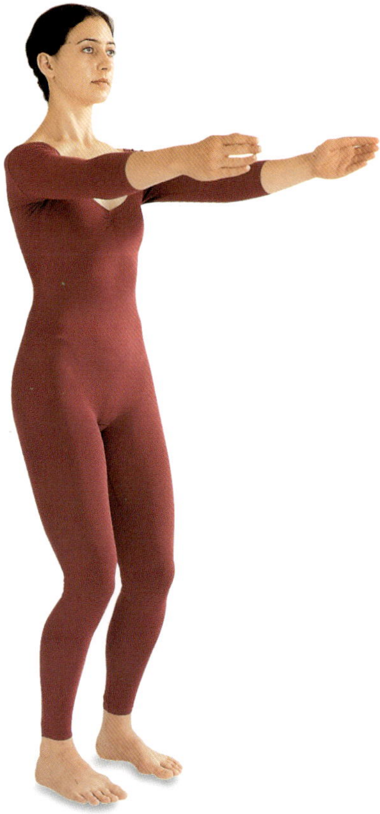

2

Inhale, then as you exhale very slowly, lift your arms in front of you to shoulder height. Your palms should be facing each other. Keep your arms straight out but don't lock your elbows. At the same time, bend your knees slowly to an angle of about 45 degrees. Keep your weight evenly distributed on your feet: do not rock forward or backward. Don't forget to use the thoracic breathing technique (see page 28).

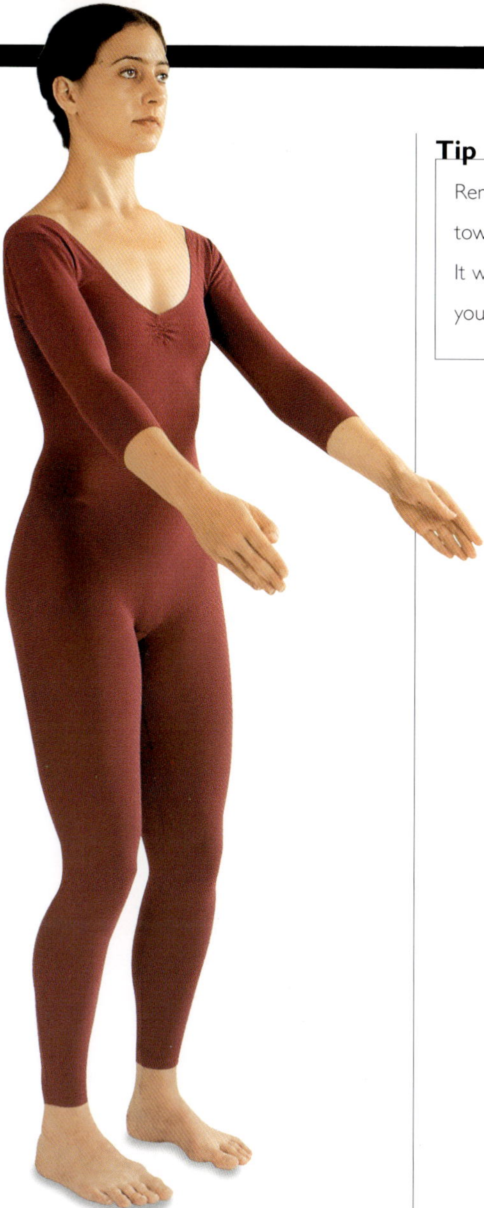

3

When your arms are straight out in front in line with your shoulders, inhale and slowly lower your arms again until your palms are touching the outsides of your thighs. At the same time, straighten your legs until you are standing upright, but do not lock your knees. The movement should be slow, gentle, and controlled throughout.

Tip

Remember to keep pulling in your navel toward your spine throughout this exercise. It will help to protect your back and keep your posture correct and strong.

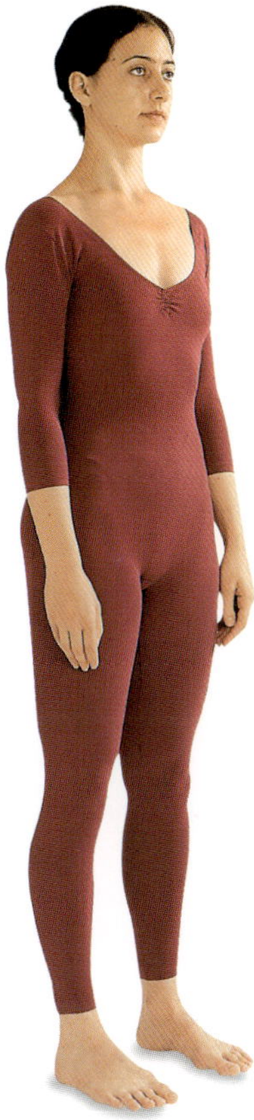

4

Repeat this exercise, raising and lowering the arms and bending and straightening the knees 10 times, making sure that you do not pause between each repetition. The whole exercise should form one continuous movement throughout. Then, pause and relax for a minute or so.

Chest stretch

The chest stretch helps to develop stability and good posture while enhancing smooth movement and coordination. It also gently stretches and tones the chest, shoulders, and upper arms. You will need a rope or a long piece of cloth such as a scarf. Alternatively, you could use a broom handle or other lightweight pole. Maintain rhythmic breathing throughout, using the thoracic method (see page 28).

Caution

Avoid this exercise if you have weak or injured shoulders or neck muscles. If you are in doubt about its suitability, seek professional medical advice first.

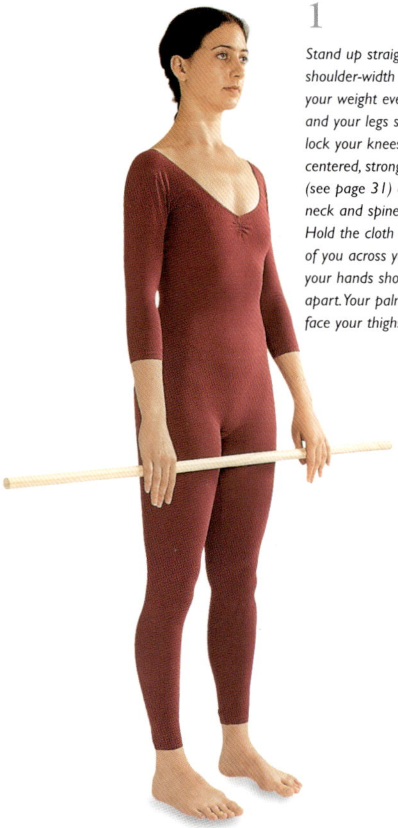

1

Stand up straight, feet shoulder-width apart. Keep your weight evenly distributed and your legs straight; do not lock your knees. Maintain a centered, strong powerhouse (see page 31) and keep the neck and spine in alignment. Hold the cloth or pole in front of you across your thighs, with your hands shoulder-width apart. Your palms should face your thighs.

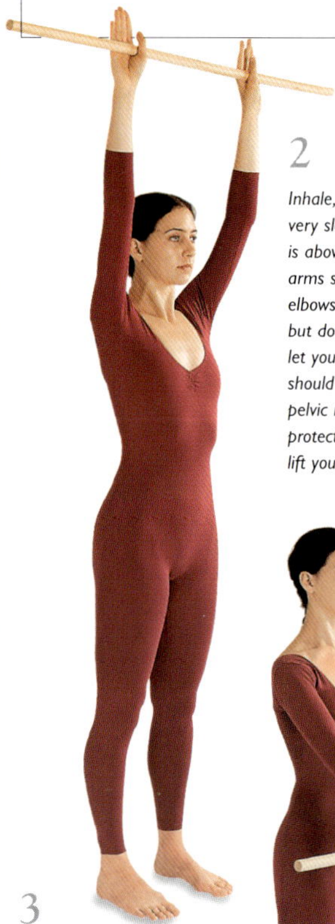

2

Inhale, then as you exhale very slowly, lift the pole until it is above your head. Keep your arms straight but do not lock your elbows. Keep your shoulders down but do not tense them. Do not let your back arch as you lift. You should also keep pulling in your pelvic muscles: this will help to protect your lower back as you lift your arms upward.

3

When your arms are outstretched above your head as far as they will comfortably go, inhale and slowly bring them back down until they are touching your thighs again. Do not let your arms drop: keep the movement slow, gentle, and controlled. Repeat this exercise 10 times, without pausing between each repetition.

Spinal release

This exercise is very effective for releasing tension, improving circulation, and increasing flexibility in the spine. You should try to repeat it at the end of your workout too because it is very relaxing and will help you to shake off any remaining tension in your body.

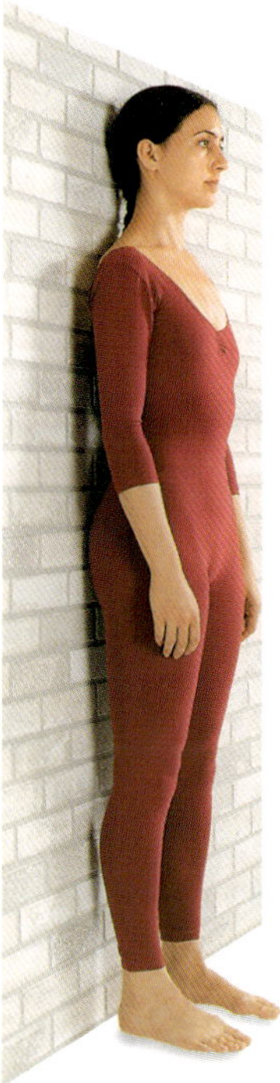

1

Stand up straight, with your back against a wall and your feet shoulder-width apart. Your weight should be evenly distributed over your feet. Keep your legs straight, but do not lock your knees. Pull your navel in toward your spine, then pull up your pelvic floor muscles and hold at 25 percent tension. Allow the base of your spine to fall toward the floor, without moving the pelvis forward. Your neck and spine should be aligned. If you can, keep your shoulders in contact with the wall, or get them as near to it as you can without straining. Your heels should be near to the wall but not touching it. Your body should stand straight—if your heels are too far away or too near, your body will curve. Let your arms hang down, hands resting on the outsides of your thighs. Use the thoracic breathing technique *(see page 28).*

Caution

Do not attempt this if you have high or low blood pressure. If you feel pain, tingling, or dizziness, stop and seek medical advice.

2

Exhale, and very slowly let your chin drop down toward your collarbone. The movement should be controlled and gentle, so do not let your chin fall heavily. Continue the slow movement downward by gradually letting your shoulders come off the wall, then letting your body roll down slowly, bending down from your shoulders and then from your waist. Roll down as far as you can, keeping your buttocks in contact with the wall. Let your head and arms hang down.

3

When you have bent down as far as you can comfortably go, inhale and then gradually straighten up, unrolling your body bit by bit. The whole movement should be slow and smooth. When you have returned to your starting position, take a couple of moments to check your posture (see step 1). Repeat six times.

Sitting exercises

In this section we will be looking at several different exercises you can do while you are sitting down. Once again, good posture is vital here. Practiced correctly, these exercises will help all your body systems to function more efficiently, which in turn will improve your health and lead to a greater sense of well-being.

Learning how to sit correctly

You can practice correct posture whenever you are sitting down—such as when you are traveling or working. If your job involves hours of sitting in front of a computer or at a checkout, use the time to develop good habits. You can also practice when sitting watching the TV, eating in a restaurant, or at the theater. Eventually sitting correctly will become natural.

Sitting correctly the Pilates way

Adopting a good sitting posture is not difficult, but if you have developed bad habits, such as slumping while sitting, it may take practice. For this exercise you will need a chair.

Tip

Your lower back should not arch too much, either forward or backward. Sit sideways in front of a mirror so you can check.

1

Sit upright with your lower back supported against the back of the chair. Do not lean your upper back into the chair and try not to slump or lean forward; you should sit erect but not bolt upright or you will not be able to sit comfortably for long periods of time.

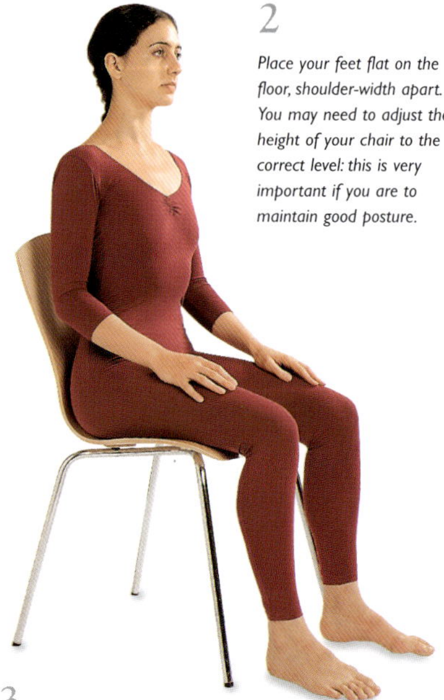

2

Place your feet flat on the floor, shoulder-width apart. You may need to adjust the height of your chair to the correct level: this is very important if you are to maintain good posture.

3

Keep your shoulder blades down, but do not strain. Put your palms on your thighs and do not lean back into the chair. Your head, neck, and spine should be aligned and your head central. Keep your powerhouse strong by pulling in your navel toward your spine and pulling up your pelvic floor muscles, holding at 25 percent tension.

Side stretches

These stretches are good for getting the lower back moving and for toning the waist. You need a chair with a straight back.

Caution

Do not do this exercise if your lower back or shoulders are weak or injured.

1

Sit facing the chair's back, legs straddling the chair. Make sure that you are sitting erect: your body should not be leaning. Put your palms on the top of the chair's back, keep your arms relaxed, and ensure that your feet are flat on the floor. Pull in your navel toward your spine and pull up your pelvic floor muscles, holding them at about 25 per cent of the tension throughout this exercise. Breathe rhythmically, using thoracic breathing (see page 28).

2

Exhale, stretch your left arm out to the left and raise it to shoulder height, palm upward. Keep raising your arm until it is over your head, palm facing inward. At the same time, move your right shoulder downward so you are leaning to the right.

3

Feel the stretch down your left side. When you have leant over as far as is comfortable, breathe in and straighten up slowly, resting your palm on the chair back again. Repeat on the other side. Then repeat this exercise 10 times.

Tip

Remember not to pause between repetitions but to keep your movements slow, continuous, and as smooth as possible.

Spinal twists

This gentle exercise helps to increase the flexibility of your spine, especially in the lower back area. You will need a stool or chair without arms to practice this exercise.

1

Sit erect on the stool or chair. Put your feet flat on the floor, shoulder-width apart, and place your palms on your thighs. Pull in your navel toward your spine and pull up your pelvic floor muscles. Hold at 25 per cent of the tension throughout this exercise. Breathe rhythmically, using thoracic breathing (see page 28).

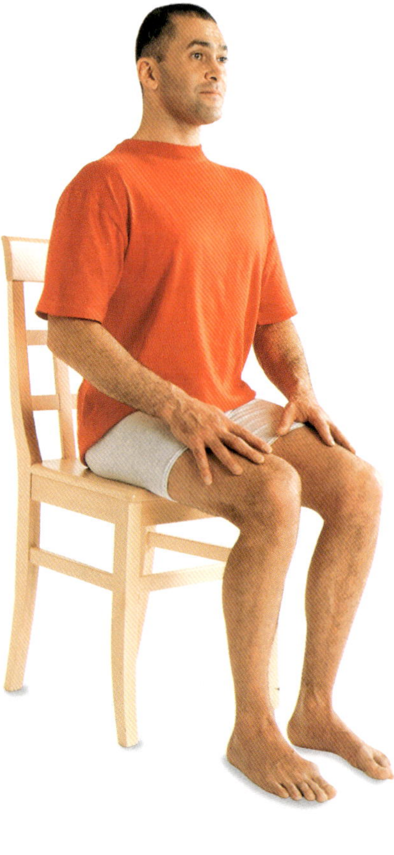

Caution

Do not do this exercise if you have a weak or injured lower back or neck.

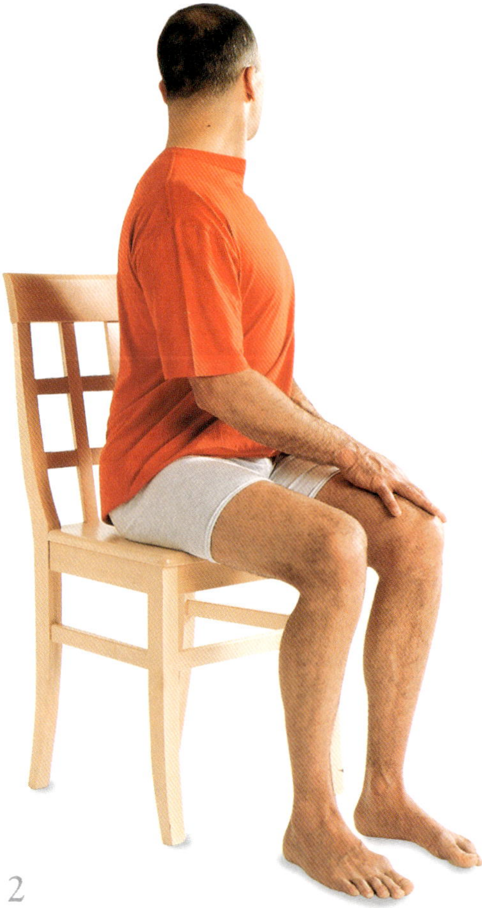

2

Exhale and, as you do so, very slowly turn your head to the left so that you are looking over your left shoulder. As your head turns, let your spine follow the turn to give more of a twist. Move your right hand and place your right palm on your left thigh next to your left hand.

3

When you have twisted round as far as is comfortable, inhale and slowly start to unwind, starting with your head and then letting your spine follow. At the same time, move your right hand back to its original position. You should now be facing the front again.

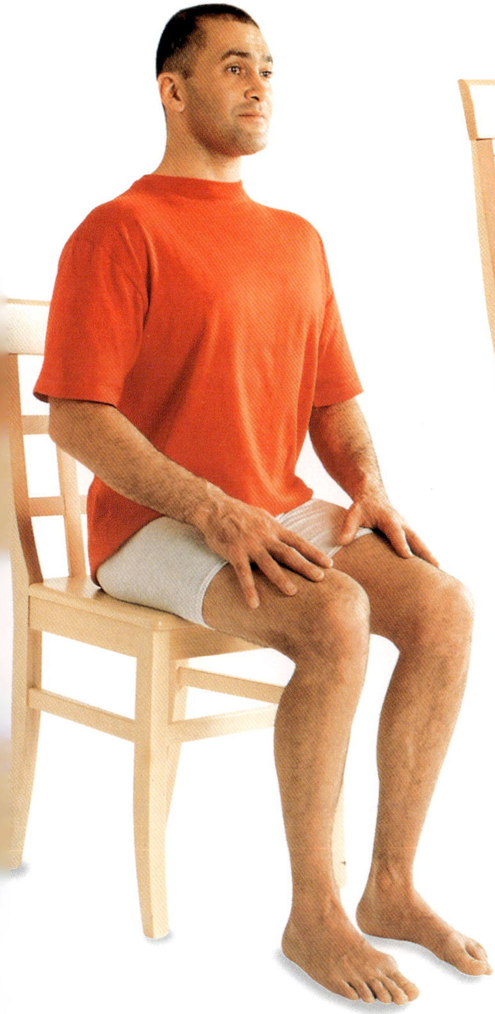

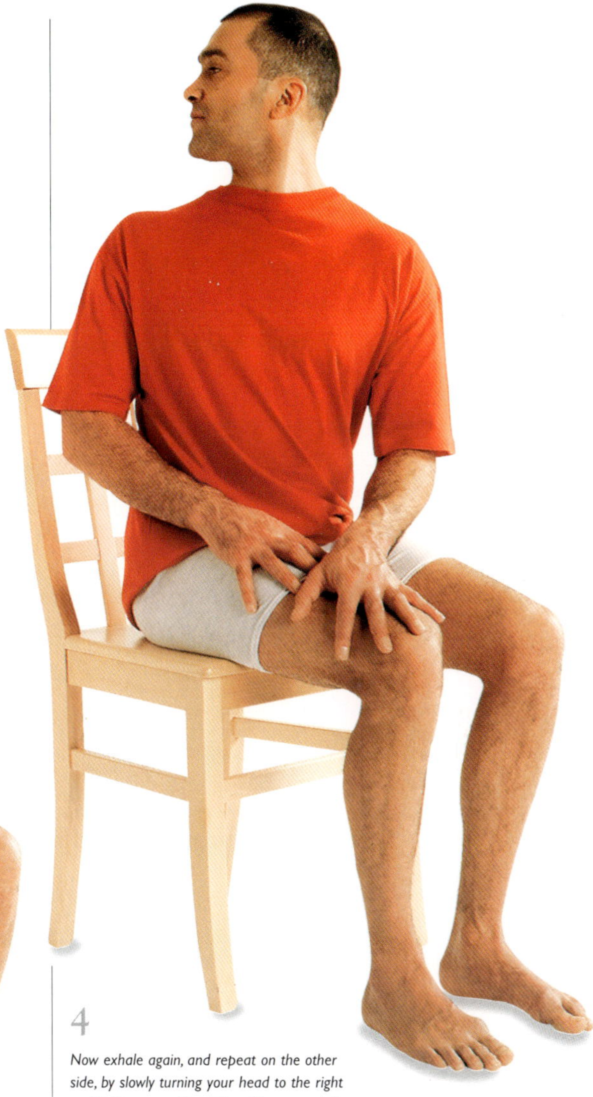

4

Now exhale again, and repeat on the other side, by slowly turning your head to the right and letting your spine follow. Move your left palm and place it on your right thigh next to your right hand. When you have twisted round as far as is comfortable, inhale and slowly start to unwind until you are facing the front again and your left hand is back on your left thigh. Repeat this exercise 10 times to both sides.

Matwork

Most workouts in the Pilates system focus on matwork, or floor exercises. In this section we will look at some of the exercises you can do on the floor. There are many others, so if you would like to explore Pilates further, we would recommend that you seek out a qualified Pilates instructor or studio near to you (some useful addresses and websites are given on page 67). When you have finished these exercises, try doing the Spinal twists again (see pages 52–53), to release any remaining tension.

Equipment

You do not need any special equipment for these exercises, but you will need to practice them on a thick carpet or rug to help protect your spine. As you progress onto a more challenging program, you may decide to buy a thick sports mat, but this is not essential. For these exercises, you will also need a couple of small cushions or pillows, or two small towels that you can fold easily.

Correct posture

Adopting and maintaining the correct posture is just as important for matwork as it is for the standing and sitting exercises. It will enable all your body systems to function at optimum efficiency, so that you can get the most benefit out of your exercise program. For all the floor exercises, you need to make sure your spine and pelvis are in "neutral"; the exercise on page 55 shows you how to do this.

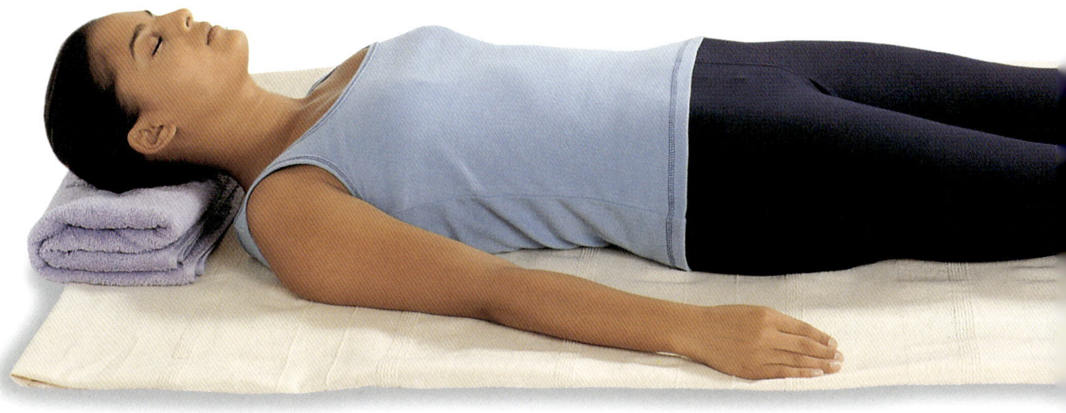

Neutral spine and pelvis

This method will help you to find the most relaxing position for your spine and pelvis while you are working on the floor. You will need a small pillow or cushion, or a small folded towel, to place under your head.

Caution

If you feel any discomfort or pain in your lower back while you are doing this exercise, stop immediately and seek advice from your doctor or another qualified medical practitioner as soon as possible.

1

Lie on your back on the floor, your head on the pillow or towel. Bend your knees and place your feet on the floor, 10 inches (25 cm) apart. Your palms should be flat and your arms by your sides.

2

Pull in your navel and pull up your pelvic floor, then hold them at 25 per cent of the tension. Breathe rhythmically, using the thoracic breathing method (see page 28). Gently push your lower back toward the floor as far as possible without discomfort. Then relax and let it rise to a comfortable position.

3

Now, arch your lower back by pushing it upward. Do not move your buttocks or upper back from the floor. When you have arched your lower back as far as it will comfortably go, let it sink back gently toward the floor. The neutral position for the spine and pelvis is between these points, neither pushed too low nor arched too high. A slight curve upward is natural: you should be able to slide your hand between your lower back and the floor. Keep your abdominal muscles pulled in. You should maintain your neutral position for your spine and pelvis throughout the floor exercises.

Lumbar twists

These lumbar twists are excellent for improving spinal mobility while keeping your powerhouse strong and centered. You will need a small pillow or folded towel to place under your head for this exercise.

Caution

Do not allow your back to arch excessively, and remember to keep your abdominal muscles pulled in toward your spine.

1

Lie on your back and place your head on the pillow or towel. Bend your knees and put your feet flat on the floor, 10 inches (25 cm) apart. Stretch your arms out to the sides at right-angles to your body, palms facing upward. Do not lock your elbows.

2

Pull in your navel toward your spine and pull up your pelvic floor. Hold them in that position, then release them slightly and hold them at about 25 per cent of the tension. Remember to breathe rhythmically, using the thoracic breathing method (see page 28). You should also have your spine and pelvis in the neutral position (see page 55).

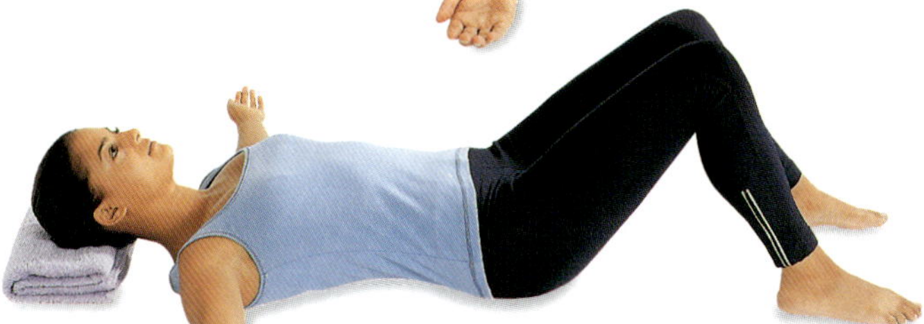

3

Exhale, and slowly turn your head to the right until your right cheek is flat on the pillow or towel. At the same time, very slowly move your knees to the left and let them descend gently toward the floor. If they cannot reach the floor, do not worry; just let them descend as far as they will comfortably go.

4

Inhale and bring your knees back up to their starting position, and at the same time move your head back up until you are looking up at the ceiling.

5

Now exhale and slowly turn your head to the left until your left cheek is flat on the pillow or towel. While you are doing this, very slowly move your knees to the right and allow them to descend very slowly and gently toward the floor, as far as they will comfortably go.

6

Inhale and bring your knees back up to their starting position, and at the same time move your head back up until your are looking up at the ceiling. Repeat this exercise on both sides 10 times.

Tip

Remember that your movements should be controlled, so do not let your knees fall to the floor. Lower them as slowly as possible.

Chest stretches

This exercise helps you to stretch out your chest and neck muscles, and tones the upper back and spine. You will need two small pillows, cushions, or folded towels.

Caution

Avoid this exercise if you have a weak neck or back or have any injuries in these areas.

1

Lie on your back with your head on a pillow or towel. Bend your knees, feet flat on the floor and 10 inches (25 cm) apart. Hold a pillow or towel between your knees. Stretch your arms out to the sides, palms facing upward.

2

Pull in your navel toward your spine and pull up your pelvic floor. Hold them in that position, then release them slightly and hold them at about 25 percent of the tension. Breathe rhythmically, using the thoracic breathing method (see page 28). You should also have your spine and pelvis engaged in the neutral position (see page 55).

3

Exhale, and slowly turn your body to the right, until your right cheek is flat on the pillow or towel and your knees are on the floor to the right. Slowly lift up your left arm and move it over to the right until it is resting over your right arm in line with your right shoulder. Your arms should be straight but do not lock your elbows. You should be lying on your right side, with your knees bent.

4

Inhale and slowly lift up your left arm, and let it stretch out behind you in line with your left shoulder. Let your head turn toward the left to maximize the stretch, but keep your knees where they are. You should now feel the stretch in your upper body, from the waist upward. Now exhale and lift up your left arm, and move it back over to the right and let it rest on your right arm again. At the same time, move your head back to the right. You should now be lying on your right side once again, with your knees bent. Repeat this exercise 10 times in total.

Tip

Do not let your arms or knees fall heavily to the floor. Lower them as slowly as you can to get the most out of this exercise.

5

Repeat the exercise, but this time turn your body to the left and lift up your right arm and rest it on your left. You should be lying on your left side, knees bent and arms stretched out in line with your left shoulder.

6

Inhale and slowly lift up your right arm, and let it stretch out behind you in line with your right shoulder. Let your head turn toward the right to maximize the stretch, but keep your knees where they are. Now exhale and lift up your right arm, and move it back over to the left and let it rest on your left arm again. At the same time, move your head back to the left. You should now be lying on your left side once again, with your knees bent. Repeat this exercise on this side 10 times.

Backward swimming

This exercise helps to improve muscular coordination and provides a healthy stretch for the legs, arms and stomach. You will need a small pillow, cushion, or folded towel.

1

Lie on your back on the floor and place your head on the pillow or towel. Bend your knees and put your feet flat on the floor, about 10 inches (25 cm) apart. Let your arms rest by your sides, with your palms flat on the floor.

2

Pull in your navel toward your spine and pull up your pelvic floor. Hold them in that position, then release them slightly and hold them at about 25 percent of the tension. Remember to breathe rhythmically, using the thoracic breathing method (see page 28). You should also be keeping your spine and pelvis in the neutral position (see page 55).

3

Exhale and slowly stretch out your right leg until it is flat on the floor, but do not lock the knee. At the same time, lift your left arm and move it up and over your head in a semi-circular motion, letting it rest on the floor behind you. Keep your lower back in the neutral position: do not let it rise upward as you stretch your arm. Make sure that you do not stretch out your arm too much—the elbow should still be soft rather than locked.

4

When you have extended your arm as far as feels comfortable, inhale and slowly lift your left arm again, moving it back in a semicircular motion the other way until it is resting by your side with your palm flat on the floor. At the same time, bring your right leg back up to its starting position, with the knee bent and the foot flat on the floor.

Tip

Keep your head centered and do not let it drop to the side during this exercise. Keep looking up at the ceiling as you move.

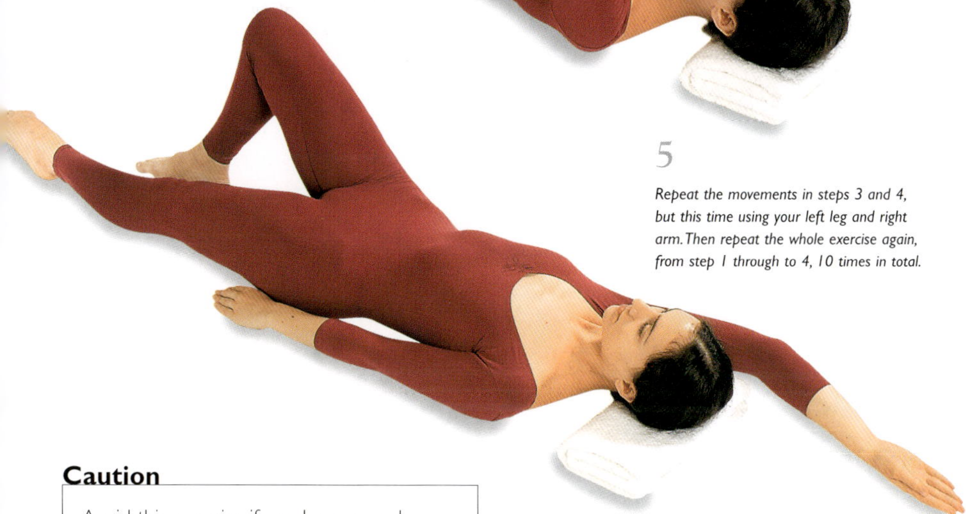

5

Repeat the movements in steps 3 and 4, but this time using your left leg and right arm. Then repeat the whole exercise again, from step 1 through to 4, 10 times in total.

Caution

Avoid this exercise if you have a weak lower back or any injuries in this area.

Hip and thigh toner

This excellent exercise helps to stretch and tone the quadriceps, or thigh muscles. It will improve flexibility and increase strength at the front of your hip and the knee. You will need a small pillow, cushion, or folded towel.

1

Lie on the floor on your left side, and extend your left arm out on the floor behind your head with your left palm flat on the floor. Place the pillow or towel on the upper part of your left arm, and then rest the left side of your head on it. Allow your right arm to rest in front of your body in line with your shoulder, with the palm flat on the floor. Bend your knees to an angle of about 45 degrees.

2

Pull in your navel toward your spine and pull up your pelvic floor. Hold them in that position, then release them slightly and hold them at about 25 percent of the tension. Keep breathing rhythmically, using the thoracic breathing method (see page 28).

3

Exhale, and slowly use your right arm to reach for your right foot. Inhale as you reach and grasp your foot. As you exhale, slowly and gently pull your foot as close toward your buttocks as feels comfortable. You should feel a stretch down the front of the right thigh. Keep the movement slow and smooth: do not jerk when you grasp and pull the foot.

Caution

If you feel any pain in your hip, thigh, or knee during this exercise, stop at once and seek qualified medical advice.

4

Now inhale and gently release the stretch on the leg, moving the leg back toward its original position. Repeat this stretch 10 times in total, exhaling on each stretch.

5

Now repeat this exercise another 10 times, but this time lying on your right side, using your left hand to stretch your left leg.

Tip

Keep your abdominal muscles pulled in throughout. Do not let your back arch or your head turn away from the pillow.

GLOSSARY

Adrenaline
A hormone secreted by the adrenal gland, which prepares the body for "fight-or-flight." It has widespread effects on the muscles, circulations and sugar metabolism.

Alignment
Positioned in a straight line.

Biceps
This term is most often used for the muscles at the front of the upper arms, but there are also biceps at the back of the thighs.

Carbon dioxide
A colorless gas formed in the tissues during metabolism, which is carried in the blood to the lungs and then exhaled.

Centering
This term refers to the technique of centering the body by strengthening and stabilizing the powerhouse (the area from the abdominal muscles to the buttocks, which stretches round the body at the back and the front).

Cervical lordosis
A postural problem of the spine that occurs in the neck area. The muscles at the back of the neck contract, while those at the front overexpand. The chin protrudes forward and over time this condition can cause inflammation of the joints, including arthritis.

Ch'i
According to Chinese tradition, this energy, or "life force", permeates everything—it is within and around all things, living or otherwise.

Cortisol
This is a steroid hormone produced in the body that is important for normal stress-response and carbohydrate metabolism.

Deltoids
These are the thick triangular muscles that cover the shoulder joints—they are responsible for raising up the arms from the sides of the body.

Ectomorph
One of three basic body shapes—the other two are endomorph and mesomorph. Ectomorph people tend to be light and delicate, often tall and thin with long limbs. This body shape is often linked to an alert, inhibited, and intellectual personality.

Endomorph
One of the three basic body shapes. People with this body shape will be heavy or rounded, and may have trouble keeping their body weight down. This shape is quite often linked to placidity, a relaxed attitude and hedonism.

Endorphins
"Happy" chemicals that occur naturally in the brain and have pain-relieving qualities. They are also responsible for feelings of pleasure.

Fight-or-flight response
A process that prepares the body for physical effort. When the body is under extreme stress, it gears up to meet the immediate threat by releasing adrenaline and other hormones into the system. The heartbeat, metabolism and breathing become more rapid, and any bodily function that is not essential to immediate survival—including the immune system and digestion processes—are automatically shut down.

Gluteus maximus
These paired muscles are located within the fleshy part of the buttocks.

Gluteus minimus
These are the paired muscles situated above the fleshy part of the buttocks.

Levator scapulis
Muscles at the sides and back of the neck.

Leucocytes
White blood cells that help to protect the body against foreign substances and disease.

Lumbar lordosis
A postural problem of the spine in which the abdominal muscles are weakened, pulling the stomach forward and creating an unnatural inward curve in the lower back.

Lymph
The name for the fluid present in the lymphatic system (a network of vessels). Lymph carries leucocytes, or white blood cells, which play a key role in helping the body to fight off disease.

Mesomorph
One of the three basic body shapes. People with this body shape will be athletic or muscular, with large chests, limbs, and muscles. This body shape is sometimes associated with an aggressive tendency. Mesomorphs are often athletic and excel at sports.

Powerhouse
The area from the abdominal muscles to the buttocks, stretching round the body. In Pilates, this is the area from which all energy and effort travel outward.

Quadriceps
Muscles situated in the thighs.

Rickets
A disease of childhood in which the bones do not harden and become soft and malformed. It is caused by a deficiency of vitamin D.

Swayback
A postural problem where the thoracic spine becomes distorted and results in weak ligaments and muscles.

T'ai Chi Ch'uan
This is a flowing form of movement, working on mind, body, and spirit, which dates back to China at least 2,000 years.

T'an Tien
The Chinese word for the reservoir of ch'i energy situated in the abdominal area.

Thoracic breathing
Sometimes known as "lateral breathing." This technique involves breathing into the back and lower ribs: as the air goes into the lungs, the back and sides of the rib cage expand, then they contract as the air is exhaled. In this way, the abdomen can stay contracted and tight and yet not interfere with the intake of breath.

Thoracic kyphosis
This is a postural problem that causes excessive outward curvature of the spine and eventual hunching of the back.

Thoracic straight spine
This is a postural problem that causes the spine to straighten as a result of muscle contraction. It causes pain in the arms and strain in the chest area.

Traditional Chinese medicine
TCM is an ancient Chinese system of healing that bases diagnosis on a person's pattern of symptoms rather than on a named disease. It incorporates Chinese herbalism and acupuncture into its treatments.

Trapezius
A flat, triangular muscle covering the back of the neck and the shoulders.

Triceps
Muscles at the back of the upper arms.

Visceroptosis
A postural problem that causes a weak, bloated abdomen and impaired circulation.

Yoga
A school of Hindu philosophy, which incorporates physical and mental techniques in its approach to personal health. There are many forms of yoga; the most well-known is hatha yoga, which is mainly concerned with well-being and uses physical exercises to achieve this. The practice of yoga can be traced to India as far back as 4,000 years.

Useful addresses and websites

The Pilates Center

4800 Baseline Road, Suite D206

Boulder, CO 80303

Telephone: 303 494 3400

Fax: 303 494 5151

info@thepilatescenter.com

The Pilates Center of Austin

5555 N. Lamar Boulevard, Suite E103

Austin, TX 78751

Telephone: 512 467 8009

info@pilatescenterofaustin.com

Alternative Health & Fitness Concepts

2016 Walnut Street, 2nd floor

Philadelphia, PA 19103

1-877-9 Pilates

Telephone: 215 567 4969

Fax: 215 567 4881

Pilates Method Alliance

2631 Lincoln Avenue

Miami, FL 33133

Telephone: 866 573 4945

www.pilatesmethodalliance.org

Body Balance

1009 North Rush Street, 4th floor

Chicago, IL 60611

Telephone: 312 440 9558

www.bodybalanceltd.com

Every Body Pilates

454 Common St.

Belmont, MA 02478

Telephone: 617 484 3311

www.everybodypilates.com

yoga

Introduction

If this section of the book inspires you to explore the system of yoga, it could become your first step toward the liberating journey of self-realization. Many people find that they choose yoga as a fitness program, to increase their flexibility and improve their muscle tone, but also gain a great deal from the philosophy behind it.

The benefits of yoga far surpass a simple physical fitness routine. The mind and body are linked, and it could be said that if the body is out of alignment, the mind cannot be in control.

Stretching, purifying, and healing the body bring balance and harmony to the mind, thus creating health, happiness, and fulfillment. It is important to learn to let go of the negative conditioning of the past, in order to become more conscious of how the emotional content of the thoughts you have today will determine your future reality.

Bringing the body, mind, and spirit into balance and harmony is the ultimate aim of yoga.

So what begins as a simple quest for a fitness program can lead to a greater understanding of "where I am coming from," and a much healthier lifestyle.

The true meaning of self-realization may take years to achieve, but yoga will shape your present, and create a positive future along the way—it's a fascinating journey.

As we spiral off into the "New Age of Aquarius," the energy around us is beginning to vibrate at a higher frequency. Time is speeding up and we need to find a way to calm down, and slow down.

There is unrest and turmoil in all parts of our planet, and there has never been a more urgent need for us to restore the balance of nature and heal ourselves.

Yoga has been practiced in India for thousands of years, and the stunning natural beauty of Kerala, above, makes it a fitting setting for this life-enhancing practice.

On a more "down-to-earth" level, yoga is an easy, undemanding, and enjoyable way of becoming healthier and stronger.

Yoga is generally thought of in the West as a means of gaining a sense of physical and mental well-being. In addition, it can have a beneficial effect on a variety of medical conditions, such as high blood pressure.

By allocating time every day to a sequence of yoga postures, you can help to purge the mind and body, and achieve a state of deep relaxation. This can result in greater self-esteem, because you will have a sense of achievement and an inner calm that will help to dispel the worries of the day.

The deep breathing and physical exercise required for yoga will help you to deal with a raft of complaints, such as pain of the joints and muscles, anxiety, stress, postural problems, and bowel tone and function problems.

All that is needed is a willingness to commit yourself to positive change, and to allow the many powerful benefits to start working through you.

When you start out on a program of yoga you will discover a range of benefits:

- more balanced emotions
- a greater level of fitness
- clearer thoughts
- improved inner calm
- a positive, healthy outlook on life.

PART I: BACKGROUND

Why yoga?

If you want to relax and become balanced, centered, and calm, yoga will lead you there. If you want to achieve peace of mind and discover your hidden potential, yoga is the answer. Yoga will also help improve your physical health, tone your muscles and internal organs, relieve inner tension, reduce weight, and strengthen your bones.

Yoga is for everyone

Forget about your fitness level. Forget about your age. Let go of your preconceived notions of what yoga is about. Yoga is for everyone. Yoga is a non-competitive, personal, and enjoyable activity that can produce truly amazing results. You start at the beginning and you continue at your own pace. Whether you are a total beginner or an advanced practitioner, the benefits of yoga are many. With commitment, time, and effort, yoga can change you as much or as little as you desire.

Practicing in a class can aid your motivation but it is important to respect your own body and work at your own pace rather than compare yourself to other students.

Yoga as art, science, and philosophy of life

The origins of yoga are shrouded in the mists of time. It is believed that the ancient wisdom known as "the supreme science of life" was revealed to the great sages of ancient India three to four thousand years ago. This vast body of knowledge, when practiced through the system of yoga, can lead to greater health, mental control, and, ultimately, self-realization.

Society today reflects the belief that disease, struggle, and strife are natural to the human condition. Negative conditioning promotes ignorance, which prevents us from

Oneness of all things

The word "yoga" means "union": union of mind, body and spirit—the union between us and the intelligent cosmic spirit of creation—"The Oneness of all Things."

experiencing our true potential. These negative thoughts get stored in our bodies, causing blockages that disrupt the balance of health. The aging of the body is largely an artificial process caused by stress, poor diet, ingestion of toxins, and exposure to the harmful rays of the sun. By purifying the body and keeping it supple, we can reduce the process of cell deterioration.

Yoga today

In our ever-changing world with its frenetic pace of life, technological advances, and financial pressures, more and more of us are turning toward the principles of yoga. Recent scientific studies have shown that the regular practice of yoga decreases problems with breathing, digestion, and blood pressure, eliminates stress and tension, and helps people suffering with arthritis and arteriosclerosis. The results of a six-month study showed a dramatic increase in lung capacity, the ability to handle stress, and a reduction in body weight, cholesterol, and blood-sugar levels.

Yoga provides a natural counter-balance to the stresses of modern life and can help you to achieve a sense of inner calm.

Harmony and balance with hatha yoga

There are many forms of yoga, but hatha yoga is the one most commonly practiced in the West. Hatha yoga concentrates on the physical body as the way toward self-realization. It teaches us that gaining control over the body is the key to controlling the mind.

Yoga is a magical fitness program that helps balance emotions, sharpen the intellect, and bring peace of mind. The attention to the physical body with the emphasis on the postures is what makes this particular form of yoga so popular in our culture. You do not have to be spiritual to practice yoga. Start with the physical exercises—the postures—and see where they lead you. If you make the choice to practice regularly, not only will your body become more flexible, so will your mind. As we open our minds to the philosophy of yoga, we become open to life's possibilities. We learn to let go of the past and leave the baggage behind. Resistance will then break down so that new energy can flow into the empty spaces. Ultimately, with a little patience, discipline, and practice, you will find yourself changing.

Practicing the physical poses of yoga helps you to open up your body. Slowly, your mind will become more flexible and open too.

Ha (Sun) Tha (Moon)

Hatha yoga emphasizes balancing the opposing forces in the body, such as masculine energy (the sun) and feminine energy (the moon), left and right, inhalation and exhalation, joy and sadness, and so on, thereby restoring the body to its natural equilibrium. Forward bends are followed by backward bends, standing postures by the inversions, contractions by expansions, and movements to the left by movements to the right.

The five principles of yoga

1 Relaxation

Rests your entire system and releases tension in the muscles. Exercise followed by relaxation dislodges blockages in the system and restores the body's normal energy flow. It helps to calm the mind.

2 Exercise—the asanas

The yoga postures (known as asanas) help to stretch and tone all the muscles and strengthen bones and ligaments. Asanas improve circulation and keep the spine, muscles, and joints more flexible. They also help to relieve depression by increasing "feel-good" endorphins in the body.

3 Breath control—pranayama

Breathing techniques, or pranayama, increase the capacity of the lungs, enabling you to breathe more fully. They help to strengthen the internal organs, improve mental control, and deepen your ability to relax.

4 A nourishing diet

A well-balanced, nourishing diet will boost the immune system, insure better health, and help to calm the mind. As a result, your body will become more resistant to illness and disease and you will feel a greater sense of general well-being and health.

5 Positive thinking and meditation

Yoga promotes positive thinking as one of its most important principles. It will train your mind to purify your thoughts so that a more confident you emerges. Meditation will ultimately lead to self-realization—the real purpose of yoga.

Making a commitment to a healthier lifestyle

The word "commitment" implies discipline and finding the time to develop a regular practice. "Yet another routine to fit into an already hectic lifestyle," you may say in despair. The very word "commitment" can be off-putting. But wouldn't it be good to take some time to slow down, take a deep breath, and let out all the tension?

Once you begin to realize the benefits of a system that not only promotes well-being but also reduces the accumulated stress of your working day, the discipline no longer seems such a chore. The mind will soon become accustomed to accepting yoga practice as a part of everyday life—a natural and enjoyable habit. Forget about the problem of finding the time. You will achieve more in each day when your mind is focused, your pulse is normal, your blood pressure is regulated, your muscles are more relaxed, and your breathing patterns are steady. The more often you consciously allow yourself to become centered and balanced, the more empowered and successful you will become. You can't afford not to find the time. All that is then required is peace, quiet, and commitment. It doesn't matter how out of shape or inflexible you may be to begin with, your increased vitality will definitely lighten the schedule of your day. Don't forget—your health and happiness are your responsibility.

Once you start to incorporate yoga into your daily life, it will quickly become an enjoyable and natural habit rather than a chore.

Creating your own plan

Reading is an excellent start to finding out what yoga is about. The deeper your understanding of the yoga philosophy, the more you will be able to focus on how yoga can be of benefit to you. You can apply all you know to your own personalized program. Over time, however, the best way to learn is with a teacher who can give you proper guidance, answer your questions, and help you fine-tune the postures. You could begin by committing yourself to a class once a week, and then perhaps make a plan to practice one or two half-hour sessions at home. The most important objective is to practice regularly. Stick to a plan and soon the benefits will become obvious. Remember that yoga is not about guilt. Some yoga is better than no yoga. No two bodies are alike and no particular technique is suitable for everyone. You may need to experiment for a while with different styles of teaching until you find your own particular path.

Guidelines for practicing yoga

- Ideally the session should take place somewhere quiet and peaceful. To avoid unexpected interruptions, disconnect the telephone, turn off the mobile phone, and remove your watch.
- Work on a non-slip mat that is long enough for your entire body to rest on comfortably.
- Practice barefoot and in light, comfortable clothing.
- Don't practice on a full stomach. You will need to wait for up to four hours after a large meal, and two hours after a snack.
- Remove contact lenses and tie up long hair.
- If it is cold, work in a heated room. As you become more adept you will be able to generate your own body heat.
- Start at the appropriate level and go at your own pace. Yoga is not about competition.
- A yoga session always requires a warm-up period. Your muscles need to become more fluid before you attempt the complex stretches.
- Do not force yourself into the postures. Push yourself just to the "edge" of the discomfort, breathe into the muscles involved, and hold the position for a few breaths. With practice you will ease yourself deeper and deeper into the posture until one day—whoosh—the break-through will occur!

PART 2: YOGA IN ACTION

From the unknown to the known

The Universal Mind choreographs everything that is happening with ultimate intelligence. It permeates every fiber of existence, and everything that is alive is an expression of this intelligence. Our bodies and all we perceive is the transformation of this consciousness from the unknown and invisible into the known and visible.

The process of creation is how Divinity expresses itself. The physical universe is pure consciousness (energy) in motion. When we see that our true nature is universal intelligence expressing itself, we begin to realize the unlimited potential of who and what we are.

What is prana?

Prana is the subtle force that animates all manifestations of creation. We extract this "life current" from the oxygen we breathe and it then circulates throughout our bodies. By practicing yoga, more prana is obtained and stored and one feels greater connection to the "oneness of all things."

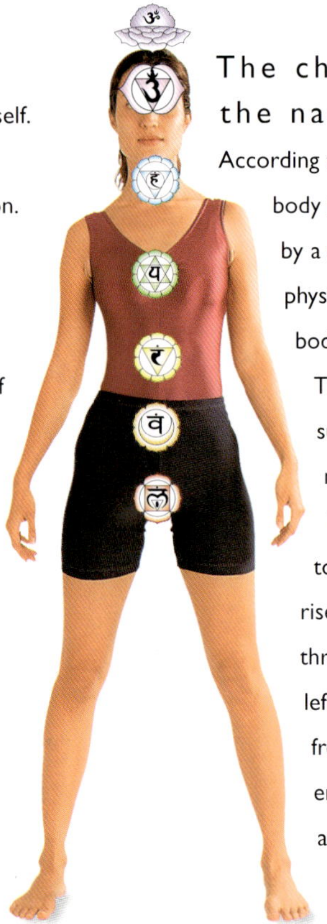

The seven chakras are storehouses for prana, which links the physical and astral bodies.

The chakras and the nadis

According to the yogic sages, our physical body is encircled and interpenetrated by a subtle, astral body. Just as a physical body has nerves, the astral body has its counterparts, the nadis. There are 72,000 nadis—the sushumna, ida, and pingala are most important.

The sushumna nadi corresponds to the spinal column; the ida nadi rises from the base of the spine through the trunk and ends in the left nostril; the pingala nadi rises from the base of the spine and ends in the right nostril. The ida and pingala nadis are said to criss-cross as they rise and the points at which they cross over are where the chakras are located.

The seven chakras of the astral body

There are seven main chakras (wheels of energy) in the astral body and many nadis come together here. Six chakras are found along the sushumna, which follows the spinal column, and the seventh is found at the crown. Chakras store prana; the energy becomes finer as it moves up from the base of the chakras to the crown.

Sahasrara or crown chakra

The crown chakra absorbs the violet ray and is the spiritual center where true wisdom and understanding reside. Opening this chakra through meditation practices can—after much time and effort—lead to the ultimate goals of self-realization and enlightenment.

Ajna or brow chakra

The sixth chakra is located between the eyebrows at the point known as the "third eye." It is associated with the color indigo and it is in this chakra that conscious and unconscious knowledge meet. Opening the third eye and allowing universal energy to flow freely through it will put you in touch with your innate intuitive and psychic powers.

Vishuddha or throat chakra

The fifth chakra, situated at the base of the skull, is linked to the glandular system and to expression. Blocked energy in this area creates difficulties with communication.

Manipura or solar plexus chakra

The third chakra, in the solar plexus area, draws in the yellow ray. It has to do with how we create balance within ourselves. Since it relates to the digestive system, it is an important center for healing and the main store for prana.

Swadhishtana or sexual chakra

This chakra is located just behind the genitals. It absorbs the orange ray and is concerned with our passions and sexuality. When we allow energy to flow freely here, this area of our lives will be positive. However, blocked energy can result in sexual or reproductive problems.

Muladhara or root chakra

At the base of the spine, this chakra draws in the red ray. It is concerned with our ability to survive and adapt and gives us stability. Too much or too little energy here can block us and make us afraid of change.

Yogic breathing

Yogic breathing, or pranayama, revitalizes the entire body, balances the emotions, and promotes clarity of mind. All the breathing exercises described here are performed sitting down, keeping the spine, neck, and head in a straight line. This will facilitate the flow of prana and create the space for the lungs to expand more fully.

Full yogic breathing

1

Sit cross-legged (sitting on a cushion relieves tension in the lower back and knees). Place one hand on the rib cage, the other on the abdomen. Keep your back straight and shoulders relaxed.

2

Make sure that you breathe through your nose with your mouth closed. Inhale slowly, feeling the abdomen expanding first, then the rib cage, and finally feel the air filling the entire chest area.

3

As you exhale, the air will leave the lower lungs first, then the rib cage area, and lastly the chest. Check that you fill your entire lungs with air and that your breathing is slow, rhythmic, and deep.

Breathe for life

According to yogic belief, life expectancy is linked to the frequency of respiration. The tortoise, which is a reptile, breathes very slowly and lives a long life. A small mammal, such as a rat, breathes faster and has a much shorter life. If we can learn to slow down our breathing, yogis believe that we can add years onto our lives.

Ujjayi breathing—*the key to conscious breathing*

The main type of breathing practiced is known as the ujjayi (pronounced ooh-jai-yee) breathing. In Sanskrit, *uj* means "to expand" and *jayi* means "success"—so we practice the ujjayi method of breathing "to expand and flow into our success." It is characterized by a soft, deep, hollow sound coming from the throat.

Ujjayi breathing is not difficult to learn. All you need to do is narrow the vocal chords slightly as you inhale through the nose with the mouth closed. As the breath passes through the restricted epiglottis, the breath will vibrate at the back of the throat. Slowly draw in long breaths. As you exhale, you should hear a throaty sound. The narrowing of the valve in the throat will (once you have got the hang of it) help regulate the intake of oxygen and the throaty sound will bring your attention to the breathing process.

Benefits of ujjayi breathing

Ujjayi breathing cools the mind, soothes the nerves, and strengthens the abdomen. It is a useful tool that can be used in all aspects of your daily life. It helps you to reduce stress, develop mindfulness, and appreciate the beauty of life in all its detail.

Anuloma viloma—*alternate nostril breathing*

The benefit of practicing this exercise is that it strengthens the whole respiratory system and rids the body of toxins that have built up through stress and pollution. Try to practice alternate nostril breathing every day.

1

Sit cross-legged on the floor with your eyes closed.

2

Close the right nostril with the right thumb and, slowly and smoothly, exhale through the left nostril for a count of four.

3

Continuing to keep the right nostril closed, inhale through the left nostril, again slowly and smoothly for a count of four. Stay centered and breathe slowly and deeply.

4

Close your left nostril with the third or ring finger of your right hand. Turn the first two fingers inward to touch the base of the thumb.

5

Continuing to keep both of your nostrils closed, retain your breath in your lungs for as long as you possibly can.

6

Release the right nostril and exhale slowly, with control to a count of four.

7

Inhale through the right nostril, use the thumb to close it, hold for a count of four, then exhale through the left nostril. This completes one round of alternate nostril breathing. Repeat this exercise 10 times.

Kapalabhati

Kapalabhati means "skull shining" and its effects are to clear the mind. The forced exhalation rids the lower lungs of stale air, clearing space for fresh oxygen to cleanse the respiratory system. The movement of the diaphragm tones the stomach, heart, and liver.

1

Sit up straight with your legs either crossed or in the half lotus position (see page 108). If you are naturally flexible, you can try this exercise in the full lotus position (see page 109).

2

Inhale slowly and smoothly, then exhale, contracting your abdominal muscles sharply, raising the diaphragm, and forcing the air out.

3

Inhale and relax the muscles, allowing the lungs to fill with air. Then exhale again sharply.

4

Repeat step 2 about 20 times, slowly and rhythmically.

5

Then, inhale and exhale in the same way but this time hold your breath between the inhalation and exhalation for as long as you can. Again, repeat about 20 times. Exhalation should be short and active; the inhalation is longer and passive. As a guide, inhale to a count of eight, and exhale to a count of one.

Asanas

In yoga, the word asana means "posture." The movements are gentle and take into account the entire being. They form part of a psycho-physical system intended to awaken individuals to the experience of their full potential. Performed regularly, the postures have a profound effect in freeing a person from fear and conditioning.

Asanas are performed slowly and meditatively using deep abdominal breathing. They are designed to make the body strong enough to hold the positions for a sufficient period of time without discomfort. The real work occurs when you are holding the pose. The idea is to keep still while the position is maintained, to breathe consciously into the pose, and to focus your attention on the rhythmic sound of your breathing. Body and mind will then naturally move into stillness and equilibrium. Once you are comfortable in a position, you can take yourself in deeper by stretching just a little further.

It has been said that there are as many yoga postures as there are creatures in the world, but of course it is only practical for us to concentrate on a few. Not only does the practice of yoga require you to mold your body into a particular pose (many of them mimic animals), it also asks you to identify with the qualities of the pose you are

Paying conscious attention to your breathing helps you to stretch fully into a yoga pose.

performing. So for example, when you are performing the Cat posture, you should feel yourself possessing the qualities of a cat as you move into the exercise; try to feel as you imagine a cat would feel; feel the arch of your back and the stretch of your spine.

Benefits of asanas

The various postures of a basic yoga session will stretch, strengthen, and tone every muscle in the body, and there are many other benefits to be gained from the practice of asanas. Some postures will work on a particular organ of the body, while others will help regulate the endocrine system. The twisting, bending, and stretching movements increase flexibility of the muscles and joints as well as massaging the internal organs and glands. They also improve the circulation, insuring that a rich supply of nutrients and oxygen reaches all the cells of the body. The most important work of the yoga asanas, however, is in strengthening and purifying the nervous system, especially the spinal cord and spinal nerves, because these correspond to the channels for prana in the astral body. The increase of pranic energy will help to awaken the spiritual potential.

The loss of vitality and the ill-health we suffer are caused by the running down of the body systems due to neglect, under-stimulation, laziness, and unhealthy lifestyle.

The power of the mind

Before entering into a posture, visualize yourself performing it perfectly. Then, with focus and control, move into the pose.

Regular practice of the asanas will promote a state of mental well-being and physical health. The techniques are designed to maximize vitality and youthfulness, reduce stress, depression, and hypertension, improve concentration, and help balance the emotions.

When you start practicing yoga, it will be the physical experience that will affect you. As you gradually develop and progress, you will begin to experience the sensation of pranic energy as it starts to flow more freely through the channels.

Start at the beginning: breathe slowly and allow yourself to build on the small, gradual changes you will notice as you persevere with your program.

Mudra and mantra magic

Technically, mudras refer to a variety of yoga postures designed to prevent energy escaping from the body. They also refer to certain hand gestures performed during pranayama (see page 80) and meditation. The word "mudra" means "seal."

Yoga mudra

This mudra is excellent for improving the functioning of the liver, spleen, kidneys, pancreas, bladder, and uterus. The yoga mudra also helps to relieve constipation.

Caution

It is very important that you do not attempt this exercise if you are pregnant or suffering from any abdominal problem.

1

Kneel on the floor and sit back on your heels. Place your hands or fingertips on your heels and keep your head and trunk erect but relaxed. Exhale.

2

On an inhalation, raise your hands in front of you to the level of your waist, then fold your fingers over your thumbs to make a fist and place both fists on either side of your navel.

3

Exhale and then, keeping your buttocks on your heels, stretch your spine from your hips by slowly bringing your head toward the floor. Hold, with your forehead on the floor, and breathe for a minute, relaxing the abdomen. Come up and rest on your heels, palms on your thighs.

Attaining wisdom—Jnana mudra

Sit with your hands resting on your knees, palms facing upward. Bring the left index finger to touch the middle of the left thumb, and the right index finger to the middle of the right thumb. This mudra opens one up to the beauty of life and promotes harmony.

Aswini mudra

Practicing this mudra daily strengthens the pelvic muscles that control the bladder and rectum. It is an especially good exercise for women. Start with 30 seconds and build up to five minutes. You can kneel, stand, or sit.

1

Lie on your back with your knees bent. Breathe rhythmically for about 20 seconds. Now contract the sphincter muscles (at the opening of your rectum), hold the tension for a count of five, breathing rhythmically while you do so, and then relax. Repeat six times. Women should simultaneously contract and relax the vaginal muscles.

2

Pull the sphincter and all the pelvic floor muscles inward and upward. Hold the tension for a count of three, breathing rhythmically while you do so, and relax. Practice this exercise for up to half a minute in total.

The Divine Om mudra

Sit with your palms facing upward, hands resting on the knees. Join the tip of the right thumb with the tip of the right index finger and repeat on your left. The two circles created represent the cycle of Divinity.

Mantras

Mantras are sounds that resonate in the body and evoke energy. The chanting of mantras calms the mind, awakens the senses, and stimulates the chakras. Through repetition, mantras can help the mind on its quest toward enlightenment.

Yogic mantras

- The highest mantra of all is "Om." Yogis believe that this is the sound by which the universe was created. It means "all that is"—infinity and eternity.
- The natural sound of the breath—SOHAM (pronounced SO-HAM) is also a mantra. It means "I Am that I Am," signifying that the Divine has no limits.
- OM NAMAH SIVAYA (pronounced OM NA-MAH SHE-VA YA) is a mantra that helps to conquer the ego, which blocks the pathway to self-fulfillment.

Let yourself go—relax

No matter where we live, today's world is stressful. We are bombarded with stimuli, perhaps pressured by money problems, insecure in our jobs, overworked, underpaid, controlled by the system, anxious about the future. You could say we are overloaded as we struggle to keep up with the pace of living in the 21st century.

As a result of all these pressures, we spend most of our time in a state of mental and physical tension. We clench our jaws, frown, hold our breath, and tighten our muscles. The consistent contraction of our muscles drains our energy, causing fatigue. We suffer from bad backs, headaches, poor digestion, heart problems, and a string of stress-related illnesses.

We need to learn to let go, to breathe out and relax. The art of total relaxation is a gift that you can offer yourself.

Relaxation is an essential part of yoga practice. Most people find it difficult to relax because they have never learned how to do it. To relax the body and focus the mind, you need to be either lying down or sitting up with your back and neck properly aligned. This allows the neuroelectrical system and the blood circulation to function efficiently.

Tension causes contraction of the muscles and contraction causes constriction, which leads to energy becoming blocked in the body. Once you consciously start to release the tension—the tightness, the holding on to protect yourself—you will begin to experience yourself expanding both mentally and physically. Relaxation is our natural state of being and the more familiar you become with being relaxed, the more it will spill out into your everyday life. You will start to become more aware of situations and circumstances that cause you to contract and close down and you will no longer wish to be at the mercy of your environment.

Even when lying down, we can hold onto body tension. Make yourself as comfortable as possible—a folded towel under the head helps relieve tension in the neck—then simply allow the ground to support you.

Once your body is relaxed, you need to relax your mind by letting go of all your preoccupations, fears, worries, and anxieties through paying attention to your breath. Slower, deeper breathing will lead you to a calm and centered space. Allow yourself to let go, relax, and enjoy the sensation of surrender.

As the body starts to relax, certain physiological changes will occur—the pulse rate will drop and tension will be released. Relaxation will bring mind and body into balance, reduce fatigue, release and expel toxins, and revitalize the entire system. When you truly start to experience yourself in stillness, you will feel calm and peaceful and you will begin to open up to a new awareness of who you really are. A few minutes of deep relaxation will be more effective in reducing tiredness than a whole night of restless sleep.

A yoga session should always begin with a period of relaxation. The body will also need to rest between postures to recover from the exertions of the exercise and to give the mind space to prepare for the next pose.

Savasana—the Corpse pose

This posture is one of the most important of all the asanas, for only when we truly learn to relax can we allow energy to flow freely through our body. Relaxing can be one of the most difficult poses for us to master. You just lie on the floor and relax. The essence of peace comes from within and the aim of Savasana is to relax the body so completely that the mind is set free and energy can flow freely.

The underlying purpose of yoga is to unite the self with the Absolute, to become conscious of "I AM" in the infinite and eternal "NOW," to achieve enlightenment. The Corpse pose teaches us to relax so completely that our bodies become irrelevant, like a corpse—dead—for it is only when we understand death that we begin to understand life. We need to turn our attention inward because it is from within that the journey toward self-realization begins. Master Savasana and you will have mastered your mind.

1

Make sure that you are warm enough. Lie down comfortably on your back and close your eyes.

2

Turn your legs in and out and then let them flop out to the sides. Your feet should be about 2 ft (60 cm) apart. Thighs, knees, and toes are turned outward. Turn your arms and let them fall out at a 45-degree angle to your body. Palms are upturned.

3

Turn your head gently from side to side and then return it to the center. Make sure that you are lying symmetrically on the floor.

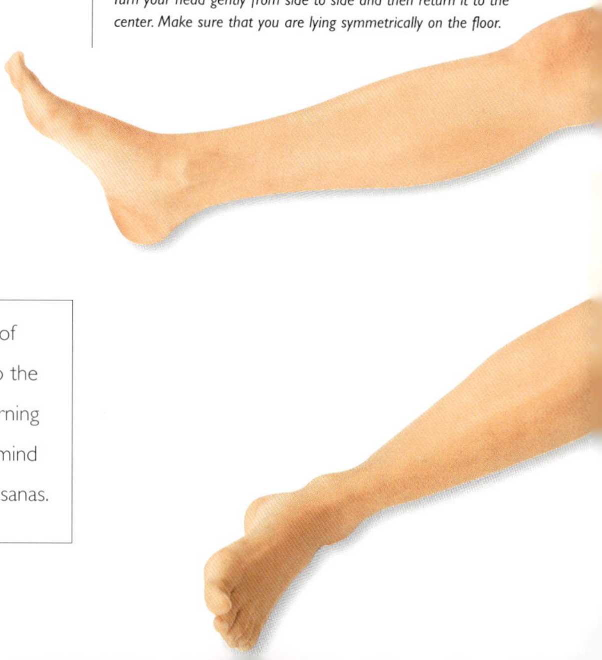

Find the inner quiet

Let yourself go, drop all the anxieties of the day and allow yourself to sink into the peaceful pool of your quiet mind. Learning how to relax both the body and the mind deepens the beneficial effects of the asanas.

4

Relax your feet. Now, take your attention to your calves and feel them relax. Next, relax your thighs, then let your hips relax onto the floor. Work up to your buttocks, relax them, then your lower back, your abdomen, your middle and upper back, and your chest. Relax your shoulders and feel the tension dropping out onto the floor. Then, relax your arms, hands, and neck. Let your eyes relax into their sockets and feel your face muscles and scalp becoming soft and relaxed.

5

Mentally scan over your body for any tension; whenever you find a tense muscle, tighten it first, then relax it. Scan your awareness around and through your body, and be alert to any discomfort. Allow yourself to "melt" into the floor.

6

Breathe into your abdomen and with each exhalation feel the weight of your body sinking deeper into the floor. Focus your attention by listening to the sound of your breath. Enjoy the sensation of the weight of your body being fully supported by the floor beneath you.

7

If your mind starts to wander, gently bring yourself back to stillness by concentrating on the slow rhythm of your breathing. The length of the inhalation, exhalation, and the pause between them should be the same. The pause should follow the exhalation.

8

Relax in the Corpse pose for five minutes, then take a deep breath in and start to stretch—a wonderful, invigorating full-body stretch. Bend your knees, roll over onto your right side, and come up to sitting position.

The final pose

It is important to end every yoga session with about 10 minutes' relaxation in the Corpse pose. Don't forget the essence of yoga is going within to experience yourself.

Warming up

Before beginning any yoga program, it is important to ease yourself into it by warming up the muscles and loosening the joints before moving on to the asanas.

Neck rolls

For this exercise you should sit cross-legged, with your back straight but relaxed. Rotating the neck slowly will help to release blocked energy in the neck, shoulders and upper back. Take care to work through the exercise slowly and gently, and stop if you feel any pain.

1

Hang your head forward so that your chin rests on your chest for a few moments. Then, slowly drop your head back as far as you comfortably can and feel the stretch. Repeat this 5–6 times.

2

Now, take your right ear down to your right shoulder. Hold for a few moments. Bring your head back to the center, then take your left ear down to your left shoulder. Return to the center. Repeat on both sides.

3

Turn your head slowly to look over your right shoulder. Look back as far as possible. Return to the center and then turn your head to look over your left shoulder. Repeat this stretch 5–6 times.

4

Drop your chin to your chest and then slowly rotate your head in a clockwise direction 2–3 times. Bring your head back to the center and then gently rotate it counter-clockwise 2–3 times.

Shoulder rotation

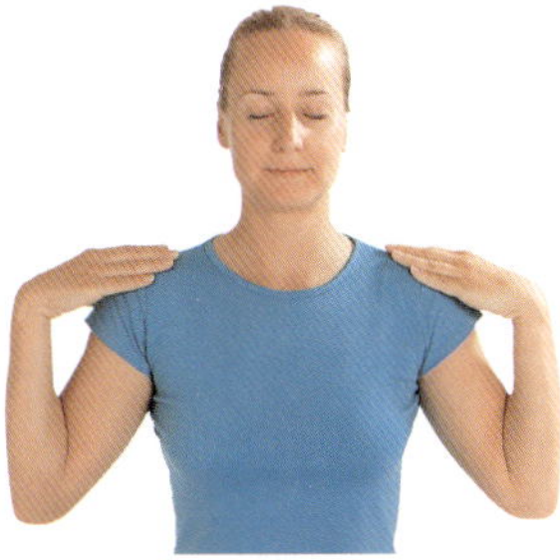

1

Sit cross-legged on the floor. Place both of your hands gently on your shoulders with your elbows pointing downward.

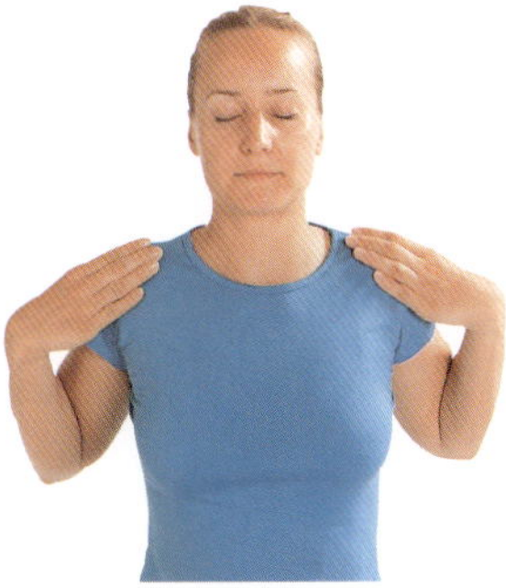

2

Inhale and slowly rotate your arms backward, trying to close up your shoulder blades as you do this. Go only as far as feels comfortable.

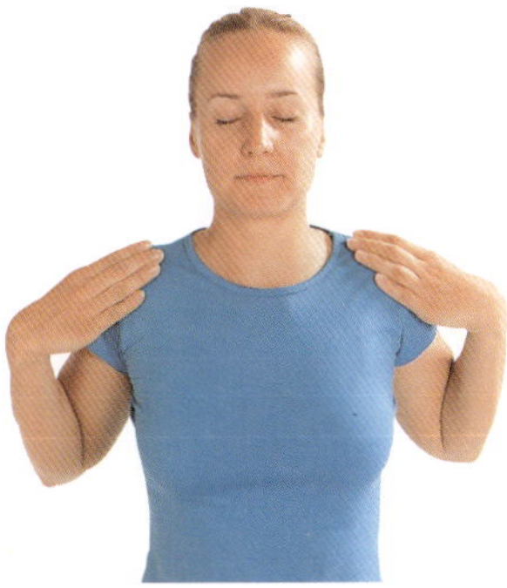

3

Exhale and bring your arms forward, making big rotations with your elbows. Repeat the movement eight times.

Leg stretches

1

Sit on the floor with your legs stretched out in front of you, heels together.

2

Gently bend the right knee and bring your arms forward (without tensing the shoulders). Take hold of your toes with both hands.

3

Straighten the leg and raise it up as far as possible. Bend the leg, relax and repeat. Change legs and repeat twice.

Bilikasana—*the Cat*

For this posture, visualize yourself as a cat arching and stretching its back.

1

Kneel on all fours with your arms shoulder-width apart.

2

Exhale and arch your back up as high as possible. Keep your head between your arms and look toward your navel. Hold this pose for a count of two.

3

Inhale and slowly hollow your back into a concave position. Raise your head and look up. Hold for a count of two. Repeat this sequence 5–10 times. The two movements should flow one into the other.

Uttanasana—*Forward Extension*

This is an excellent posture for releasing the shoulders and stretching the hamstrings.

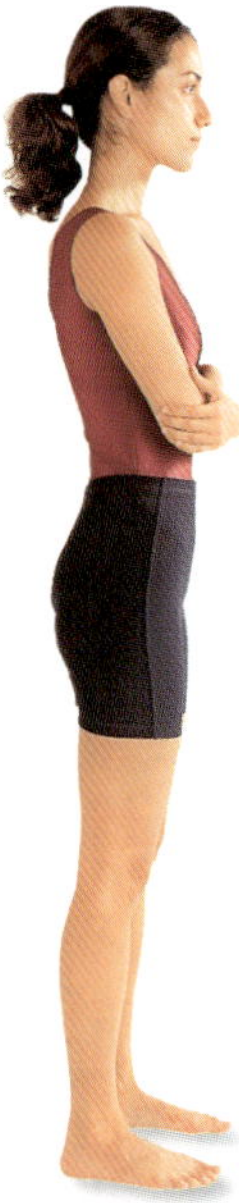

1

Stand with your feet about 1 ft (30 cm) apart. Exhale and catch hold of your elbows so that your right hand is holding your left elbow and vice versa.

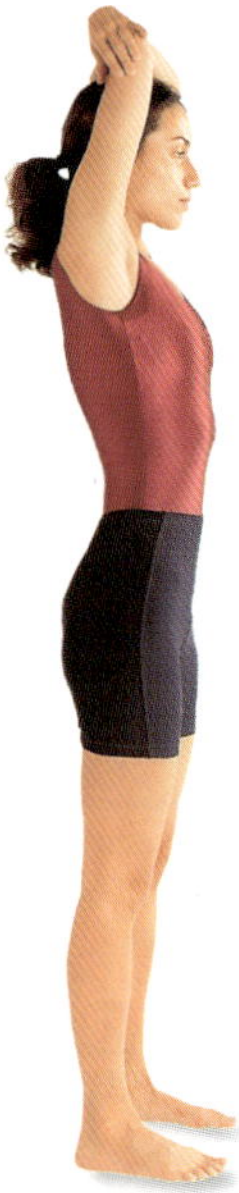

2

Inhale and take your arms up over your head, still holding your elbows. Draw your waist slightly back. Feel a strong stretch up through the back of your legs.

3

Exhale and slowly bend downward bringing your arms as close to your chest as possible. Pull your elbows toward your body and down to bring your trunk as far down as possible. Now bring your hips farther forward to keep your legs vertical.

4

Keep your knees straight (but not locked) and your leg muscles pulled up. Relax your head. Blood will now rush to your head, nourishing your brain with nutrients. Remain in this position for about 30 seconds, remembering to breathe slowly and smoothly.

Tadasana—*Mountain pose*

This is the basic standing posture. It involves bringing the energies of body and mind into stillness and balance.

1

Stand with your feet together, your big toes and heels touching. Your arms should hang loosely by your sides, palms facing inward.

2

Lift your body, extending upward from the base of your spine. Your shoulders should be relaxed with your chest open. Look straight ahead.

3

Pull up your thigh muscles from your knees. Make sure that you are equally balanced and root your feet into the floor.

4

Using the ujjayi method of breathing (see page 81), take a few slow, rhythmic breaths. Remain focused and balanced.

Namaste mudra—*the Prayer position*

Place the palms together with the fingers extending upward as in the prayer position. Now bring your hands to your heart as a gesture of peace and respect, and to honor the light within.

Surya Namaskar—*the Sun Salutations*

This graceful sequence is done as one continuous movement to the rhythm of your breath. It is an excellent warming-up exercise.

1

Stand in Tadasana (Mountain pose—see page 95). Take a few, deep ujjayi breaths (see page 81). Exhale and bring your hands together in Namaste, the prayer position (see page 95).

2

Inhale and stretch your arms up, with your hands open. Bend back from the waist, hips forward.

3

Exhale and bend forward. Place your hands beside your feet. Bend your knees if you need to.

4

Inhale. Take the left leg back, left knee touching the floor. The hands and right leg are in front. Arch your back, lift your chin, and look up.

5

Retain your breath and take the right leg back. Support your weight on your hands and toes. The head, back, and legs make a straight line.

6

As you exhale, lower your knees to the floor. Let your chest, then your forehead touch the floor. Your hands should be flat on the ground.

7

Inhale, lower the hips to floor, and arch the spine back. Look up, tilting the head back. (This is Cobra pose—see pages 48–49).

8

Exhale, roll your weight onto your feet and raise up the hips. Push your heels down and hang your head (Downward-facing Dog pose—see page 100).

9

Inhale, step back with the right leg, right knee on the floor. The left leg is in front, knee bent and foot flat. Look up and back (this mirrors step 4).

10

Exhale and, without moving your hands, move the back leg forward, then bend down from the waist as in step 3.

11

Inhale, straighten, and raise the arms. Stretch back from the waist, as in step 2.

12

Exhale and come back to Tadasana (see step 1).

Benefits of Sun Salutations

- Focus and calm the mind
- Strengthen major organs and muscles
- Stimulate digestion
- Increase flexibility of the spine and joints

The standing postures

The standing postures are about developing strength, power, and balance. They teach us how to stand with presence and self-assurance and how to remain centered in the moment. You will notice that the times you lose balance in these poses will be times when your concentration wavers and you are no longer focused.

Pada Hasthasana—*the Standing Forward Bend*

"You are only as young as your spine." This is an excellent pose for improving posture and promoting youthful vitality.

1

Stand with your legs together, the weight of your body on the balls of your feet. Inhale and stretch your arms above your head. Extend your body from the base of your spine to your fingertips. Pull up the muscles of your thighs from your kneecaps. Your hips should be pointing upward and your knees straight.

2

Exhale and bend forward, catching the backs of your legs with your hands. Keep your body weight centered and your legs straight. Do not drop the hips. Take your forehead toward your legs. You may wish to extend further by taking hold of your big toes with your respective thumbs. Hold for five ujjayi breaths *(see page 81)**, then inhale and straighten up slowly.*

Benefits of Pada Hasthasana

- Invigorates the nervous system
- Stretches muscles at the back of the legs
- Takes nourishing blood to the brain
- Lengthens the spine, improving suppleness and elasticity
- Tones muscles on the back of the body

Trikonasana—*the Triangle Pose*

This posture has many variations that can be learned once you have become more familiar with the basic practice. It involves an intense stretch all along the side of the body, from your feet to the tips of your fingers.

1

Stand in Tadasana (see page 95). Exhale and relax. Your feet should be slightly more than shoulder-width apart.

2

Inhale, and stretch the left arm up alongside the left ear.

Benefits of Trikonasana

- A complete lateral stretch
- Tones spinal nerves and abdominal organs
- Improves digestion; stimulates circulation
- Reduces pain in the lower back

3

Exhale and bend the body from the waist to the right. Slide the right hand down the right leg as far as you can. Breathe and hold for 30 seconds. Keep the legs and arms straight. Press the left leg onto the floor; make both legs strong.

4

Return to the center and repeat on the other side. Work toward holding the posture for 1–2 minutes at a time on each side.

Adho Mukha Shvanasana—*Downward-facing Dog*

It doesn't take much imagination to visualize the way in which a dog stretches its spine when it first stands up after lying down for some time. This posture is one that most people will recognize as a classic yoga pose. The trick is to concentrate on lengthening and stretching out the lower back, rather than rounding the back. Remember to feel yourself as a dog stretching forward. Besides stretching the spine and hamstrings, the Downward-facing Dog pose brings heat to the body and gives the heart a rest.

1

Go down to the floor on your hands and knees.

2

Lift up your tailbone and bring your knees off the floor so that your body forms an upside down "V" shape. Your hands should be shoulder-width apart, fingers open, with your weight evenly distributed on your palms and all 10 fingers. Keep your arms straight.

3

Now take your head between your arms and look to your navel. Point your hips upward. Slowly take your heels to the floor and straighten your legs. Hold the position, taking five ujjayi breaths (see page 81).

4

If you have trouble getting your heels on the floor, try concentrating on the seated forward bends (see pages 102–105) to help loosen the backs of your legs first. Eventually you will master this posture and it will feel very relaxing, but it can seem quite hard work at first.

Parsvottanasana—*Extreme Sideways Stretch*

This is an excellent exercise for toning your abdomen, correcting drooping shoulders and developing flexibility of hips, spine, and wrists.

1

Stand in Tadasana (see page 95). Join the palms behind your back in the Prayer position (Namaste).

2

Inhale. Take the feet 3 ft (1 m) apart. Turn the left in 45 degrees and the right 90 degrees to the right. Turn trunk and hips to right; bend back from the tailbone.

3

Exhale and bend forward over your right leg. Make sure that both of your legs are straight and that the hips are level. Try to get your chin as close to your shin as possible. Hold, taking five ujjayi breaths (see page 81).

4

Inhale and come up. Without releasing the hands turn to the front, line up your feet, and repeat on the other side.

Namaste—*the Prayer Position*

Join the palms behind the back, fingers upward. Move the hands up between the shoulders, palms together and elbows and shoulders down.

Virabhadrasana—*the Warrior pose*

Think of the strength, balance, and nobility of a warrior. Feel the power as your hands stretch up to the sun and your feet root to the earth.

1

Exhale and stand with your feet about 3–4 ft (1–1.2 m) apart. Turn your right foot inward to the left about 45 degrees, and turn the left foot outward about 90 degrees to the right. Bend the left leg and turn your body to the right. The right leg should be straight behind you.

2

Inhale and lift the arms above your head, palms facing inward. Look ahead. Relax the shoulders and face. Keep the arms straight and bring your palms together. Push down on the back foot, keeping the leg strong. Take five ujjayi breaths (see page 15). Push up with your front leg, turn and repeat on the other side.

Focusing inward with forward bends

The forward bends are excellent for helping you focus inward—you bend forward and your heart moves inward. They are great for stretching out and loosening up the muscles in the lower back and for lengthening the hamstrings.

Paschimothanasana—*the Forward Bend*

This is a stretch all the way up the back of the body, from calves to thighs, along the spine, and up to the head. It works to rejuvenate the system.

1

Sit up on the floor with your head, neck and back in a straight line. Your legs should be together flat on the floor, with your toes pointing toward your body.

2

Inhale and stretch both arms above your head. Stretch up from the base of your spine.

3

Exhale and bend forward from your hips to catch hold of your feet, ankles, or shins, whichever feels most comfortable to you. Inhale, and look upward, moving your chin forward and up. Keeping hold of your feet, lift your back up, stretching up through your spine and pushing forward with your abdomen to avoid rounding your back.

Benefits of Paschimothanasana

- Stimulates and tones the digestive system, helping to counteract obesity, relieving constipation, and regulating the pancreatic function
- Strengthens the hamstrings
- Increases the elasticity of the lower back
- Energizes the nervous system
- Greatly improves the ability to concentrate and focus the mind

4

Exhale and bend forward, bringing your chest to meet your legs. Hold the position, taking five ujjayi breaths (see page 81), and then come up slowly.

Janu Shirshasana—*Sitting One Leg pose*

The benefits of this posture are much the same as for the previous one (the Forward Bend). However, this position will also work on opening up the hips.

Tips

- Make sure that you bend forward from the hips and not from the waist. This applies to all the forward-bending poses.
- Be patient with yourself if at first your body feels stiff and unyielding. With regular practice you will gradually start to stretch out and open up.
- Remember, yoga is not about the ego. Forget about being competitive.

1

Bend your right leg and place the foot against the top of the left inner thigh. Your right knee should now be forming an angle of almost 90 degrees to your left leg. Sit on the floor with your left leg straight out in front of you and your toes pointing upward.

2

Inhale and raise your arms above your head. Then exhale and slowly bend forward over your left leg. Catch hold of your ankle. For those of you who are more flexible, grasp your foot with your hands.

3

Inhale and lift up your back from the base of your spine as in the Forward Bend (see step 3 on page 103). Look up.

4

Exhale and bend forward. Again try not to round your back. Take five deep breaths. Repeat the sequence with right leg forward.

Mudhasana—*the Pose of the Child*

This is a wonderful relaxing posture; it makes you feel safe and nurtured, as if you are back in the womb. It stimulates respiration, relieves lower back pain, and releases tension in the shoulders. It is an excellent position for counterposing backward bends and for relaxing the body between postures.

1

Kneel on the floor and sit back on your heels. Your buttocks should touch your heels. Use a pillow between your buttocks and the backs of your legs if it feels more comfortable.

2

Bend forward, taking your forehead to the floor. Your buttocks should still be on your heels. Your hands should be resting beside your body with your palms facing upward.

3

Relax and breathe into your abdomen. Feel the tension dropping out from your shoulders onto the floor.

This simple posture can help you connect to childhood feelings of safety, trust, and a willingness to embrace your experience.

While you are still seated

Too much time spent sitting in chairs means that many people develop poor posture. The following seated poses work to open up the hips and flex the spine and so can help to counteract long-held bad habits. As with all yoga poses, it is important to move into the postures slowly, working to the capacity of your own body and using your breath and focus to help you deepen and lengthen into each pose.

Bhadrasana—*the Butterfly*

While you are doing this exercise, imagine a butterfly gently resting its wings on a lotus leaf. The Butterfly posture opens up the hips, loosens ankles and knees, and provides a stretch for the inner thighs.

1

Sit on the floor with your head up and your back straight yet relaxed. Using your hands, bring the soles of your feet together and, holding onto the toes, draw your heels close to your body.

2

Exhale and gently work your thighs down to the floor. Try not to use your elbows to help you by pushing at this stage. Feel a strong stretch on the inner thighs and hips.

3

Inhale and move the thighs up. As you exhale, move them down again. Repeat about 10 times.

4

Exhale and now you can use your elbows to push your knees and thighs toward the floor. Take your head to meet your toes. Breathe into the position, hold for 10 seconds, then relax.

Maricyasana—*the Spinal Twist*

Align your spine, massage the internal organs, and force out toxins with the Spinal Twist.

Benefits of Maricyasana

- Tones the liver, spleen, and intestines
- Decreases back and hip pain
- Improves the nervous system
- Frees the joints and helps stimulate kundalini energy

1

When you have completed this pose, return to the starting position and twist to the other side, reversing the legs and arm. Sit on the floor with both legs straight in front of you. Bend your right leg and take your right foot outside your left leg.

2

Turn your upper body to the right. Place your left hand near the base of your spine.

3

Bend your left arm and place your left elbow on the outside of your right knee. Keep your shoulders level.

4

Lift your spine and, looking behind you, twist in the direction you are facing. Don't over twist your neck.

Padmasana—
the Lotus pose

The lotus flower has its roots in the mud and stretches up through the water to blossom into a beautiful flower, its petals facing the heavens above. Padmasana represents the flower with its leaves open in the light. The Lotus position opens your chest and stimulates the heart chakra. It is revered as a position for meditation and pranayama (see pages 80–83) because it promotes focus.

Caution

Respect the limitations of your body and do not force yourself into this or any other yoga posture. It can be easy to damage the knees in Lotus, which requires flexible hips. Half Lotus (step 2) and Butterfly pose help to open up the hips and you should master these postures before attempting the full Lotus. It can take people many years to master the advanced position of Lotus.

1

Sit erect on the floor with both legs extended forward.

2

Bend your left leg and place the left foot so that it rests at the top of the right thigh with the heel up.

Seated posture tip

Remember to keep your head, neck, and back in a straight line, to promote good breathing and a free flow of energy.

3

Bend the right leg over the left leg. Place the right foot so that it rests at the top of the left thigh with the heel up.

4

Relax the arms and place the hands on the knees in the Om mudra position (see page 87).

5

Breathe rhythmically, using the ujjayi method (see page 81). Beginners may find this position difficult. If it is uncomfortable for you, try sitting in the Half Lotus, with only one foot on the top of the opposite thigh; the other should just have the heel upturned and as close into the body as possible. Repeat on the other side.

Improving focus with the balancing postures

Good posture and balance are essential to good health. If your body isn't properly aligned, you will be out of balance; energy will become blocked in certain areas, causing physical and emotional problems. It doesn't look too good either! Yoga will teach you how to get in touch with the poise and strength of your "inner warrior."

Vrikshasana—*the Tree*

Practicing this asana can bring you a wonderful feeling of inner peace. The balancing postures promote mental concentration, focus, and physical balance. For this exercise, visualize yourself as a tree that is firmly rooted to the earth with branches growing up toward the sun. Keep your breathing regular and steady so as not to disturb your balance.

1

Stand straight and get yourself balanced on your left foot. Bend the right knee and place the left foot against the opposite thigh with the knee pointing outward. Do not lean forward. The right foot should be flat against the left thigh; the left leg should be straight.

Tip

Focusing on something steady in front of you—such as a fixed point on a wall—can help you to maintain good balance.

2

Focus on a point in front of you. Now bring both palms together at the chest in Namaste, the prayer position (see page 95). Balance and breathe, using the ujjayi method (see page 81).

3

Keeping both palms together, extend the arms above the head and stretch to your fingertips. Hold the position for about 30 seconds, breathing gently. Now go back to step 1 and repeat the exercise with the right leg straight and the left leg bent. You can gradually increase the time that you hold this posture to up to three minutes.

Natarajasasana—
the Cosmic Dancer

The god Shiva as Natarajasasana, the cosmic dancer, destroys and recreates the universe with each step he takes. He destroys the old to make room for the new and symbolizes the flow of energy. This posture develops focus and balance and stretches the upper body.

Tips

- Keep the weight firmly on the left leg.
- Keep the arm straight, alongside the ear.
- Remember to breathe as you hold the pose, keeping your breath steady.

1

Stand with your head and body erect. Bend the left knee and take hold of the ankle behind you with your left hand. Lift the foot up until it is as close to your buttocks as possible. Press down firmly with the right leg and find your point of balance.

2

Inhale and stretch your right arm up straight alongside your right ear. To help maintain balance, focus on a point in front of you.

3

Breathe normally and stretch the left foot away from the buttocks behind you, as far back as you can, still keeping hold of the ankle.

4

Focus on a point on the floor just in front of your body. Keeping the right arm alongside your ear, bring the weight of your body forward until both the chest and the arm are parallel to the floor. Hold the pose for 5–6 breaths and then repeat on the other side.

Squat on Heels and Toes

Although not a classic yoga pose, this exercise helps to improve balance and gives a good stretch to the ankles, heels, and foot arches.

1

Stand tall with your feet level and shoulder-width apart. Stretch your arms out straight in front of you and look ahead.

2

Keeping your back straight, squat down on your toes, allowing your heels to rise up. Hold the position for a count of two.

3

Rock back on your heels, come back onto your ankles and stand up straight. Repeat the movement slowly 5–6 times.

Tips

- Make sure you keep your back straight as you squat down onto your toes.
- Keep your knees together as you bend.
- Hands and arms should be held straight in front of you throughout the exercise.

Opening the heart and strengthening the back

The back-strengthening postures in this section stretch out the front of the body, open the chest area, and strengthen the back of the body. On a subtle level, tightness in the front of the shoulders and the chest indicates a protective psychological mechanism against emotions. The heart chakra is blocked through fear of feeling, and energy is unable to flow through freely. When we begin to stretch out and breathe into the chest area with the backbending postures, we open up the heart. While the forward bends are about conquering ego, the backward bends open us up to confronting our fears.

Bhujangasana—*Cobra pose*

The Cobra pose helps to align the spinal disks, strengthen the back, and open up the heart chakra. It also energizes the nervous system. To perform this exercise, visualize the graceful movement of this powerful and flexible creature. Don't use your arms to support yourself—snakes do not have arms.

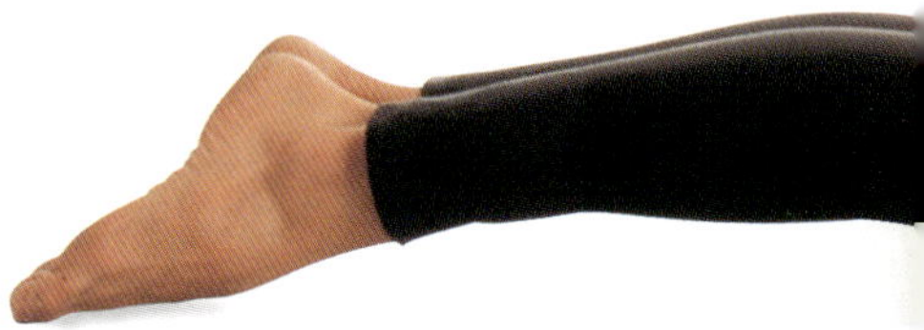

1

Lie on your stomach with your heels and toes together. Place your hands on the floor on either side of your chest, fingers pointing forward with the tips in line with your shoulders. Your forehead should be on the floor.

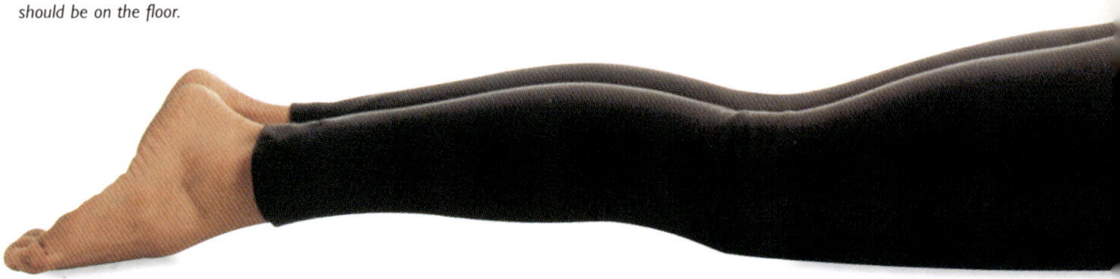

Benefits of Bhujangasana

- Massages and tones all the back muscles
- Expands lungs and chest area
- Helps ease menstrual problems
- Pressure on the abdomen massages all the internal organs
- Increases flexibility of the spine and rejuvenates spinal nerves
- Awakens kundalini energy, the "coiled serpent" that lies at the base of the spine

2

Inhale, lifting your forehead, chin, shoulders, and lastly your chest off the floor. Keep the hips pressed down to the floor. Elbows should be slightly bent and shoulders relaxed. Roll the body up and back. Breathe and hold the position for 10–15 seconds, then relax back to the floor.

Dhanurasana—*the Bow*

For this exercise, imagine your body as an archer's bow about to launch an arrow. This is a high-energy posture that massages the back, tones the stomach, improves concentration, and keeps the spine supple. Regular practice of this asana promotes energy and vitality.

The Bow

It is important to keep your arms and elbows straight in this pose. Your shoulders should be pressed down and back.

1

Lie on your front with your body straight, your arms by your sides and your forehead resting gently on the ground.

2

Bend the knees and bring the feet up. Reach back with the hands to hold the ankles. Inhale and bring your feet as high as you can, keeping them away from your body.

3

Keeping your arms straight, lift your head, chest, and thighs off the ground. Hold your head back and look upward to lift your chest higher. Hold the position and take five deep ujjayi breaths (see page 81).

Salabhasana—*the Locust posture*

This is an exercise that helps in the development of the cardiac muscles while strengthening the lower extremity of the spine. It promotes digestion and also tones the muscles of the bladder.

Tips

- The shoulders and chin should remain in contact with the floor.
- Avoid the tendency to twist the hips.

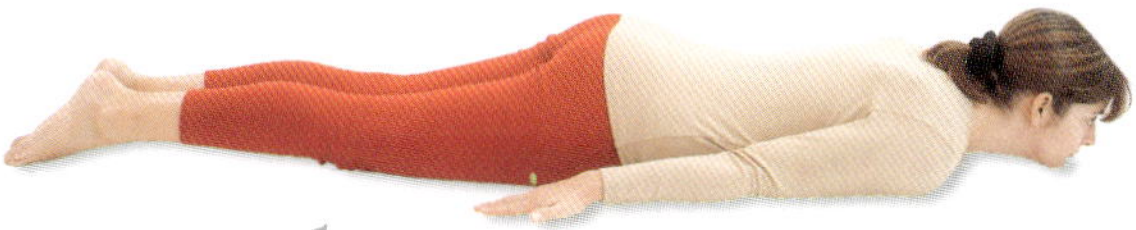

1

Lie on your front, legs straight and close together, with your chin resting on the floor. Your arms should be next to your body.

2

Inhale and raise up your left leg to an angle of 45 degrees. Keep your legs straight, toes pointed. Hold the position for two breaths.

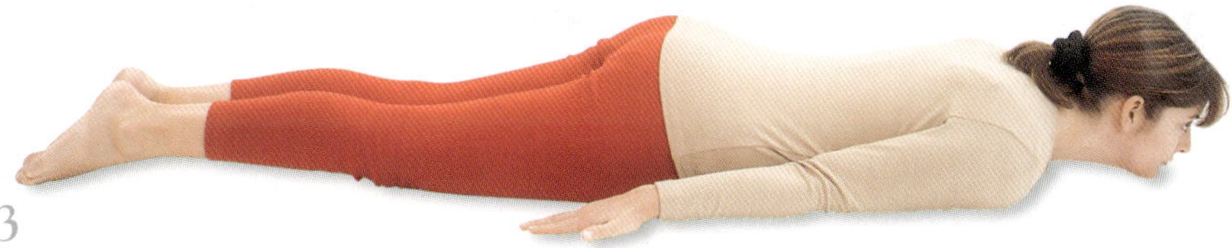

3

Exhale and gently lower your leg. Inhale and repeat on the right leg, again holding the position for two breaths.

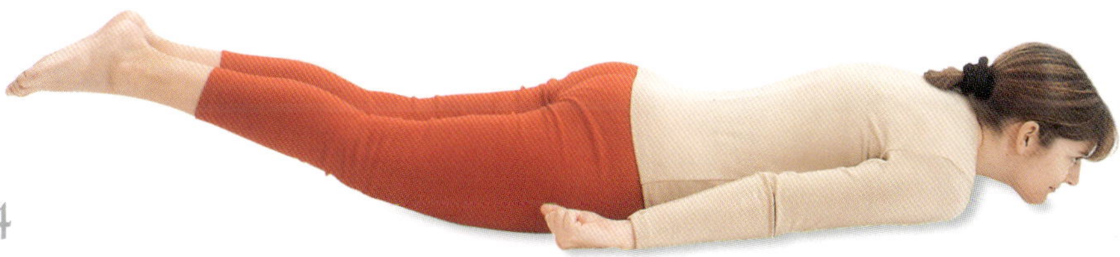

4

Inhale, and this time raise up both legs to an angle of 45 degrees. Again keep your legs straight, together and with toes pointed. Hold the posture for five ujjayi breaths (see page 81). Exhale and lower your legs. Relax.

Ustrasana—*the Camel*

The Camel works on opening up the chest and releasing the shoulders. You should feel a strong stretch to the thighs, abdomen, and the rib muscles. This pose can also help people who are suffering from sciatica—inflammation of the sciatic nerve that runs from the hip down the back of the leg.

1

Kneel on the floor with your feet slightly apart behind you and your back, neck, and head forming a straight line.

2

Stretch your hips and thighs forward and reach your arms back toward your heels. Visualize your thighs pressed up against a wall in front of you. Your spine extends upward as you lean back.

3

As you bend backward, try to catch hold of your heels with your hands. Tilt your head backward and look up.

4

Hold the position for five steady breaths. On an exhalation, come up slowly, preventing your spine from twisting as you do.

Tip

If you find that you can't grasp your heels to begin with, keep your hands on your hips when you lean back. Eventually you will be able to reach your heels, but be patient with yourself. Strength comes with practice.

Matsyasana—*the Fish*

The Fish stretches the spine and at the same time expands and opens the chest. The most important benefit of this posture is the regulation of the four parathyroid glands in the neck. These endocrine glands control the levels of calcium in the blood. Calcium, as we all know, strengthens bones and teeth. It is also important for the contraction of muscles and the clotting of blood.

Benefits of Matsyasana

- Corrects rounded shoulders
- Increases lung capacity and helps with breathing problems
- Relieves stress and regulates moods
- Increases prana in the neck, shoulders, lungs, stomach, and spleen
- Energizes the parathyroid glands and tones the pituitary

1

Lie flat on your back, with your legs together and your knees straight. Place your arms under your thighs with your palms facing downward.

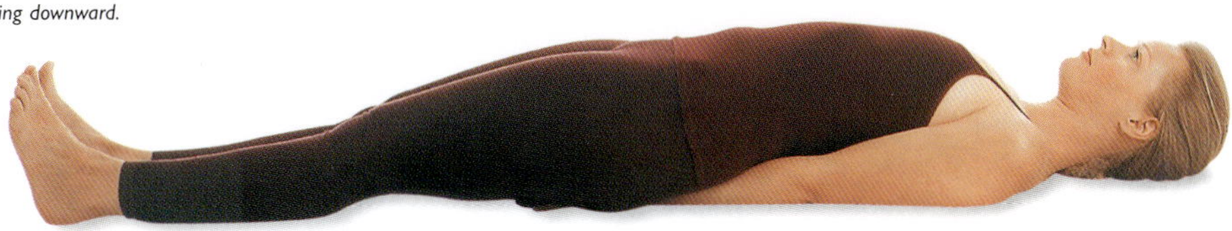

2

Bend your elbows and push them into the floor. Lift your chest upward but make sure that your legs and buttocks remain on the floor.

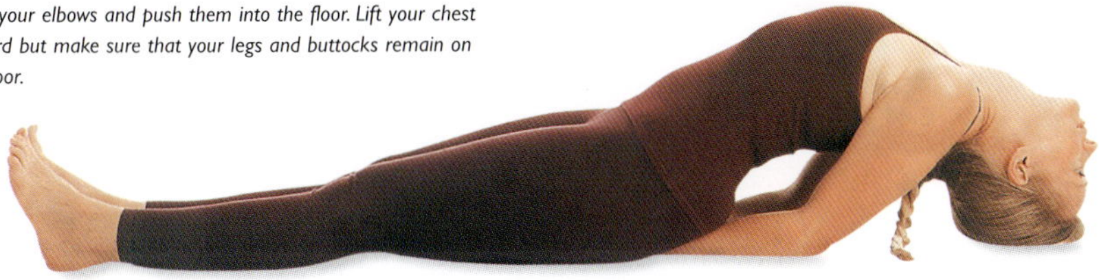

3

Take your head back and rest the top of your head on the floor, with your chest wide open. Keep your weight on your elbows. Breathe into your chest and abdomen. Hold the position for 10–20 seconds. As you gain strength, try holding it for a little longer each time.

Tips

- Check your weight is on your elbows and that they are not sticking out.
- Arch up your chest as high as possible.

The inverted postures

It is important to end a yoga session with inverted postures. They help to quieten the mind in preparation for relaxation and cool down the body. Blood flows more easily to the upper body, heart, and brain, helping to improve the circulation and combat lethargy. Being upside-down also helps to give you a different view of the world.

Sarvangasana—*the Shoulderstand*

This is an inverted posture that will invigorate and rejuvenate the whole of your body. Its most important function, however, is to stimulate the thyroid and parathyroid glands as the chin is pressed into the base of the throat. Since it limits the use of the top of the lungs, it encourages deep abdominal breathing and can promote patience, relaxation, and a feeling of letting go. You can practice the shoulderstand for many minutes.

1

Lie down on the floor with your feet together and your palms down beside your body and flat on the floor. Inhale and push down on your hands, raising your legs straight up above you.

2

Lift your hips and legs up about 45 degrees from the floor, taking care not to move your head.

Benefits of Sarvangasana

- Stretches the spine, helping to keep it strong and supple
- Regulates the thyroid and the parathyroid glands
- Helps venous blood to flow to the heart, thereby relieving varicose veins

3

Exhale and support your back with your hands, keeping your arms as close to your shoulders as possible. Thumbs are around the front of your body, fingers at the back. Lift your legs up.

Caution

Do not perform the Shoulderstand if you:

- suffer from high blood pressure
- have any eye problems
- are very overweight
- are menstruating or pregnant

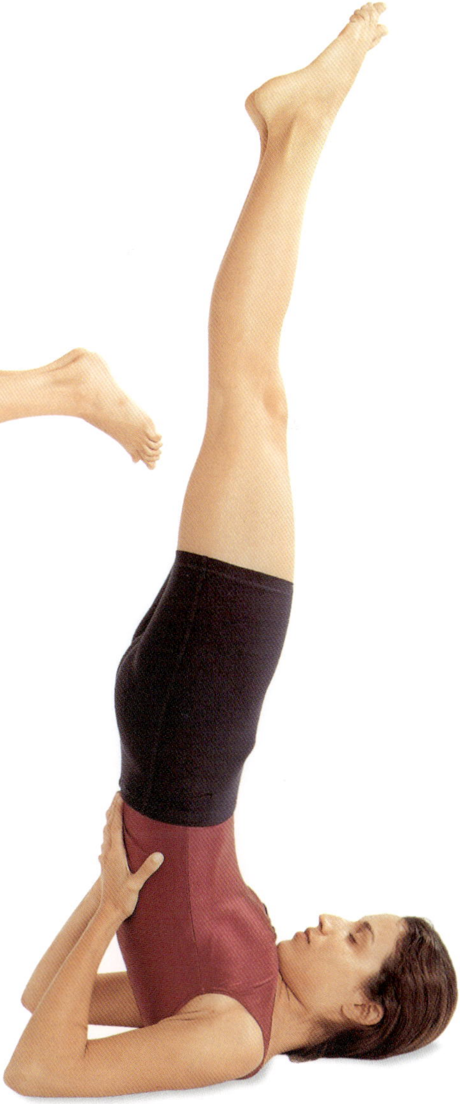

4

Straighten your back and take your legs up to a vertical position. Breathe into the posture, keeping as straight as possible by pulling in your buttocks. Keep your arms close to your body with your hands near your shoulders. Your feet should be relaxed and pointing toward the ceiling. Hold the position for five ujjayi breaths (see page 81).

Halasana—*the Plow*

Beginning from Shoulderstand (see page 120), the Plow is an extreme forward bend promoting strength and flexibility to the back and neck. Breathe rhythmically and make sure you don't twist your head or neck.

Benefits of Halasana

- Strengthens the nervous system
- Improves blood circulation
- Stimulates and massages internal organs
- Releases any tension from the shoulders and upper back region
- Decreases insomnia

1

Start from the Shoulderstand position (see page 120, step 2). Keeping your legs straight and together, exhale and, with control, take them over your head. If your legs remain straight, and you feel no strain on your neck, touch your feet onto the floor behind. Do not move your head.

2

If your feet can reach the floor, place your palms against your back. Push your heels to the floor with your toes tucked in toward your body. Press the toes firmly down, lifting your hips to give a stretch to the hamstrings. Hold the pose for about a minute. As you become stronger, you can hold the position for a longer period.

Setu Bandha Sarvangasana—*the Bridge*

This position counterposes the previous two postures, helping to release any tension that may have built up. The Bridge helps to strengthen the neck and spine and also increases your lung capacity.

1

Lie flat on the floor on your back with your knees bent and shoulder-width apart. Your arms should be alongside your body.

2

Exhale and raise your hips, supporting your lower back with your hands. Your thumbs should be around the front of your body and your fingers at the back. Keep your shoulders, neck, and head on the floor throughout the exercise.

3

Lift your hips and chest as high up as possible and breathe into the chest. You should feel a good stretch on your thighs. Keep your knees parallel with your toes pointing forward. Try to keep your neck, head, and shoulders on the floor, and breathe deeply into the chest rather than the abdomen. Hold the position for five ujjayi breaths (see page 81).

Sirshasana—*the Headstand*

This king/queen of postures stimulates the entire system; it improves circulation, nourishes the spinal column, nervous system and brain, increases memory and focus, and enhances breathing. For the Headstand, you need sufficient strength in your arms, stomach, shoulders, and neck, which can be developed through regular practice of standing postures.

Caution

- Practice the headstand with a wall behind you in case you lose balance. You should not attempt it if you:
- suffer from high blood pressure
- have any eye problems
- are very overweight
- are menstruating or pregnant

1

Begin from the Pose of the Child (see page 105). Sit back. Keep the elbows on the floor and clasp each with the opposite hand. Release the hands and interlink the fingers, making a tripod of elbows and hands.

2

Place the back of your head firmly against your clasped hands. Now straighten your legs, raising your hips upward. Push down on your elbows. Your body should take the form of an inverted "V" shape.

3

Walk the feet toward the elbows and feel your back straighten until the hips are over the head. Bend your knees and lift the feet off the ground, bringing heels to the buttocks. Keep your weight on the elbows, not the head.

4

Slowly start to straighten your knees, taking your feet up to the ceiling. Try to hold this position for 30 seconds, breathing normally. You can gradually increase it to three minutes. Come down by bending your knees, then the hips and with control take the feet down to the floor. Now relax in the Pose of the Child (see page 105).

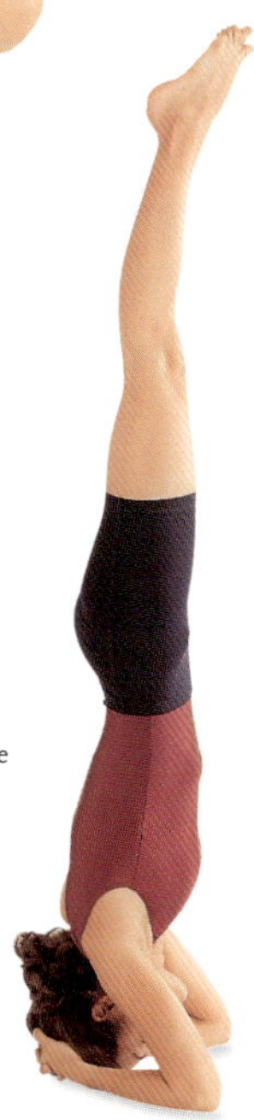

Kakasana—*the Crow*

Like the Tree (see pages 110–111), the Crow is a good exercise for improving physical and mental balance. It's fun to practice but requires focus. It may look advanced, but it is relatively easy to perform once you get your balance.

The posture will develop strength in the upper body, but the trick lies in keeping your balance as you transfer your weight onto your hands. Ensure your hips are raised, your knees resting on the upper arms and your head up. Your feet should be together and relaxed.

Benefits of Kakasana

- Stretches out the arms, wrists, and shoulders, increasing flexibility
- Strengthens the arms, shoulders, wrists, and hands
- Increases breathing capacity
- Develops mental focus and your powers of concentration
- Improves awareness and mental poise
- Promotes inner balance and improves vitality and energy

1

From a squatting position, place your palms firmly on the floor. They should be directly under your shoulders and between your knees. Spread your fingers (like the feet of a crow).

2

Bend your elbows outward, rise up on your toes and rest your knees on your outspread upper arms. Inhale, retain your breath, and gradually transfer your weight forward and onto your outspread hands.

3

Slowly lift your feet, gradually bringing the full weight of your body onto your hands. Breathe steadily and hold the position for as long as possible.

Be mindful with your thoughts

Our thoughts and beliefs serve to create our reality. Because of this, changing our thoughts can change our lives. You could say thinking is a serious responsibility. Giving any thought our attention will help it to grow. A negative thought will grow as much as a positive one and will affect our experience of life accordingly.

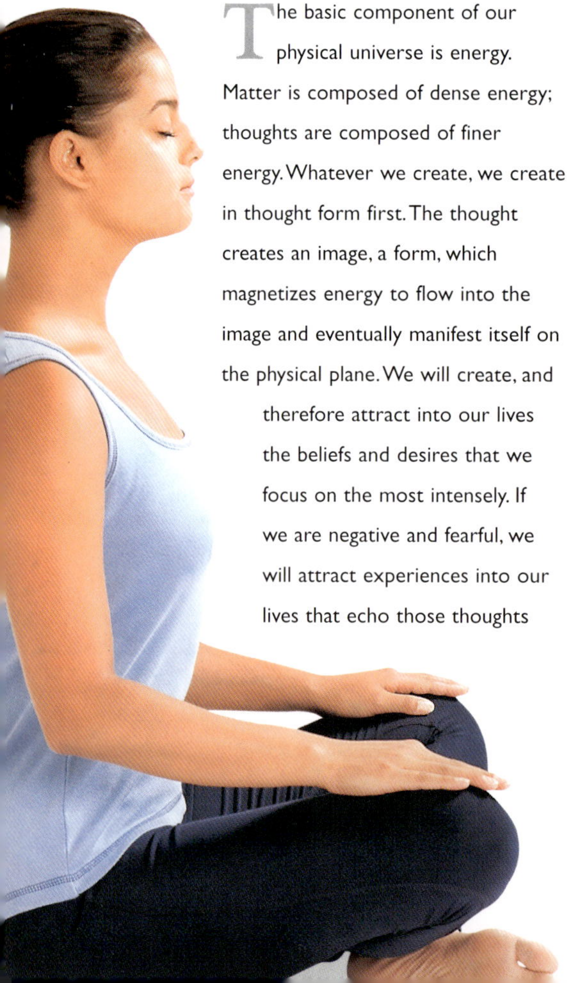

The basic component of our physical universe is energy. Matter is composed of dense energy; thoughts are composed of finer energy. Whatever we create, we create in thought form first. The thought creates an image, a form, which magnetizes energy to flow into the image and eventually manifest itself on the physical plane. We will create, and therefore attract into our lives the beliefs and desires that we focus on the most intensely. If we are negative and fearful, we will attract experiences into our lives that echo those thoughts and feelings. When we are positive in attitude, we attract more pleasure, good health, and happiness into our lives.

The practice of yoga is one that fully embraces positive thinking as one of its most important principles. It helps us to discard old thoughts, beliefs, and attitudes that no longer support us. It connects us to the intelligence and wisdom of our bodies and helps us to use the power of our minds constructively.

Our successes and failures are not caused by "the world out there," but by our inner world. By exploring our inner world and bringing it into consciousness, we can understand the hidden agendas through which we create our reality. We don't have to spend years in psychoanalysis to "find ourselves." We can relax and enjoy the process through yoga, "the ancient science of life."

Yoga gives us an opportunity to hear the wisdom of our body, find the stillness of our mind, and create a happier way of being.

Working creatively with your thoughts

To work creatively with your thoughts, you need to learn to control them. You can do this by learning to still the reactive mind and release it from negative conditioning and old patterns of behavior that no longer serve you. Meditation, mantras, affirmations, breath control, and visualization all serve as tools to help you.

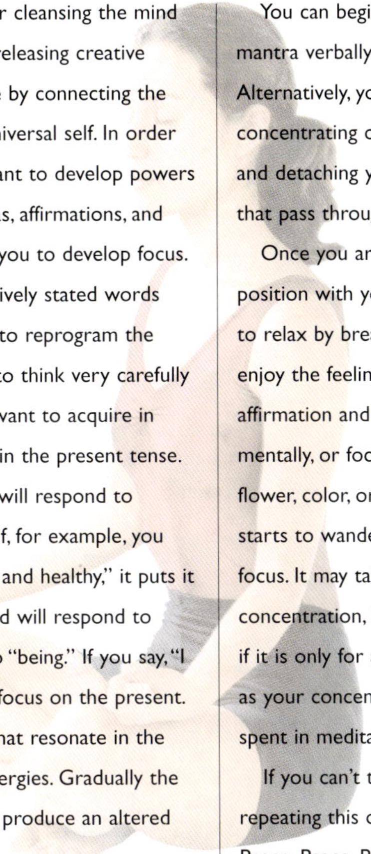

Meditation is the tool for cleansing the mind of limitations and fears, releasing creative energy, and finding peace by connecting the personal self with the universal self. In order to meditate, it is important to develop powers of concentration. Mantras, affirmations, and breath control will help you to develop focus.

Affirmations are positively stated words repeated over and over to reprogram the subconscious. You need to think very carefully about the qualities you want to acquire in yourself and state them in the present tense. The subconscious mind will respond to exactly what you tell it. If, for example, you say: "I am going to be fit and healthy," it puts it in the future, so the mind will respond to "going to be" and not to "being." If you say, "I am fit and healthy," you focus on the present.

Mantras are sounds that resonate in the body evoking certain energies. Gradually the chanting of mantras will produce an altered state of consciousness.

You can begin by constantly repeating the mantra verbally and later mentally. Alternatively, you can meditate by concentrating on the sound of your breath and detaching your mind from the thoughts that pass through.

Once you are sitting in a comfortable position with your back straight, you can begin to relax by breathing rhythmically. Let go and enjoy the feeling. Now choose a mantra or affirmation and repeat it again and again mentally, or focus on an image. It can be a flower, color, or any image. When your mind starts to wander, guide it back to the object of focus. It may take quite a while to develop concentration, but continue the practice even if it is only for a few minutes a day. Gradually, as your concentration improves, your time spent in meditation will lengthen.

If you can't think of a suitable mantra, try repeating this one: Om Shanti Shanti Shanti—Peace, Peace, Peace. Enjoy your journey!

Glossary

Adho Mukha Shvanasana
Downward-facing Dog; a forward bend.

Ajna chakra
The sixth chakra, located at the "third eye," the point between the eyebrows.

Anahata chakra
The fourth chakra, located at the heart center.

Anuloma Viloma
Alternate nostril breathing.

Asana
Physical yogic exercise. Asana is a Sanskrit word that translates as "posture."

Astral body
The subtle body containing the prana, emotions, and the mind.

Aswini mudra
A lock that strengthens the pelvic muscles.

Bhadrasana
The Butterfly pose.

Bhujangasana
The Cobra; a backbend.

Bilikasana
The Cat pose.

Chakras
Energy centers in the ethereal astral body.

Dhanurasana
The Bow; a backbend.

Gunas
These are the three qualities of nature: Sattva, Rajas, and Tamas. Everything in the universe is made up of gunas, in different proportions.

Halasana
The Sanskrit name for the Plow, an inverted posture.

Hatha yoga
The path of yoga that deals primarily with the physical body as the path to enlightenment.

Ida
One of the three main meridians in the astral body through which prana, or energy, passes. Located to the left of the sushumna.

Janu Shirshanasana
Sitting One Leg; a forward bend posture.

Kakasana
The Sanskrit name for the Crow; a balancing posture.

Kapalabhati
A cleansing exercise to clear the lungs, sinuses, and respiratory tract.

Kundalini
The cosmic energy that resides in the base chakra.

Manipura chakra
The third chakra, corresponding to the solar plexus and the main storehouse for prana.

Mantra
A magical word or phrase repeated either verbally or mentally. It is used to focus the mind during meditation.

Maricyasana
The Half Spinal Twist; a twisting position.

Matsyasana
The Fish pose; a back-bending exercise.

Mudhasana
The Pose of the Child; a forward bend.

Mudra
A hand position or yoga "seal" that channels prana.

Muladhara chakra
The lowest chakra, located at the base of the spine.

Nadis
The subtle channels in the astral body through which prana can flow.

Namaste mudra
A mudra in which the hands are placed together in the prayer position.

OM
Pronounced A-OO-M—the sacred symbol of God as the absolute; a mudra used during meditation—the sound of the universe's vibration.

Padmasana
The Lotus pose; a meditative posture which is said to resemble the lotus flower.

Parsvottasana
The Side Angle stretch; a standing posture.

Pingala
Located on the right of the sushumna and one of the three most important nadis for channeling prana in the astral body.

Prana
The life force that flows through the nadis of the astral body.

Pranayama
Breathing exercises for purifying and strengthening the mind and body.

Rajas
One of the three gunas, raja has the qualities of overactivity and passion.

Sahasrara chakra
The seventh and highest chakra; it is located at the crown of the head.

Sanskrit
The most ancient literary language of India, said to be the language of the gods.

Sarvangasana
The Shoulderstand; an inverted posture.

Sattva
One of the three gunas, sattva has the qualities of purity and lightness.

Savasana
The Corpse pose; a relaxation posture.

Setu Bandha Sarvangasana
The Bridge pose; a back-bending posture.

Shakti
The primordial cosmic energy seen in the personification of the Great Goddess, or kundalini.

Siva
Hindu god and the divine inspiration of yoga.

Surya Namaskar
The Sun Salutations.

Sushumna
A channel in the astral body corresponding to the spine and through which kundalini energy can travel.

Swadhishtana chakra
The second chakra; situated in the genital region.

Tadasana
The Mountain pose; a standing posture.

Tamas
A guna with the qualities of inertia, lethargy, and laziness.

Trikonasana
The Sanskrit name for the Triangle; a standing posture.

Ujjayi
A breathing technique that produces a throaty sound.

Uttanasana
Standing Head to Knee; a forward bend.

Virabhadrasana
The Warrior; a standing pose.

Vishuddha chakra
The fifth energy center in the astral body; it is located at the base of the throat.

Yoga mudra
A forward bend.

Yogi
A male who practices yoga.

Yogini
A female who practices yoga.

meditation

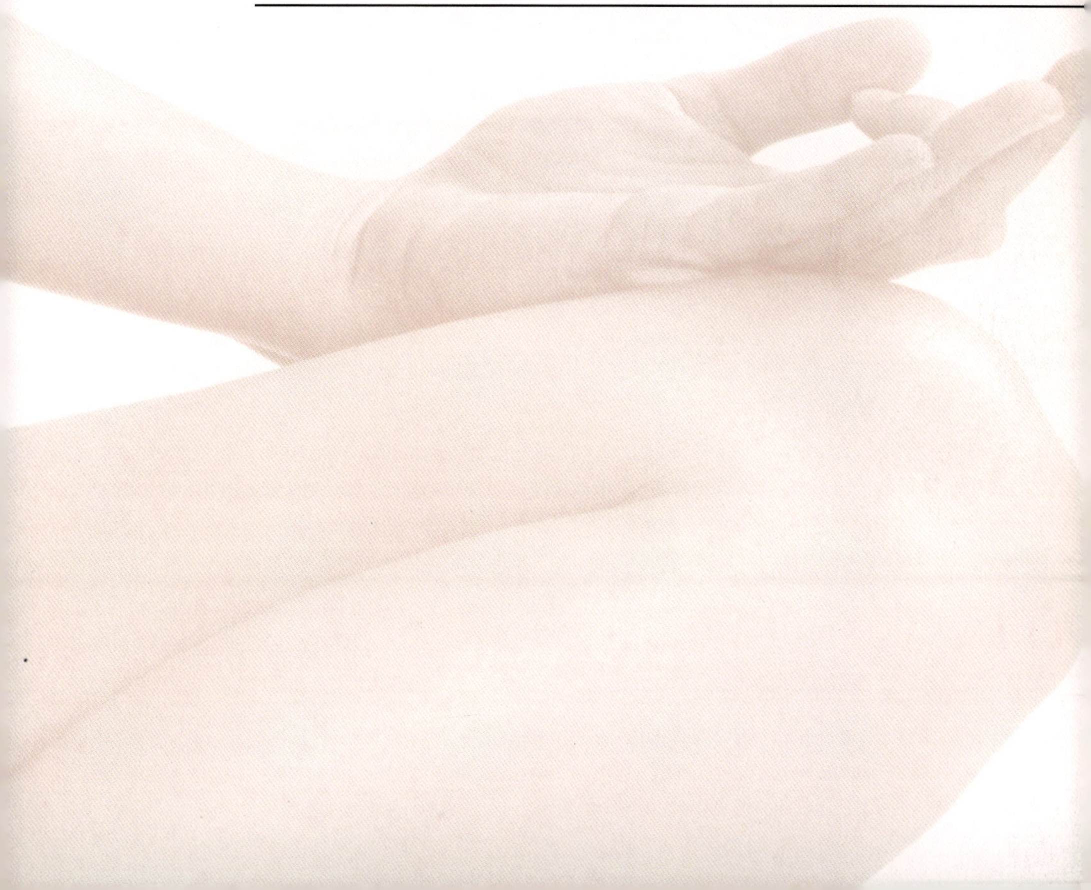

Introduction

People have used meditation for thousands of years in their quest for inner harmony. All the major religions, including Buddhism, Islam, Hinduism, and Christianity, use it in their teachings to help attain spiritual enlightenment. Meditation improves concentration, increases self-awareness, and enables us to combat stress by helping us to relax and cope. It even helps us to get on better with others. Many people who meditate improve their physical and mental well-being, and some have been able to conquer depression or addictions to drugs, caffeine, or alcohol.

The Buddha reached enlightenment through meditation and devoted the rest of his life to teaching others what he had learned.

Mind control

There is no doubt that the mind's ability to analyze, discriminate, plan, and communicate has helped us reach where we are today. Yet it can be a double-edged sword. Although the brain may help us to reason, to think creatively, and to relate to others, if we do not learn to switch it off it can overwhelm us. It can persecute us with fears about failure, our appearance, or the opinions others may have of us. Meditation can bring relief from these anxieties by helping us to silence inner chatter, to recognize and dismiss negative thoughts, and to create a feeling of peace and serenity.

"All you need is deep within you waiting to unfold and reveal itself. All you have to do is be still and take time to seek for what is within, and you will surely find it."

EILEEN CADDY

Health and work benefits

Clinical studies into the effects of meditation are encouraging: they have shown reductions in migraines, insomnia, irritable bowel syndrome, premenstrual syndrome, anxiety, and panic attacks, as well as lower levels of stress hormones, lower blood pressure, and improved circulation. They have also shown that meditation can help control pulse and respiratory rates, and increase job satisfaction and work performance. As a result, doctors are now beginning to recognize the therapeutic benefits of meditation and some are already recommending meditation exercises and relaxation techniques to their patients to help treat stress-related ailments.

Meditation is for everyone, whatever their lifestyle.

Meditation for everyone

Nowadays, meditation is no longer the preserve of mystics, yogis, and philosophers. Its value has been recognized by many well-known individuals and groups, including celebrities such as The Beatles, Tina Turner, and Richard Gere. You don't have to be religious or have huge amounts of time to meditate—you can do it no matter how old or busy you are. So, if you want to learn how to beat stress, understand more about yourself, or increase your sense of well-being, this section is for you.

We owe our advances to the power of the mind, but we need to learn how to control it.

PART I: THE BASICS

What is meditation?

Meditation is much more than simply relaxation: during relaxation the mind wanders uncontrollably, whereas during meditation the mind stays alert and focused. By using meditation to restrain the wanderings of the mind, we can bring ourselves back to full awareness and experience things as they really are.

Practicing meditation

Meditation is a time-honored method of controlling the mind and there are many different ways to do it. In fact, there are literally thousands of different meditation exercises. Many of them have one thing in common—they start with a period of relaxation, then the mind is given one point of focus and concentrates on this and nothing else. Every time the mind tries to stray onto something else, it is gently but firmly brought back to the point of focus.

Many people find this difficult to do at first, especially if they have been used to letting their minds wander without restraint, but most people can get over this with a little practice. Even if you can only manage a couple of minutes at a time, you will soon see results if you do it regularly. It doesn't need to be hard work: meditation should be enjoyable, and if you allow yourself, say, at least five minutes a day at first, you will soon find that you look forward to these periods and enjoy them as special times for yourself.

There are many different ways to meditate. Some call for exercises that focus on a particular object, such as a leaf or a sound.

There are all kinds of ways you can meditate and even a few minutes can make a difference to the way you feel.

Some use chanting, or withdrawal or expansion of the senses in some way. Others involve contemplation on a concept such as love, anger, or growing old. You can also mix different methods and approaches. For example, you may start off by focusing on your breath, and then move on to contemplate the nature of friendship.

Restoring balance

Meditation helps us to restore balance between the left and right sides of the brain. The left side of the brain deals with thinking, speaking, and writing. When we are awake and in a busy, thinking state of mind, the brain emits faster electrical patterns called "beta" waves. In this state we are able to rationalize and think about the past and future.

The right side of the brain deals with intuition, imagination, and feeling. When we are sensing something—such as listening to music—and we are in a receptive rather than an active state, the brain emits slower electrical patterns called "alpha" waves. In the alpha state we are more passive and open to our feelings. The alpha state is most likely to happen when we live in the present rather than in the future or the past. It often happens just before or after sleep (but not during sleep—when we are sleeping the brain emits other waves, called theta and delta).

When we are awake we are usually in beta most of the time, and spend only about an hour in the alpha state. Meditation helps to restore the balance by increasing our time spent in alpha: it helps us to recover feeling and to experience the world directly, in the present, before the sensations become "interpreted" by the left side of the brain.

Alpha	**Beta**
Receptive	Active
Intuition	Thought
Present	Past/future
Relaxed	Tense
Being	Doing
Listening	Talking
Imagination	Calculation

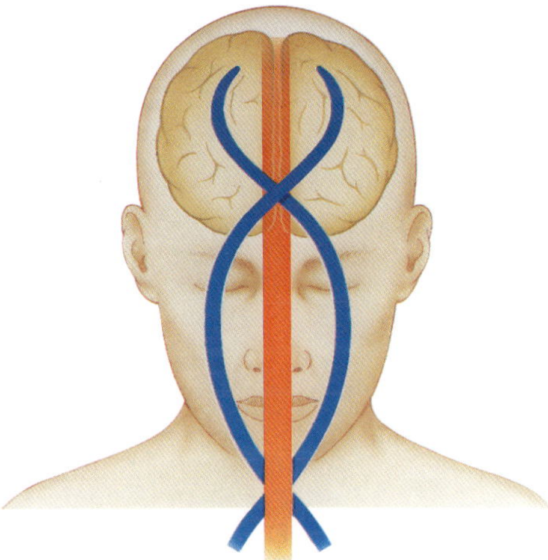

Meditation can create better balance between the thinking and emotional sides of the brain.

Finding time to meditate

If you lead a very busy life, you may be wondering how you are going to fit in enough time for regular meditation. Many of us have work and family commitments, but often all that is needed is a little planning and reorganization to help you incorporate meditation into your daily life. After a while, it will become a habit.

Meditating regularly

When the word "meditation" is mentioned, some people automatically think of ascetic hermits and monks spending days in a trance-like state in isolated caves and temples. Although some very dedicated practitioners of meditation do spend their time like that, for the majority of people there is no need to go to such extremes. You only need to meditate for a few minutes at a time, but in order to make steady and noticeable progress you should try to meditate regularly.

Effective time management

If your life is hectic and full of commitments, you may not find it easy to think about having to fit in something else, but it may help if you look on this one as a commitment to yourself. Your meditation periods are going to be times that you can spend entirely on yourself, which is a very good reason for finding the time to do it. After all, everyone is entitled to spare at least a few minutes each day for themselves.

Managing your time more effectively will have other benefits too. You may find that you are more organized and have fewer pressures and more leisure time. This will help you to be more relaxed and therefore better able to concentrate on your meditation, which in turn will help you to feel calmer, too.

A busy life is no barrier to practicing meditation; all you need is a few minutes.

Writing down a timetable of your week may help you to pinpoint times for meditation.

Saving time

Making time for meditation needn't be difficult. Start by drawing up a timetable for yourself: it doesn't have to be exact, just a timetable of a typical week laid out on a piece of paper. List all the things you normally do on a regular basis, such as going to work (include traveling time), taking the kids to school, or doing the shopping on a Saturday afternoon. Decide roughly what time you go to bed each evening, and block out time for that.

When you have got all the regular events down on paper, make a list of tasks that you should do regularly but may sometimes miss. These could include weeding the garden, for example, or filing your bills and letters. Allocate enough time for these jobs. Since they may vary from week to week, you may want to allow two or three hours at a certain time each week to catch up on these tasks before they get out of hand. After you have done this, take another look at your timetable.

You may be surprised at how much more time there is than you originally thought. Now you have to find out where the rest of the time is being spent. Perhaps you have been spending more time watching TV than you realized, for instance, or doing things for other people that they could quite easily do for themselves. If you find you have plenty of blank spaces in your timetable but can't account for them, you may find it helpful to keep a diary of all your activities for a week, and note carefully how much time you have spent on each one. You may find that the shopping actually takes you twice as long as you thought, or that you forgot to include a regular task in your schedule. A diary will help you to spot these things, and to plug the holes in your timetable.

Allocating yourself enough time for chores can make them seem more pleasurable.

Making priorities and delegating tasks

Now it is time to make a list of all the one-off jobs you have been meaning to do, but haven't found the time for yet, such as painting the front door, calling a relative, or oiling that squeaky hinge. Include everything, no matter how small. Then prioritize them by giving them numbers. For example, you could allot number 1 to the most urgent task, then number 2 to the next most urgent job, and so on. Now go back to your timetable, and allocate a period of time each week to clearing these tasks. Tick them off as you do them, and add any new ones to the list as they arise. Renumber them when necessary.

When you have done this, study your timetable and see what time you have left. Very likely you will have some spare slots for meditation, but if your timetable is still packed, then you should look carefully at what is using up all your time. If it is work, then do another timetable for work and prioritize all your tasks within it. If you still can't fit them all in, then you will have identified a problem: you are overworked! If this is the case, you should take steps to ease the situation: get help and delegate any tasks you don't need to do yourself.

If you are spending too much time doing housework or looking after other people when they are capable of doing things themselves, ask for help here too. Sometimes all that is needed is a simple request to spur people into action. If your requests are ignored, however, you may have to be firm!

Free up some time to spend on yourself.

Learn to delegate and give everyone in the household specific tasks to do.

Other time-savers

Changing a few of your everyday habits can often save a lot of time during the day. Try some of these simple techniques and see how much time you can save:

- Open your mail over the trash, and dispose of unnecessary items immediately.
- Answer letters the day they come in.
- File things away as you deal with them.
- Control the amount of time you spend on the telephone. If someone you know is a chatterbox, try calling at times when you know you can keep the call short, such as just before that person's favorite TV program. Your telephone bill and your timetable will love you for it!
- Limit your time spent watching TV: choose the programs you particularly want to watch, and then switch off the TV when you have finished watching.
- Be vigilant about people offloading jobs onto you. For example, if someone says to you "can you call so and so," explain that you haven't got time and suggest that he or she makes the telephone call instead.

These are just some of the ways by which you can make more time in your life to meditate. There are many, many more. Try some of the suggestions straight away, so that you can start planning in your meditation times and enjoy the benefits that regular practice can bring.

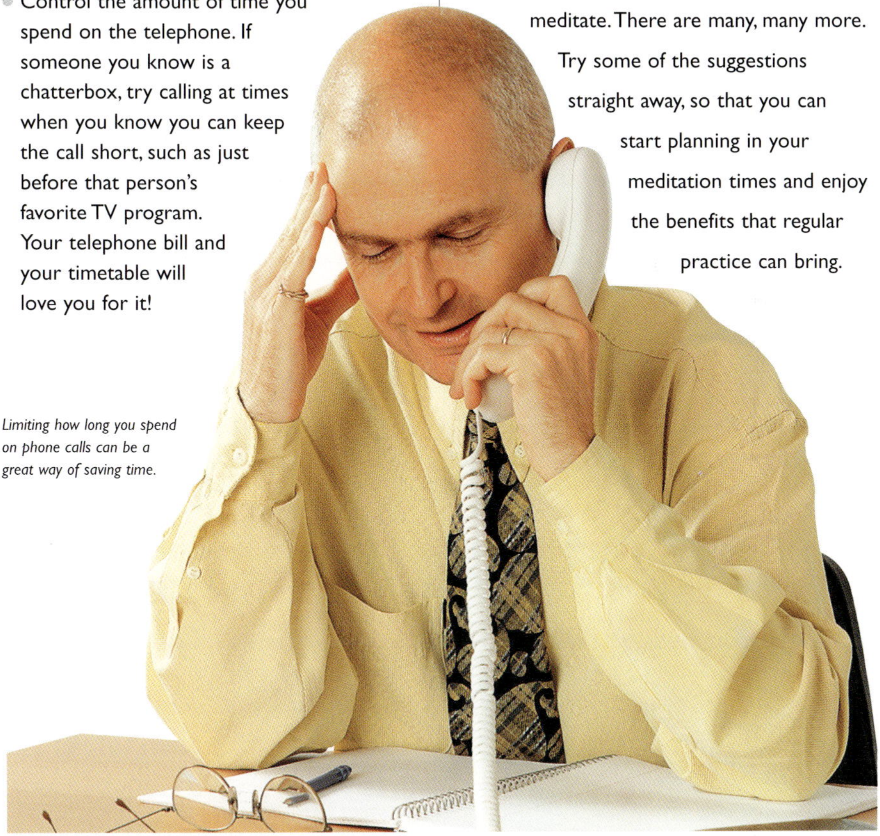

Limiting how long you spend on phone calls can be a great way of saving time.

Preparing to meditate

In an ideal world, we would each have a special place for meditation: a quiet sanctuary where, as soon as we enter it, everyday stresses melt away and we are instantly in the mood for meditation. In reality, however, most of us do not have the luxury of such a place; we may not even be able to choose where we meditate at any given time.

Creating a space for meditation

If you do not have a spare room at home that you can devote to meditation, there may be a corner or a peaceful spot in a quiet room that you can reserve for the purpose. If you keep this spot just for meditation, your brain will associate it with peaceful feelings and instantly put you in the right state of mind whenever you go there. If that's not possible, you can create the right atmosphere by adding a special chair, or by keeping some tranquil sounds on hand, such as classical music. Don't meditate in bed; it is easy to fall asleep.

Learning to improvise

If you do not have a quiet space in your home where you can meditate regularly, don't worry. There are many other places you can try—all it takes is a little improvisation. For example, if the weather is dry, why not go to your local park? Find a bench, or sit with your back to a tree, or sit on the grass in a quiet spot. If it is raining, there may be a gazebo or other small shelter that you can use.

Candles, pictures, and an aromatherapy burner can add to the ambience of your spot.

If you are lucky enough to live near beautiful scenery, you have the ideal meditation area.

The most important thing is to find a quiet spot where you will not be interrupted, even if this turns out to be a quiet nook in a city street. If the weather is bad, try your local library, a church, or even your car.

To create a good atmosphere, try listening to some peaceful music through headphones before you start and after you have finished, for example, or carry something with you, such as a flower or other inspiring object.

Your clothes should be comfortable and loose. Take some extra clothing if you are going to be outside: you feel the cold more if you sit in the same position for any length of time.

Spontaneity

Although it helps to choose a suitable spot and create the right atmosphere before you meditate, there may be times when you suddenly feel like meditating wherever you are, without any preparation at all. For example, you may suddenly feel like meditating on a train or on a bus. This is fine, and as you will see later in this book, as your concentration improves, you will find that you can meditate anywhere, even in the most crowded of situations.

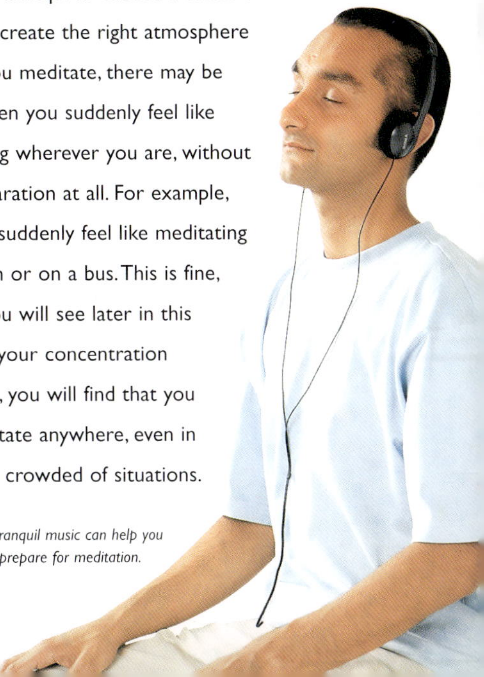

Listening to tranquil music can help you to relax and prepare for meditation.

Posture and breathing

Correct posture and breathing are essential for good meditation practice, but you don't have to torture yourself with difficult yoga stances and complicated breathing sequences. Meditation should be enjoyable. If you make sure you are comfortable, you will be able to meditate, uninterrupted, for any length of time.

Basic postures

There are many different meditation postures to choose from, but you need only concentrate on the ones given here.

Seated posture

You can use a chair, stool, or bench for this posture. Sit up, with your back straight. Hold your head and spine in alignment. Rest your hands comfortably on your knees, or on the arms of the chair. Your thighs should be parallel to the floor. If you are using a chair, make sure you do not lean against the back of it.

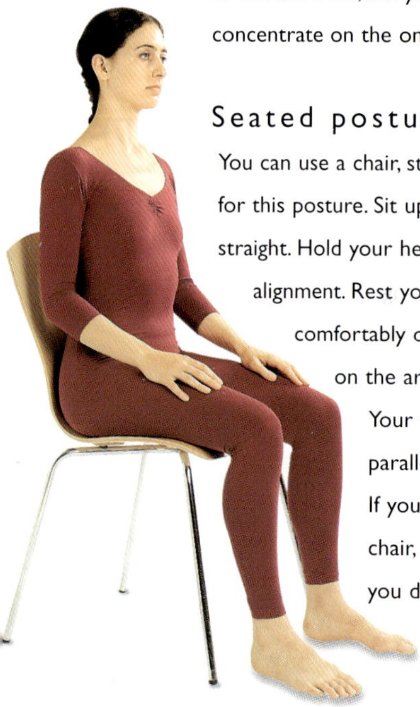

You may prefer to sit on a chair rather than the floor, but make sure you sit up straight.

Cross-legged posture

Sit on the floor and cross your legs. There is no need to raise your feet and rest them on your thighs the way the Indian yogis do—in fact you should avoid it unless you are skilled at yoga. Simply sit on the floor and cross your legs, feet tucked under your legs. Sit upright, back straight and your head and spine in alignment. Rest your hands on your knees. Sit cross-legged on a cushion if you find it more comfortable.

Take a little time to find a comfortable position before starting.

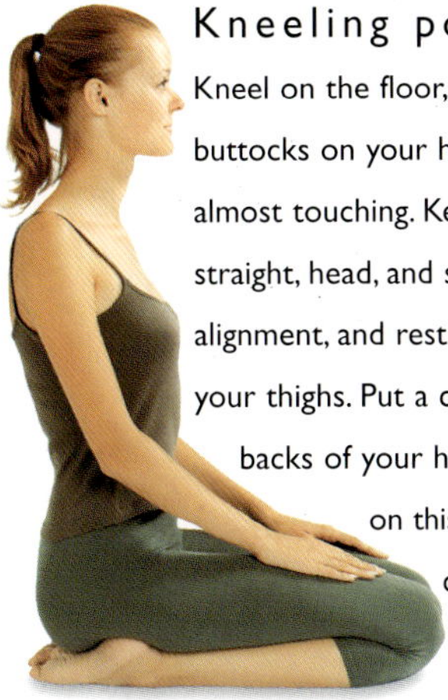

Kneeling posture

Kneel on the floor, knees together, buttocks on your heels, and toes almost touching. Keep your back straight, head, and spine in alignment, and rest your palms on your thighs. Put a cushion on the backs of your heels and rest on this if you find it comfortable.

Kneeling posture

Lying down posture

This is known as Savasana, or the Corpse posture, in yoga. Simply lie down on your back on a carpeted floor or rug. Your legs should be straight but relaxed. Let your arms rest comfortably by your sides. The lying down posture is not ideal for meditation because it is much easier to fall asleep in it. However, it can be useful if you are feeling stressed and need to relax (see page 145), or if you are very tired and need revitalizing.

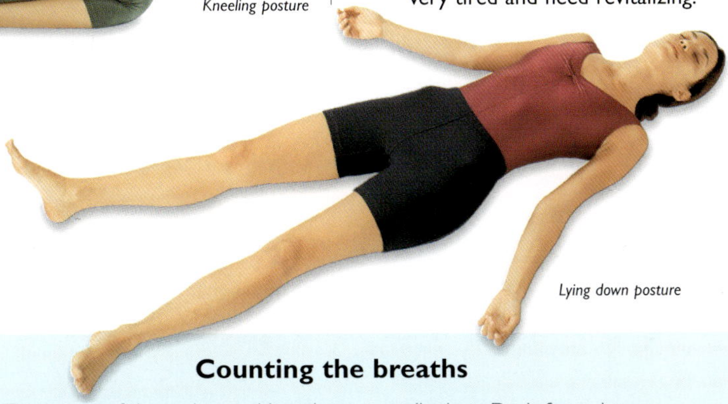

Lying down posture

Counting the breaths

This is one of the easiest and best-known meditations. Do it for as long as feels comfortable. A few minutes may be all you can manage at first, but try to build up to about 20 minutes if you can.

1 *Adopt the seated or cross-legged posture (see opposite). Close your eyes, relax your body, and breathe normally for a few breaths.*

2 *Focus your attention on your breathing. After each exhalation, but before breathing in, count silently as follows: "One" (inhale, exhale), "Two" (inhale, exhale) and so on until you reach "Five," then start again from "One."*

3 *Feel the air going in and out as you breathe. You will soon notice how your mind tries to distract you from counting, with all manner of thoughts. Just bring it gently back each time you realize you have been sidetracked. When you have finished, come back from the meditation slowly and open your eyes.*

Relaxation

Being able to relax is essential for meditation, but many people find it hard to do. Lifestyles today are more stressful than ever, with increasing work, family, and financial pressures taking their toll on our bodies and our peace of mind.

Effects of stress

Some stress is good for us: it motivates us to take action and can even help to save us from danger. Imagine that you are about to be attacked by a tiger, for example. The stress response, or "fight-or-flight" mechanism, will kick in. Adrenaline is pumped into the system, the heart, breathing, and metabolism speed up, and anti-inflammatory agents such as cortisol are released. Systems not immediately essential—such as the digestive and immune systems—close down. If you then run to escape danger, the physical action releases the stress. Your body relaxes and returns to normal.

In normal life, we do not always have an outlet for stress; we can't run out of a difficult meeting, for example. Stress chemicals stay in the body, obstructing the digestive and immune systems and depleting our energy. The long-term effects of this can lead to serious illness.

A meditation or yoga class can help you to learn the skill of total relaxation.

Learning to relax

Relaxation is vital to good health: it helps to combat stress, and gives the body time to replenish its energy. It is also essential to relax before, during, and after meditation to get into and maintain the alpha state (see page 135). Some suggestions to help you relax are:

- Try unwinding in a hot bath
- Listen to some gentle music
- Have a massage
- Join a relaxation group or yoga class

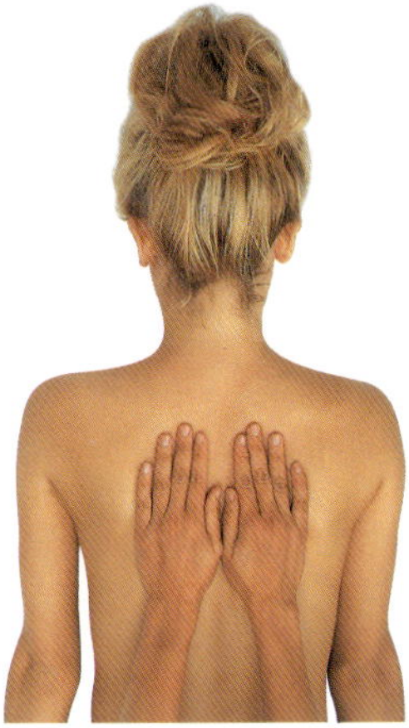

Receiving a massage can be a wonderful way of relaxing tension in your body.

Relaxing the body

You can perform this exercise on its own, or before or after other meditation exercises.

1 *Adopt the lying down posture (see page 143). Close your eyes and breathe naturally. Move your attention to the top of your head, and notice any tension there. Once you have located the tension, relax and let it go. Feel the gentle movement of your breathing.*

2 *Move your attention down to your forehead, and let any tension go from here. Relax your eyebrows and eyelids, ears, nostrils, mouth and jaw, releasing the tension as you go. Keep breathing normally.*

3 *Move your focus to your neck, then down through your shoulders, arms, and hands. Release all the tension in those areas. Then shift your concentration to your chest and heart, stomach, abdomen, buttocks, and genitals, relaxing each area as you go. Finally, move your attention to your legs and feet and remove all the tension here.*

4 *Breathe for a few moments. After a while you may find that tension has started to creep back into some parts of your body. If so, try to feel where the tension is located and consciously let it go again.*

5 *Come back from the meditation slowly and open your eyes. You will feel refreshed.*

PART 2: MEDITATION IN ACTION

Mindfulness

Many of us spend our time "sleepwalking." We perform actions automatically and are unaware of what is happening around us. While we are sitting on a bus, for example, we may be thinking about the past. As a result, precious moments in the present are lost. We may not notice the scenes passing by or who is sitting next to us. Mindfulness helps us to reclaim each moment, to live in the present so that nothing passes us by.

Taking the time to be aware helps you to connect to your experience of the moment.

Cultivating mindfulness

A certain amount of automatic activity isn't necessarily bad: it gives us time to remember things and to plan ahead. However, too much dwelling on the past or the future means that the most valuable time—the present—is lost. Cultivating mindfulness, or learning to become fully aware in the present moment, heightens our sensitivity and enables us to perform tasks more efficiently. It also makes us more observant. For example, a doctor who listens with mindfulness to a patient will be aware of everything that is happening to the patient in the present moment—even the tiniest details—which will help the doctor to be more sensitive to that patient's needs.

Most of us spend our days "lost in thought," our attention anywhere but on our actions.

To develop mindfulness, you need to keep yourself totally in the present, noticing every sensation and every detail of what is going on. If you are writing a letter mindfully, for example, you will notice everything about it: the smell of the fresh sheet of paper before you start writing, the feel of the paper against the skin of your hand, the weight of the pen and how it rests between your fingers, the flow of the ink as the shapes of the letters form, even the speed of the pen's movements, and your thoughts and feelings during the process. Nothing, no matter how small, escapes your attention. You see everything, feel everything, and with a sense of peaceful detachment. You don't try to analyze or judge anything, you just watch and feel.

Living in the present

When you are truly living in the present, everything takes on a new meaning. Colors are brighter and more vivid, objects appear in striking detail, and you can hear every note in a piece of music. Flowers smell heavenly, and every sensation is intense. You can cultivate this awareness by doing the "Mindfulness meditation."

Bringing mindfulness to the simplest action engages your senses.

Mindfulness meditation

This meditation is excellent for cultivating mindfulness. Try to do it whenever you can.

1. *Pull your mind away from wherever it is, and concentrate on what you are doing at that moment. It doesn't matter whether you are standing up, walking, or sitting down. Whatever you are doing—walking home, eating, having a shower—start doing it with all your senses. Smell the fragrance of the air around you, taste every mouthful of food you are eating, feel the sensation of water against your skin as you shower. Ask yourself what you are doing, and what you are experiencing and feeling.*

2. *After a short while, you will probably find your mind trying to distract you. Notice the thoughts that arise, but don't follow them. Let them go, and bring your mind gently back to the present moment. You will gradually find yourself moving into the peaceful alpha state (see page 135). Keep this meditation going for as long as you can.*

Mindfulness meditation helps you to see the beauty in everything from the tiniest flower to the people closest to you.

Affirmations

Affirmations are statements that you can repeat silently or out loud to yourself, over and over, until the constant repetition becomes meaningless and you are aware only of the sound of the affirmation in your head. Although repeating statements in this way may seem pointless at first, try to persevere because they are a powerful tool and can have some very positive effects on your mind and overall well-being.

Affirmations in daily life

In everyday life, people can use affirmations to reprogram their minds into a more positive way of thinking. Say a man has been asked to speak at a wedding. The "chatterer within" takes over and torments him with fears about making a fool of himself. Eventually he is so tense that he can't concentrate at all.

Thinking positively can have a beneficial effect on how you feel about yourself.

The man decides to use the affirmation "I am a good public speaker," and repeats it to himself constantly. He doesn't believe it at first but the constant repetition renders the statement meaningless and its implication doesn't jar. It starts to feel almost natural to say it, and he feels comfortable with it.

Used correctly, affirmations can help you to let go of self-doubt and embrace confidence.

Since the statement is familiar, the left side of the brain no longer needs to analyze it and it passes to the right side of the brain. The right side is not concerned with judgement, only emotion and sensation. It will accept the thought without question and transform it into a positive feeling. Fears of failure will dissipate, and a new self-confidence will emerge.

Any statement can be used as an affirmation: just make sure it gives you a good feeling, is confident in tone, and easy to say. For example:

I am very confident
I forgive myself
My body is beautiful
I am at peace
I am completely relaxed

Try writing your affirmation down, then put it in a place where you will see it often.

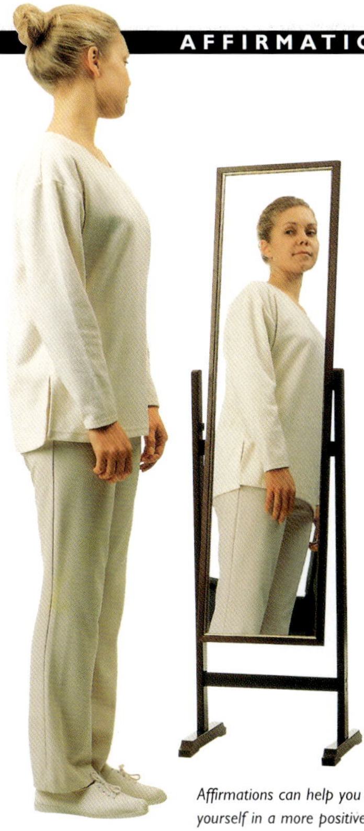

Affirmations can help you to see yourself in a more positive light.

Affirmations in meditation

In meditation, affirmations are often used for a different purpose, namely to stop the endless chatter of the brain. If, when you are meditating, you find it hard to stop your mind from distracting you, repeating a simple affirmation blocks the communication channel so that the mind cannot feed you other thoughts. It works in the same way as counting the breaths (see page 143) in that it enables you to block out distractions by concentrating on something else. Some people find affirmations easier to do than counting the breaths.

During meditation, we usually repeat affirmations while we are focusing on something else, such as sensations. Since the purpose of the affirmation is to block out invading thoughts, the meaning of the affirmation is unimportant, but it does no harm to choose to say something positive so that, after constant repetition, the idea will take root in the subconscious mind. However, remember that the main aim here is to counteract the chattering of the brain, not to feed it ideas that may distract you further.

Regular practice can help to get you used to affirmation work. Once you feel comfortable with it, try experimenting with other simple phrases that are meaningful to you.

Affirmations in action

The best time to repeat an affirmation is when you are relaxed. In this way, you will be better able to counteract the chatter of your mind, and the suggestion behind the affirmation will move from the realm of thought into the realm of feeling more quickly. If you are having trouble relaxing, perform the "Relaxing the body" exercise first (see page 145). The main thing to remember with affirmations is that you should repeat them regularly. Repeat them for as long as feels comfortable, but as a guide, start with repeating them at least three times each session, three times a day.

Other affirmations

Try the "Affirmation exercise" opposite, then try it using any other affirmations of your choice. The most suitable ones will be those that help you to counteract inner chatter; they should be easy to fit into the rhythm of your breathing. Here are some suggestions:

let it go

peace forever

wide awake

joyful and free

Feeling relaxed before you start your affirmations will help you to embrace them more quickly and effectively.

Affirmation exercise

This exercise is very effective for controlling the mind and improving concentration.

It is also a great stress reliever.

1 *Adopt either the seated, kneeling, or lying down posture (see pages 142–143). Make sure you are really relaxed before you start. If necessary, perform the "Relaxing the body" exercise first (see page 145). Let go of any tension, allowing it to fall away from your body.*

2 *Bring your attention to your breathing. Breathe in and out naturally, following the rhythm of your breath rather than trying to control it.*

3 *When you feel ready, repeat the word "RELAX" to yourself, either silently or out loud. Say the first syllable, "RE," as you breathe in, and the second syllable, "LAX" as you breathe out. Don't try to force your breathing into any particular rhythm or pattern. Just keep breathing normally and match the speed of the affirmation to your breathing.*

4 *You may find your mind tries to sway you with other thoughts. Just bring your mind gently back and continue to repeat the word "RELAX" in rhythm with your breathing. Repeat it for as long as feels comfortable.*

5 *When you have finished the exercise, notice how you feel. You will probably be more relaxed, but note any other feelings as well.*

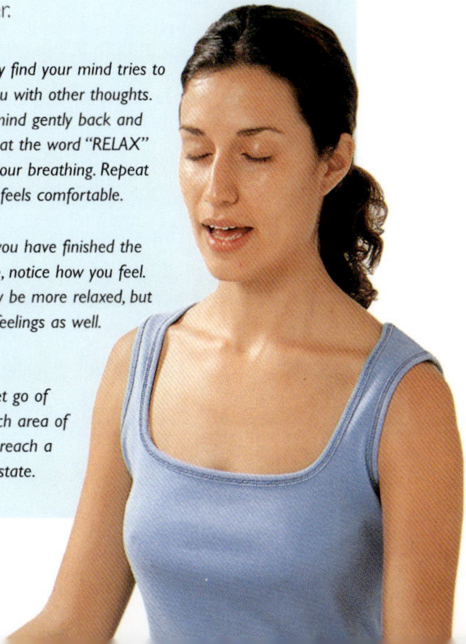

Consciously let go of tension in each area of your body to reach a truly relaxed state.

Mantras

Mantras are similar to affirmations, in that they are statements that you can repeat to yourself. Unlike affirmations, however, the sound qualities of mantras are important, and are said to resonate through the body to bring about a transformation of consciousness. Some people believe that mantras possess magical powers.

Followers of the Buddha use the mantra Om Mani Padme Hum *to evoke compassion.*

Mantras for everyone

There is no doubt that some mantras do have a magical quality about them, and they are often found in spiritual traditions. The Hindus have used mantras for thousands of years and so have Buddhists, Muslims, and Christians.

You don't have to be religious to use mantras, however. You can choose mantras that are not linked to a particular deity. Mantras can be used to induce a state of peace and tranquillity or they can be used to increase awareness, alertness, or creativity.

Well-known mantras

Probably the most famous mantra of all is OM. It is Hindu in origin and is pronounced "A-OO-M" (the "A" is sounded like the "a" in "car"). Hindus believe that OM is the sound vibration that underlies the creation of the universe. It is considered a very powerful mantra and is a good one to choose if you want to identify with the "Oneness of the universe" and all of creation.

OM MANI PADME HUM is another well-known mantra, which is often used by Buddhists to evoke compassion and dispel negative feelings toward oneself or others. This mantra is also said to help keep you alert while you relax. It is pronounced "AOOM-MANI-PADMAY-HOOM."

If you are a Christian, a popular mantra to use is ALLELUIA, pronounced "AH-LAY-LOO-YA." It is also intoned as HALLELUIA, pronounced "HAH-LAY-LOO-YA." It comes from the Hebrew *hallelu* (praise) and *Jah* (Jehovah), and means "praise God."

Mantra exercise

You can use any mantra you like for this exercise, but it helps to choose one that has a particular resonance or special quality of sound. You may only be able to do this exercise for a few minutes at first, but try to build up to at least 20 minutes.

1 *Adopt the cross-legged posture or any other seated posture (see page 142). Close your eyes and breathe naturally.*

2 *Start repeating the mantra that you have chosen. You can repeat it silently or aloud, whichever you wish. If it helps you, try repeating it in time with the natural rhythm of your breathing or your heartbeat.*

3 *Let the rhythm and sound of the mantra take you up and carry you along. If you lose your concentration, bring your mind back gently but firmly, and try repeating the mantra with more emphasis.*

4 *Come out of the meditation slowly and open your eyes.*

The power of mantras

The mantra's sound quality, even when it exists only in thought, will still resonate through the body. You can repeat a mantra in rhythm with your breath or heartbeat, or intone it freely.

At first, it is probably better to use mantras that are known to work well. Later on, you can try creating your own. Just make sure the sound resonates and hums through your body.

Here are some suggestions:

love

peace silence

one doh shhhh

ahhhh oo mmmm

Standing and walking meditation

Meditation can be done anywhere, at any time. You don't even have to be sitting or lying down. You can meditate while standing, walking, or even dancing.

Standing posture

Stand erect with your feet about 18 inches (45 cm) apart. Your feet should be parallel to each other, and your head and spine in alignment. Keep your pelvis straight so that your lower back does not curve inward. Above all, don't strain. Your standing position should be comfortable so that you can maintain the posture without getting tired.

When you stand straight, but relaxed, energy can flow freely through your body.

Golden flower meditation

This meditation is excellent for developing your powers of concentration. It is also revitalizing, and calls on the earth's energy instead of depleting your own.

1. *Adopt the standing posture (see left) and allow any tension to drop away from you. Breathe naturally and smoothly.*

2. *Imagine your spine as a straight stem. Feel it growing upward, from your lower back up between your shoulders to the back of your neck. It continues up above your head until a large, golden flower blooms. The flower head travels upward a little farther, pulling your spine straighter.*

3. *At the same time, imagine your feet as the flower's roots. Feel your feet go deeper into the earth. Between the flower above your head and the roots that are your feet, feel your spine stretch out just a little more. Your arms and hands become the leaves, as light as air.*

4. *Now imagine energy, in the form of golden-white light, traveling up from the roots that are your feet, up through your spine to the top of your head, where the golden flower shines. The light fills your body with cleansing energy, and revitalizes you. Hold this image for a few seconds.*

5. *Let the light descend through your body, into the earth. See the flower close, and the stem relax and become your spine again. Relax.*

Practicing mindfulness while walking will make you more aware of the earth's natural beauty.

Walking with mindfulness

This meditation helps to develop concentration and increases awareness. It is also very relaxing and enjoyable.

1 *While you are out walking, perhaps to or from work or simply going for a stroll, bring your mind away from thoughts of the past or the future. Focus on your breathing and walk erect, with your head and spine in alignment.*

2 *Shift your attention to your walking. Walk mindfully, focusing on each step. Notice how your weight shifts from one foot to the other, the way your arms and legs move, and how the air feels on your face.*

3 *Now expand your awareness to include everything around you. Where are you? Who or what is there with you? Listen to the sounds, and notice the smells, colors, and movements. How do you feel about this experience? Try to take in as many sensations as you can.*

The chakras

In Indian yoga, chakras are great centers of energy in the body. Although they are invisible to the eye, these spinning wheels of spiritual energy keep our bodies and spirits in balance. They store the powerful life force that yogis call prana, the Chinese call ch'i and the Japanese call ki. This dynamic energy is the precious universal life force that permeates everything; it surrounds and is within all things.

Exploring the chakras

The seven main chakras of the body are sited between the base of the spine and the top of the head. There are other chakras, but we will concentrate on those listed here. (See also pages 78–79.)

- The first, or base, chakra is located at the base of the spine. It is associated with anything of a material nature, including physical strength and structures, possessions, status in life, and survival. It is also where a dormant energy called kundalini is stored. Yogis aim to reactivate this energy and send it flowing through the chakras. When it reaches the top and all the chakras are open and in balance with one another, enlightenment is attained.

- The second chakra, or sacral chakra, is located at the level of the lower abdomen, above the genitals. It is associated with sexuality, sensuality, and reproduction.

- The third chakra, or solar plexus chakra, is located at the solar plexus area (this is high at the back of the abdomen, just between the ribs and navel). This wheel of energy governs inner power, the will, and self-confidence.

- The fourth chakra, or heart chakra, is positioned at the level of the heart. It is associated with relationships, as well as love, compassion, and emotions in general.

- The fifth chakra, or throat chakra, is located in the throat area. It is concerned with expression and communication and also with our creative impulses.

- The sixth chakra, or brow chakra, is positioned at the level of the forehead, between the eyebrows. It is associated with imagination, clarity of thought, intuition, and dreams, as well as our psychic abilities.

- The seventh chakra, or crown chakra, is situated on the top of the head. It governs understanding, higher consciousness, and our link with universal spirit and the divine.

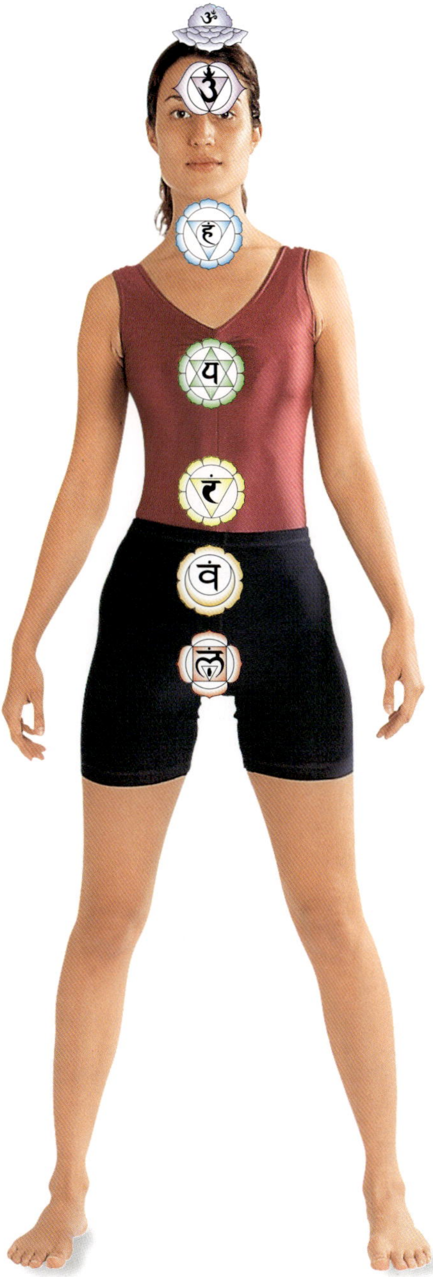

Achieving balance

An essential thing to bear in mind about the chakras is that energy should flow naturally between them and that they should be in balance with one another. Meditation can help to balance the chakras in order to ensure pure energy flow, enhance spiritual awareness, and improve overall well-being.

If a particular chakra is "blocked," it can create problems in the area with which it is associated. For example, if the second chakra is blocked, it may interfere with sexual expression or with the normal function of the reproductive system. Likewise, if the fifth chakra is blocked, it can inhibit self-expression or the flow of creativity. Very few people actually have all their chakras open and in balance and the process of attaining this state should be seen as a long-term one.

In fact, any in-depth work on opening all the chakras calls for advanced training and self-discipline and should only be done under the guidance of a suitably qualified and experienced teacher. However, if you would like to learn more about them, feel where your own chakras are, or experience a little of their energy for yourself, you can do so.

The six lower chakras ascend up the body, their positions corresponding to the spinal column. The highest chakra is located at the crown.

Petals of the lotus

When meditating on one of the chakras, it is customary to imagine it as a lotus with a certain number of petals. The lotus has special significance because although its roots are in the mud, it blossoms into a beautiful flower that opens its petals to the heavens above. If you find a lotus flower difficult to imagine, you can just visualize each chakra as a storehouse of energy. The following table gives the names and positions of the seven main chakras, together with their associated colors and number of petals.

As you work up through the chakras, you can visualize lotus flowers with open petals.

Attributes of the seven main chakras

Chakra	Indian name	Position	Attributes	Color	Gland and body system	Number of petals
Base	Muladhara	Base of spine	Material plane, status in life, survival	Red	Adrenals, skeleton, lymph, and elimination system	4
Sacral	Swadhisthana	Lower abdomen, just above genitals	Sexuality and sensuality	Orange	Gonads and reproduction system	6
Solar plexus	Manipura	Solar plexus or navel area	Inner power, will, and confidence	Yellow	Pancreas, muscles, and digestive system	10
Heart	Anahata	Heart area	Relationships, as well as love, compassion, and emotions in general	Green	Thymus, respiration, circulation, and immune system	12
Throat	Vishuddha	Throat	Expression, creativity, and communication	Turquoise and blue	Thyroid and metabolism	16
Brow	Ajna	Between eyebrows	Imagination, clarity of thought, intuition, and dreams	Indigo	Pituitary and endocrine system	2
Crown	Sahasrara	Top of head	Understanding, higher consciousness, and link with the divine	Violet	Pineal and nervous system	1,000

It can be difficult to imagine the chakras; using a CD can help you to picture them.

Locating the chakras

Contrary to popular belief, the chakras are positioned horizontally. In other words, if you are looking at a standing person face to face, the chakras are not positioned flat against the person's body like spinning buttons. They are actually on a horizontal plane, so that you can only see them side on.

If you want to see this visually, try this experiment. Hold your index finger upright in front of your eyes. Put a CD on your finger and spin it, and you will find that you can only see the CD side on—only the edge of the CD will be visible. This is how the chakras are positioned in the body. If you want to see the chakras as spinning circles, you would have to place yourself above the person's head and look down through the person's chakras from above. In this way, you would be able to see that the chakras are round.

The sushumna channel

To make things as easy to visualize as possible, you can imagine the chakras running up your spine at the back of your body, or running up the front of your body. You can also visualize them going up inside your body between the back and the front. To be more precise, however, they actually ascend up a central channel called the Sushumna, and are linked to nerve centers along the spinal cord. To check their locations at various points up the "ladder," you can refer to the table of chakras on page 158.

Try standing upright and visualizing the chakras within.

Meditating on the chakras

When you start meditating on the chakras, you will probably find some easier to sense than others. With practice, however, you should be able to feel them all.

If you find, after a few attempts at Chakra meditation (opposite), that you are having difficulty feeling the energy flow through certain chakras, it may be because the flow there is "blocked." Almost everyone will find one or more of their chakras blocked. However, you should not let blockages go untreated because they can create problems later on (see page 158 for a list of the chakras and the functions they govern).

Unblocking the chakras

If you suspect that one or more of your chakras are blocked, do not attempt to unblock them yourself. You should consult an appropriately qualified therapist as soon as possible, such as a practitioner of Ayurveda. Ayurveda is an ancient Indian healing system that aims to restore health and balance to the mind and body through herbal remedies, diet, breathing exercises, purification, meditation, yoga postures, massage, and other treatments.

A qualified Ayurvedic practitioner will be able to sense blockages in your chakras and can help to restore your natural energy flow.

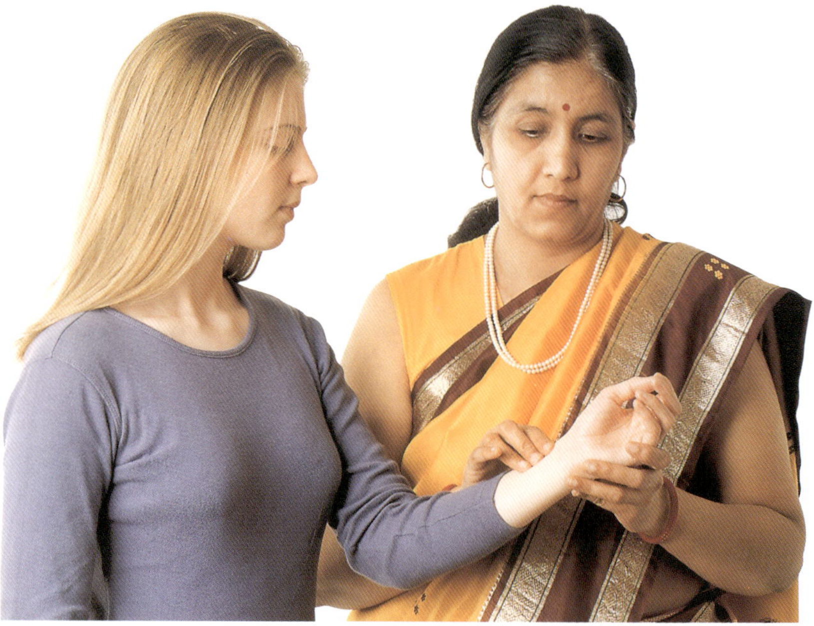

Chakra meditation

For this meditation, choose a quiet place where you will not be disturbed. Your clothing should be loose and comfortable. You may find it helps to close your eyes.

1 *Adopt the seated or cross-legged posture (see pages 142–143). Make sure that you are sitting upright with your spine straight and your head and spine in alignment. However, don't strain. Your posture should be comfortable and you should feel relaxed. Take three deep breaths, then breathe naturally.*

2 *Using your mind, try to sense the chakra at the base of your spine. You can imagine it as a lotus with the corresponding number of petals (see table on page 158), or as a spinning wheel or storehouse of energy. Choose the image that feels right for you, and sense the energy within it. What does it feel like to you?*

3 *Move your attention up to the next chakra in the lower abdomen, just above your genital area. Again feel the energy within it. Does the energy feel different compared to the energy of the base chakra?*

4 *If you have trouble feeling the energy flow in one or more of your chakras, try to "breathe" energy into the affected area. In other words, as you inhale and exhale, imagine that your breath is revitalizing the chakra concerned and filling it with life-giving energy.*

5 *Move your attention up through the other chakras, through the solar plexus or navel area, then the heart, then the throat, and up to the forehead, between the eyes. Feel the subtle differences of energy between the chakras as you move your attention through them. Finally, move your concentration to the top of your head and feel the chakra there. What does the energy feel like?*

6 *Gradually wind down your meditation, let your body relax even further, and then take a couple of deep breaths before finishing the exercise.*

Working through the chakras can help you to become more in tune with your energy.

Visualization

Visualization is an extremely powerful technique that uses the imagination to create particular states of mind and being. It is becoming increasingly popular nowadays and can be used for a wide variety of purposes, such as improving the concentration and training the mind, or increasing self-confidence and problem-solving. It can even be used for healing or for helping to achieve spiritual enlightenment.

How visualization works

Visualization goes far beyond just the imagination. Although it uses the imagination to create mental images of things, it goes much further because it involves all the senses, and not just sight, smell, touch, hearing, and taste, but the emotions as well. What's more, some visualizations can even manifest themselves on a physical level.

As an example of this, try to remember a situation that you found particularly frightening. It could be a terrifying car ride, for example, or a lonely walk late at night in a dark, secluded street. If you can't remember one, what about any phobias you might have? For example, if you are frightened of spiders, imagine one jumping onto your hand or into your hair. If you are afraid of heights, imagine jumping out of an airplane.

If you visualize this clearly enough, so that you can recall that past experience in detail, or feel the spider moving in your hair, you will find that your body responds to this stress and you will notice some physical reactions taking place. For example, you will probably tense up and your pulse will get quicker. You might also find that you are breathing more rapidly. If the stress is strong enough, you might even find yourself sweating or shivering.

For some people, the very thought of spiders may elicit the same feelings and body sensations as seeing them in the flesh.

The reason your body is responding in this way is that our bodies do not distinguish between things we visualize and reality itself.

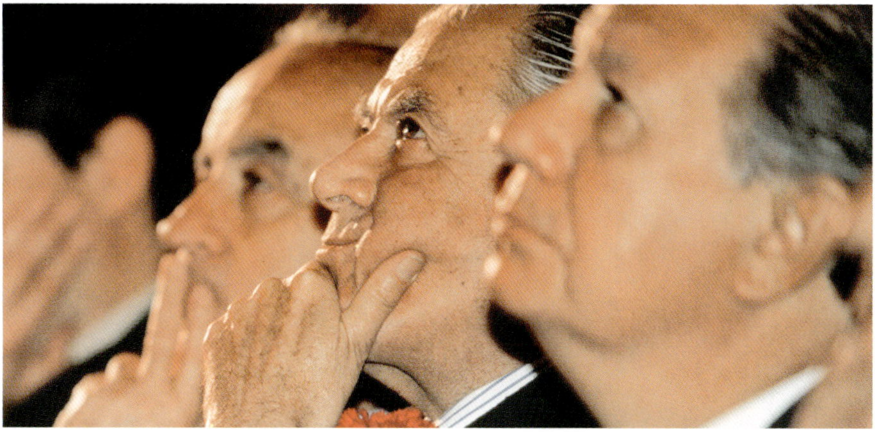

A person nervous of public speaking may find visualizing an attentive audience helpful.

So if the situation you are visualizing is stressful enough, it will trigger the body's "fight-or-flight" mechanism (see page 144).

As we have already seen, when the "fight-or-flight" response kicks in, your body will shut down all the systems that are not essential to immediate survival, adrenaline and anti-inflammatory agents will be pumped into the system, and your body will be poised for potentially life-saving flight.

Benefits of visualization

The good news about this is that you can use visualization to achieve beneficial effects. For example, when we daydream about something that makes us happy, the brain produces endorphins and other pleasure-giving chemicals, and our bodies experience the physical sensations of joy. We can use visualization to achieve the same effects.

If we now go back to our man with the fear of public speaking (see page 148), we can easily see how he could use visualization to help himself over his fear. He could simply visualize himself in front of his audience, speaking confidently and clearly. The audience is smiling and hanging onto every word he says. He is enjoying himself and feeling very calm and comfortable. At the end of his speech, the audience applauds enthusiastically. If he keeps on visualizing this situation in the same positive way, eventually the right side of his brain (see page 135) will come to associate the thought of public speaking with pleasure and he will find that his fear disappears.

So visualization is not just all in the mind. Although it starts in the mind, it can have profoundly physical effects.

Making visualization work for you

As mentioned earlier, visualization can be hugely beneficial and can help you to achieve all kinds of things. If you want to conquer a fear, you can use visualization to help you, as our man with the fear of public speaking could have done (see page 148). If you want to cure an addiction, perhaps to give up smoking, drinking, or caffeine, or you would like to increase your self-confidence, you can use visualization to help with that, too.

The main thing to bear in mind with visualization is that you should endeavor to do it as clearly and in as much detail as possible. You also need to keep doing it, in order to reinforce the message you are giving to the right side of your brain. This side of the brain, you will recall, is the side that deals with feelings and intuition rather than thinking and speaking. It will receive your visualizations without question and transform them into feelings, once you get them past the left side of the brain (see page 135). Practice and repetition will help you achieve this.

Using the power of visualization

Visualization involves using two different kinds of imagery: active and receptive. Active imagery can be any image that is chosen and focused on for a particular purpose. Receptive imagery, on the other hand, involves allowing images to arise from the subconscious mind and following where they lead. Some people prefer the discipline of active imagery, while others feel more comfortable letting images surface in their own way. Some people feel comfortable using both types of imagery.

Whichever imagery you find you prefer, you can use either active or receptive images to help train the mind. If you would like to find out how easy or difficult it is for you to visualize something, and whether you prefer active or receptive imagery, try the "Visualization skills" exercise (opposite).

You can use visualization skills to sharpen and focus your mind or for specific results, such as to unleash your creative potential.

Visualization skills

This meditation is excellent for assessing and sharpening your powers of visualization. Practice in a quiet place when you know you won't be disturbed.

1 *Adopt any posture that feels comfortable (see pages 142–143). The seated or cross-legged postures are best, but the lying down posture can also be used if you are not tired. Breathe naturally and close your eyes.*

2 *Try to visualize an oak leaf. What is it like? Try to see it in your mind's eye as though it really exists. See it in as much detail as you can. Notice everything about it: its color, shape, and texture. Notice every fine line on it. Turn the leaf over and study the other side. If you can bring in the other senses, so much the better. Rub the oak leaf between your fingers. What does it feel like? Can you hear the sound of your fingers rubbing the leaf? Put the leaf to your nose: can you smell it?*

3 *Open your eyes. Write down every sensation and detail. Repeat this exercise with the following objects: a coin, a rose, and an ice-cream.*

Active or receptive?

What did you notice about each of the objects you have just visualized? Was the leaf vibrant or withered? Smooth or crumbly? What did you do with the coin? Was the rose hard to visualize? Could you taste the ice-cream? If you could only keep the object in view for a short time, you need to keep practicing until you can hold each image for extended periods.

If you found you couldn't visualize these objects at all, don't worry: many people find visualization hard but master it with practice.

Alternatively, you may have found that your brain substituted different images, such as a dahlia instead of a rose. If so, you may be more comfortable with the flexibility of receptive imagery. Receptive images can be just as revealing as active ones, and both will help you to train your mind. Eventually, you should aim to be at ease with both types.

Writing down your experience can help you to see how best to use visualization.

Increasing your understanding

Images are the language of your subconscious mind. If you can learn to communicate with your subconscious mind using and interpreting these images, you will have found a way to communicate with your subconscious and use the understanding it can bring. For example, if you want to understand other people or a situation you find confusing, you can ask your subconscious mind to help you. You will need to use receptive imagery to do this—in other words, you will need to let images arise freely.

So the next time you are in a situation you find difficult to understand, try the "Gaining insight" experiment below.

Gaining insight

Try this technique to help you understand a particular feeling or situation.

1. *Adopt the seated or cross-legged posture (see pages 142–143). Alternatively, you can do this meditation in the standing posture (see page 154). Relax into your chosen posture and breathe naturally for a few moments.*

2. *Close your eyes, and hold the feeling or situation you want to explore in your concentration for a few moments. When you are ready, ask your subconscious mind to produce an image that describes either the situation or the feeling that you are trying to understand.*

Don't worry if the image that appears makes little sense at first; it may take you time to uncover the meaning of the animal, flower, or other symbol your mind chooses.

3. *Let the image surface. At first it may seem to have nothing to do with what you are asking. Persevere—it may take practice to understand the symbols of your mind. Perhaps your image is of a barking dog—then you realize the person you are trying to fathom is "all bark and no bite."*

4. *Once you have your image, and have studied it, close down the meditation and open your eyes. Think about the insights you have gained. You can continue to think about the image when you are not meditating.*

Sacred space

Visualization can help you to find a sacred space, a sanctuary you can go to in order to rest and receive comfort if you need it. If you also need to seek guidance, you can use visualization to help you find a guide there.

There are many guided meditations to help you with this. Some are available on tape and talk you through the visualization so that you can concentrate on responding to the imagery. In "Sanctuary meditation" (below), you will need to use active and receptive imagery. When you have finished, think about what you saw and heard. It may take time before you fully understand it, or you may understand it immediately.

Sanctuary meditation

You can do this meditation whenever you like. Choose a quiet place where you will not be disturbed.

1 *Adopt the seated or cross-legged posture (see pages 142–143), whichever feels most comfortable to you. Once you have adopted your posture, take a few moments to relax into it and breathe naturally.*

2 *Close your eyes, and see yourself walking in a wood. You are following a small stream. You can hear the water flowing gently, trickling over rocks, and you can see patches of shining blue sky between the leaves of the trees. Squirrels run up the trunks of the trees in front of you. What color are the squirrels? Birds are warbling in the branches over your head, and you can hear the crunch of twigs and leaves under your feet as you walk. You feel very comfortable, and very relaxed.*

3 *Up ahead, the trees part and you enter a large clearing. The stream flows through the clearing, and you can smell the heady scent of woodland flowers as you emerge into the glade. The clearing is peaceful, except for the sound of the water and occasional birdsong.*

4 *Lie down on the ground here, and relax totally. Soak in the warm sun. You are perfectly safe here and free to do as you wish. Stay here as long as you like, until you feel both rested and refreshed.*

5 *Now is the time, if you want to, to meet your guide. Relax, and wait for your guide to enter the glade from the trees on the far side. Your guide may be a man, a woman, or an animal. When you have greeted each other, pay special attention to anything your guide says. You can also use this time to ask questions on everyday or spiritual matters.*

6 *When you have finished, thank your guide and make your way out of the clearing, and into the wood. Gradually close down your meditation and come back to everyday consciousness. Open your eyes.*

If your guide didn't come to you this time, don't worry. Your guide will appear when the time is right.

Meditation for healing

An increasing number of doctors now believe that, in addition to having a well-balanced diet and taking enough physical exercise, practicing meditation can lead to better health and improvements in our overall lifestyle and well-being.

How meditation helps

Meditation has wide-ranging benefits: it can help us to think more clearly and improve our energy levels so that we work more efficiently and tire less. It can help us to relax and create a distance from stressful situations so that we remain more in control and less overwhelmed by negative emotions. It can also help us to understand ourselves and to accept situations.

The mind has the power to affect the body. Just thinking about a stressful situation can trigger adverse reactions.

In addition to improving our quality of life and making us happier, the relaxation that meditation brings can help to improve our physical health. Positive thinking can encourage the production of endorphins and other "feel-good" chemicals. We should never underestimate the mind's power to bring about change in the body, and we should try to think positively as much as possible.

Visualization for healing

This is where visualization comes in. As we have already seen, our bodies do not distinguish between things we visualize and reality itself (see page 162). So if we use visualization correctly, it can bring about positive changes within the body that can help us treat minor ailments and put us back on the road to good health.

Many people believe that visualization can also be beneficial in the treatment of more serious or long-standing complaints, but it must be emphasized that it should not be used to replace medical treatment: if you have a serious or persistent ailment, you should always consult a qualified medical practitioner. There is no reason, however, why you should not use visualization alongside any medical treatment you are currently having. You could visualize, for example, a drug working more effectively, or you could see yourself feeling fit and radiant. Discuss your plans with your doctor first, to make sure that you are working together on this.

Current research

Research is still under way into the possible effects of meditation on our health but, as mentioned earlier, a growing number of conventional doctors are now recommending relaxation and meditation exercises to their patients in order to help them combat stress and stress-related illnesses (see page 133). Clinical studies continue, but in the meantime there is a growing belief that meditation practice, alongside changes in diet and lifestyle, can help to do the following:

- Reduce migraines
- Combat insomnia
- Ease irritable bowel syndrome
- Soothe premenstrual syndrome
- Calm anxiety and reduce panic attacks
- Lower levels of stress hormones
- Improve circulation
- Regulate the pulse
- Lower blood pressure
- Control respiration
- Ease stomach cramps
- Aid digestion
- Ease depression
- Improve memory

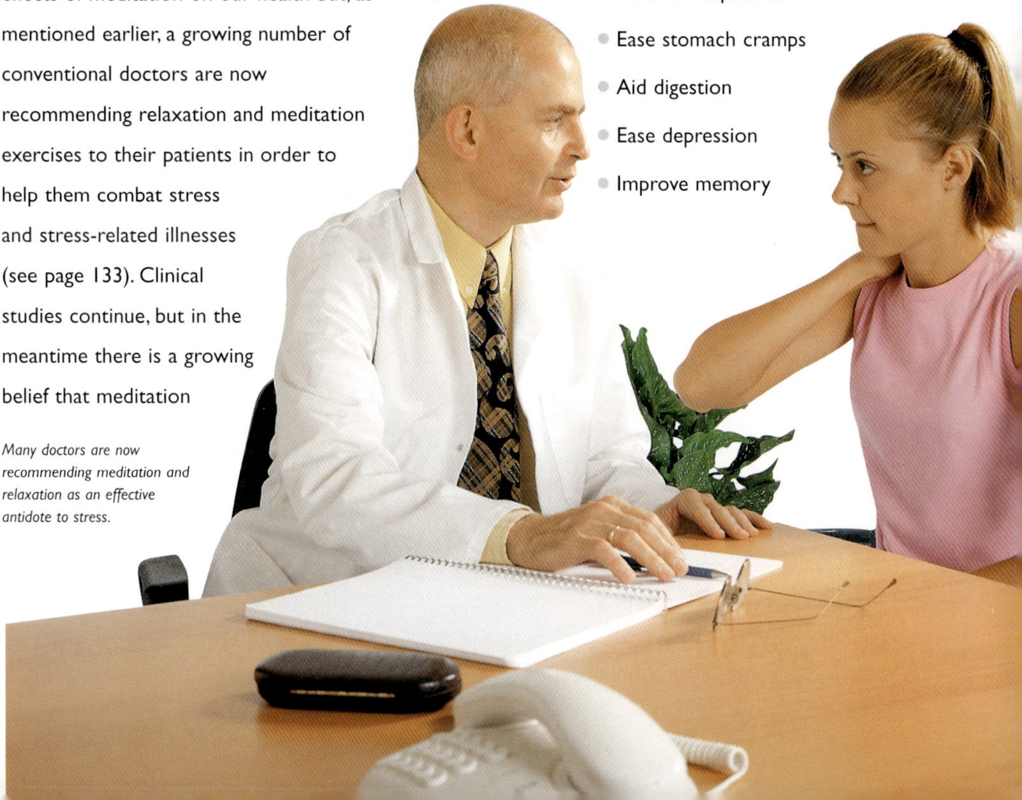

Many doctors are now recommending meditation and relaxation as an effective antidote to stress.

Deities from all religions are shown meditating, illustrating its importance in spiritual practice. However, meditation is also used to aid mental, emotional, and physical well-being.

Personal development

In addition to its many physical health benefits, meditation practice can also be of use in psychotherapy, especially in those areas that focus on personal development and self-understanding. Through meditation, many of us have learned that it is possible to understand ourselves better and the nature of our relationships with other people. With regular practice, we can increase our confidence and self-esteem, let go of past hurts, and enjoy life more, both in our work and in our social lives. We can learn how to conquer fear and dispel doubts, and we can transform that critical inner voice within us into a valuable and supportive friend.

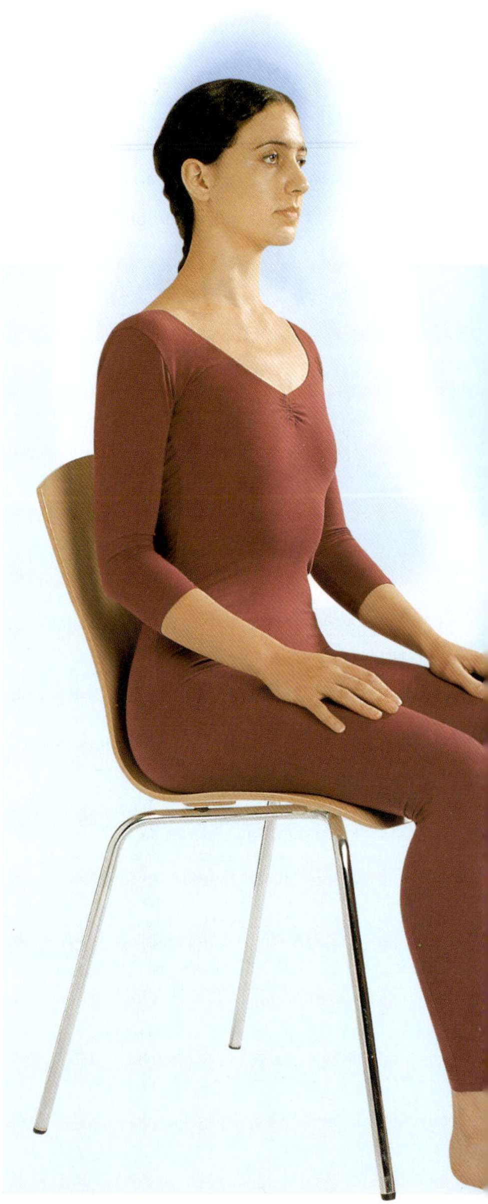

Using visualization for healing

You don't have to wait until you feel ill to do healing visualizations. In fact, it is often a good idea to do it when you are feeling well. Good health needs to be protected and, in addition to a balanced, healthy diet and plenty of exercise and restful sleep, visualization can help you to maintain your good health and guard against illness and disease. It can also help you to become more in touch with your body and physical changes. The "Healing the body" exercise below can be used to heal part of the body or to maintain good health.

Healing the body

This exercise is excellent for purifying and healing and for revitalizing the whole body. Make sure that your clothing is loose and comfortable before you start the exercise.

1 *Adopt the seated or lying down posture (see pages 142–143), whichever feels most comfortable. If necessary, you can also do this visualization while you are standing or walking (see page 154).*

2 *Allow your body to relax and breathe naturally. If you are not walking, close your eyes if it helps you to concentrate.*

3 *Check over your body and release any tension you are holding. Start with the top of your head, then move your attention to your forehead. Relax your eyebrows and eyelids, ears, nostrils, mouth and jaw, then your neck, shoulders, arms, and hands. Shift your concentration to your chest and heart, then stomach, abdomen, buttocks, and genitals, and finally your legs and feet.*

4 *When you are relaxed, begin the healing. Imagine you are standing under a shower of whiteish-blue light. The light comes in through the top of your head, then washes through your body, clearing it of impurities. Feel the light wash through your head and into your neck, outward through the shoulders until it fills your arms and hands. Let the light continue down through your chest, back, and torso, and down through your legs and into your feet. Feel the light taking out all the impurities and toxins from your body, and if any parts of your body need special healing, focus on them and let the light purify them. Continue until you feel that your whole body has been cleansed. You may need to do this several times before you feel completely purified.*

5 *When the light has cleansed and purified you, let it take the impurities from your body out through the soles of your feet and into the earth beneath you, where they are cleansed until they disappear.*

6 *Let the light flow back up through your feet and into your body, charging it with vibrant, healing energy. Feel it rush up your legs and torso, setting the whole length of your spine tingling. Feel it flow into your heart and chest, outward into your arms and hands, and up into your shoulders and neck. Finally, let it flood up into your face to the top of your head. If any parts of your body need special healing, let the vibrant light flow in and heal them. Hold the image of your whole body flooded with healing light, then let the light ascend up through the top of your head and out into the universe.*

7 *Give yourself a few moments to relax and take a few deep, smooth breaths. When you are ready, close the meditation and open your eyes.*

Note

If you find the whiteish-blue light hard to visualize, imagine pure water instead, such as water from a healing spa, or anything else that signifies a purifying force to you. If you are religious, you could visualize holy water or the healing breath of a deity.

Color and light

The powers of color and light can have a great influence on us and on many aspects of our daily lives. Colors can affect our moods and are associated with particular emotions: red, for instance, is often linked with anger, blue with peace and relaxation, and yellow with mental clarity. We also attribute different qualities to colors: for example, we associate wealth and abundance with gold. Light is also very powerful: it can affect our moods, how things appear, and how we view things around us.

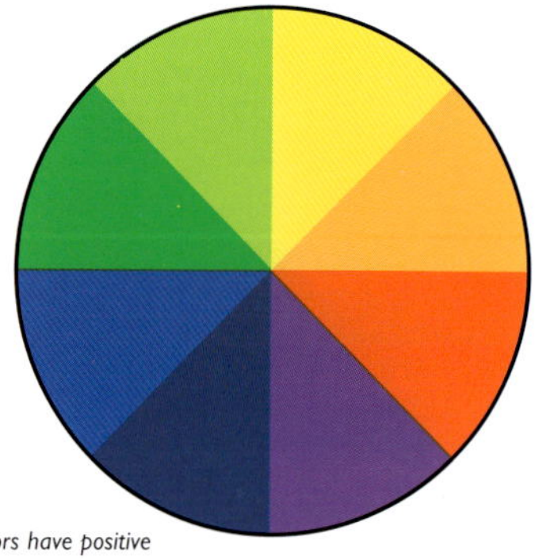

All colors have positive and negative qualities.

The power of color

It is important to have a healthy balance of all the colors in your life. If one color is missing, it could represent an aspect of your life that you find difficult to accept. For example, if there is an absence of blue in your wardrobe and home, you could be having problems with communication and with creativity. Likewise, if you have an excess of a particular color, the energy associated with that color may be dominating your life at the expense of other energies. You can use colors to energize your body and spirit and to create balance in your surroundings. You can also use them for healing, by utilizing their special qualities. Interpretations of color energies vary between people, cultures, therapies, and religions, but here the chart opposite shows some of the most popular interpretations from around the world.

Both the color of gold and the metal itself are associated with wealth.

Colors and their attributes

Color	In balance	Out of balance
Red	The material world, status in life, survival, courage, physical strength, and vitality	Greed, anger, cruelty, vulgarity, and violence
Pink	Empathy, warmth, stimulation, and loyalty	Selfishness, fickleness, and egotism
Orange	Sexual energy, sensuality, happiness, optimism, and friendship	Loss of sexual energy or obsession with sex, and fatigue, and pessimism
Yellow	Self-esteem, willpower, determination, confidence, inner power, mental energy, intellect, and mental alertness	Lack of mental clarity and concentration, stubbornness, inflexibility, and deviousness
Green	Emotions, including love and sympathy, relationships, harmony, freedom, growth, and renewal	Jealousy, possessiveness, insecurity, dislike of change, and dwelling on the past
Turquoise	Healing, eloquence and self-expression, independence, and protection	Allergies and other immune system disorders, tendency to be easily influenced, restricted self-expression, and vulnerability
Blue	Communication, creativity, inspiration, expression, peace, trust, devotion, sincerity, and relaxation	Insincerity, suspicion, distrust, sadness, and inability to communicate
Indigo	Imagination, intuition, clarity of thought, dreams, mystery, and secrecy	Paranoia, nightmares, confusion, and deceit
Violet	Understanding, higher consciousness, spiritual development, link with the divine, idealism, reverence, and commitment	Misunderstanding and misinterpretation, fanaticism, domination, adherence to outmoded beliefs, and lack of faith
Silver	Clairvoyance, the subconscious mind, fluidity, and transformation	Suggestibility and lack of stability
Gold	Wealth, abundance, spirituality, higher ideals, pleasure, and leisure	Avarice, poverty, apathy, laziness, and excessive pleasure-seeking
White	Order, completion, clarity, purity, wholeness, simplicity, and innocence	Rigidity, extremism, obsessive cleanliness, puritanism, and naivety
Brown	Stability and centeredness, resourceful, and nurturing	Depression, dullness, and inability to change
Black	Deep power, self-knowledge, discernment, and judgment	Tyranny, prejudice, blindness, and refusal to compromise

Finding the right balance

As you will see from the chart on page 173, it is possible to have too much of a color or not enough of it. Meditation will help you to harmonize these color energies.

The "Exploring color meditation" (below) will help you to become familiar with different color energies. You can also take it a step further and explore your own feelings about each color as its energies emerge.

Exploring further

You can build on the meditation below by using different shades of a color. For example, if your blue is pale this time, next time imagine a deeper or darker blue. Try to spot changes in their energies and note your feelings about them. Noting your feelings is useful because some colors may have different qualities for you than the ones described in the table (see page 173).

Exploring color meditation

This exercise is very good for improving your concentration and mental focus. It will also give you an insight into the different energies of different colors and what those energies mean to you as an individual.

1. *Adopt a seated or cross-legged posture (see pages 142–143) or a standing posture (see page 148).*
2. *Breathe naturally and, if it helps you to concentrate, close your eyes.*
3. *Think of the color red. Visualize a red bubble of energy all around you. Feel the red bubble expanding and contracting as you breathe in and out How does the energy feel? Does the red feel light, dark, bright, or dull?*
4. *Now think of the color pink. Once again, visualize yourself inside a pink bubble. What shade of pink is your bubble? What feelings does it trigger? How does the energy feel?*
5. *Now do the same with the following colors: orange, yellow, green, turquoise, indigo, violet, silver, gold, white, brown, and black.*
6. *When you have finished, close down the meditation. Note any feelings you had about the colors and their energies, particularly any strong likes or dislikes you experienced.*

As you focus on each color, be aware of any feelings they evoke within you.

Using color to solve your problems

Attributing colors to people or situations can help you understand them better. For example, if you are having trouble with a colleague, visualize the person and ask your subconscious for a color to describe that person. If green arises, consider if there is jealousy between you. Once you see what energies are at work, you will be able to improve things.

Color and the chakras

Meditating on different colors and the seven main chakras is a useful way of strengthening your visualization skills and discovering the power of your chakras.

As mentioned earlier, each chakra is associated with a particular color and energy quality (see page 158). You can explore these energies and help to unlock them using the "Chakra color meditation."

Chakra color meditation

Use this meditation to help you energize the chakras and identify with their different qualities and associated colors.

1 *Adopt a seated or cross-legged posture (see pages 142–143). Make sure that you are sitting upright with your back straight and your head and spine in alignment. Relax and breathe naturally.*

2 *Visualize the first chakra at the base of your spine. Imagine the color red flowing into that area: sense the energy of this powerful color revitalizing your chakra. What does it feel like?*

3 *Move your attention up to the next chakra, the sacral chakra in the lower abdomen, just above your genital area. Visualize vibrant orange flowing into this area and feel it energizing the chakra. Does the energy feel different from the energy of the base chakra?*

4 *Work your way up through the other chakras, using yellow in the solar plexus or navel area, then green at the heart, blue at the throat, indigo between the eyes and then violet on the top of your head. How do all the energies differ from one another?*

5 *When you have finished, take a couple of deep breaths and gradually close down your visualization. Open your eyes.*

Visualizing your chakras and the colors associated with them can be a very powerful practice.

Meditating on the power of light

Visualizing light in your meditation is a very powerful way of utilizing its special qualities. Light can be very energizing and healing, as we have already seen in the "Golden flower meditation" (see page 154) and the "Healing the body" meditation (see pages 170–171).

You can meditate on light in other ways too. For example, meditating on the sunlight is very uplifting and can also help treat Seasonal Affective Disorder Syndrome (SADS), or "winter blues." This condition is believed to be caused by light deprivation, which occurs especially in winter or if a person has spent long periods of time in a dark or shady place.

Using different colored lights in meditation will unlock different energies. If you would like to try this for yourself, simply do the chakra color meditation (see page 175), but instead of visualizing each colored energy, visualize light in the appropriate color for that chakra instead. So for the base chakra you would visualize red light, for the sacral chakra you would visualize orange light, and so on.

You can also meditate on light to improve your concentration. The "Candle meditation" (see opposite) is a simple exercise that will still the mind and bring peace and relaxation.

Focusing on the flame of a candle can clear your mind.

Different colored lights can unlock different energies when used in meditation.

Candle meditation

For this exercise you will need a quiet, darkened room and a lit candle. A simple white or cream candle is best.

1. *Adopt either a seated, cross-legged, or kneeling posture (see pages 142–143). Choose whichever posture you find most comfortable to sustain for a reasonable period of time. Place the lit candle in front of you.*

2. *Relax, breathe naturally, and focus your gaze on the flame. Empty your mind of all thoughts and just concentrate on the flame. Don't stare: just gaze softly at the flame and allow your eyes to blink when necessary. Let your mind slow down to a receptive, alpha state (see page 185). Whenever your mind tries to sidetrack you with other thoughts, bring it gently but firmly back to the flame.*

3. *Keep up this exercise for as long as is comfortable, then gradually close down the meditation.*

Note that this well-known exercise is primarily intended to help you build up concentration and mental focus. However, you can also adapt it to help you develop other qualities. For example, you can also use a candle of a particular color if you want to explore a specific energy. Perhaps you might like to use a green candle to help you reconnect with feelings of love and harmony after an argument (see page 173 for the colors and their energies). You can also use this exercise to sharpen your visualization skills: simply close your eyes at the end of step 2 and try to see the candle in your mind's eye, in as much detail as possible. Then gradually close down the visualization.

The flickering flame of a candle gives the restless mind something to focus on. This helps you to quieten the inner chatter and develop your concentration skills.

The power of sound

Towards the end of the nineteenth century, American doctors discovered that some types of music could stimulate blood flow. Since then, there has been increased medical interest in the therapeutic qualities of sound.

How sound affects us

Just as color and light can influence our moods, sound has the power to affect our emotions. It can reach deep inside us and alter the way we feel and even the way we react in a given situation. Sound is made up of waves of pressure that resonate at different frequencies. These different levels of sound affect us in different ways. For example, a high-pitched sound, such as a scream, will set our nerves on edge and make us tense, whereas the gentle sound of water trickling from a fountain will soothe and relax us. In the same way, gentle, beautiful music is calming and can inspire creativity, whereas loud, thudding music is irritating and will leave us feeling stressed. In extreme cases, very loud music can even cause headache and damage the hearing.

There are exceptions to this. There are times, for instance, when irritating or chaotic sounds can energize us or inspire our creativity. For example, the bewitching sounds of Ravel's concerto "Bolero" were inspired by the interminable sawing rhythm of a mill. However, these cases are very much the exceptions, and it is better to try to improve the quality of sound around us whenever possible so that we can become more relaxed and avoid increasing the amount of unnecessary stress in our lives. This helps us to function more efficiently and enjoy a better quality of life and a greater level of happiness.

People are drawn to waterfalls because the sound of running water has a soothing effect.

Classical music tends to have a soothing and even inspirational effect on the mind.

Sound as healer

Research is still under way into the therapeutic potential of sound, but there is a growing belief that certain sound waves can affect the pulse, respiration, and blood pressure, and improve mental clarity. Sound therapists now use machines to send healing sound waves to ailing parts of the body, and to help autistic patients to hear properly.

Research in both the US and Europe during the 1980s and 1990s showed that music could be used to reduce stress levels and help patients to recover from illnesses more quickly. Music therapists are increasingly being asked to help treat patients with learning difficulties and other mental and physical disabilities. They use music to encourage patients to find ways of expressing themselves and even to give pain relief.

Using the qualities of sound

There are many ways to use sound in your meditation practice. For example, you can have beautiful music playing in the background. I have found that instrumental pieces work best for this, and would recommend gentle classical or New Age music. Sounds of nature, such as sounds of the seashore, also create the right atmosphere. Whichever sounds you choose, try meditating on each sound with mindfulness (see page 146). In other words, be aware of every sound as it happens. In this way, your appreciation of the sounds will be intense.

Using sound to solve your problems

Like color (see page 147), sound can help you to understand people or situations. If you are finding it hard to understand someone, hold that person in your mind's eye and ask your subconscious to describe him or her with a sound. If it's a whisper, it could suggest the person is timid or unsure. If it's a roar, then perhaps the person is overbearing or insensitive. The sound and your interpretation of it give an indication of your feelings and put you in a better position to improve your relationship.

Sound within the body

Chants or mantras (see page 152) help to still the mind and create a sense of tranquillity and peace. The vibrations are felt throughout the body and can lead to a state of bliss and euphoria. Experiment with a few sounds and mantras and feel the effects different sound vibrations have within your body.

The "Chakra sound meditation" links sound vibrations with the seven main chakras (see page 156). Like the "Chakra color meditation" (see page 175), this will help you identify with your chakras and unlock their power.

Chakra sound meditation

This meditation is best performed in a silent place where no other sounds will be able to disturb your concentration.

1 *Adopt the seated or cross-legged posture (see pages 142–143). Relax and breathe naturally. Visualize the chakra at the base of your spine. Make a long sound "DOH" in as low a key as you can. Imagine the "DOH" is coming from the chakra itself. Let it vibrate for 10 seconds at least. What does it feel like?*

2 *Move your attention to the sacral chakra in the lower abdomen. Make a long sound "RAY," in a slightly higher key. Hold it for at least 10 seconds, and try to imagine it coming from the chakra itself. How does the energy of this sound differ from the energy of the "DOH?"*

Practicing chanting with other people can intensify the power of the sounds.

3 *Shift your attention to the solar plexus or navel area, and make a long sound "MI," as in "see," in a slightly higher key than the "RAY." Again, and throughout the meditation, hold the sound for at least 10 seconds. How does it feel?*

4 *Now focus on the heart chakra, and make a long sound "FAH," as in "far." Sound it in a slightly higher key than the "MI." Feel the vibrations coming from your heart area. How does this energy feel?*

5 *Now, do the same for the throat chakra, using the sound "SOH" in a slightly higher key. Can you feel the differences in energy as the tones become higher?*

6 *Shift your attention to the chakra on your forehead, and make a long sound "LAH" in a slightly higher key. Then move your focus to the crown chakra and make the sound "TI," as in "tee." This should be the highest pitched sound of all. How does it feel?*

7 *Finally, be absolutely still. Hear the sounds your body makes from within. Pay special attention to them, because they will help you to forge greater awareness of your body. Then, breathe deeply and close the meditation.*

Note

You can use any sounds of your choice for this as long as they are of one syllable, resonate in the body, and get progressively higher as you work up the chakras.

Using fragrances in meditation

Since ancient times we have been aware of the emotive power of fragrances. We have used incense and fragrant oils in our rituals for thousands of years. They have the power to change our mood and can evoke images and memories of places far away.

How fragrances affect us

Your sense of smell is very sensitive and acts as an early warning system that helps you to detect threats to your safety. For example, if there is smoke in your home, your nose alerts you so that you can check for fire.

What happens is that the nose detects a smell, and then the mind associates it with an image or idea. So if the nose detects smoke, the brain will associate it with fire and burning. This link between the nose detecting a smell and then the brain producing an image in response to it is what gives smells their power to inspire the imagination.

Smell is the most evocative of the senses. A simple aroma, such as a lemon or perfume, can instantly conjure up an image of a special place or person.

The physical effects of fragrances

What we smell can also affect the body. This is because our bodies do not distinguish between things we visualize and reality itself (see page 162). If we think about something that makes us happy, the brain produces pleasure-giving chemicals, and we feel physical sensations of joy (see page 163).

In this way, what we smell can affect us physically. The smell is detected in the nose, then interpreted by the brain, which produces an image or idea, and that idea triggers a response in the body. We should therefore not underestimate the powerful effects that scents can have on us. They can lift our moods or depress us, comfort us, or irritate us.

Healing fragrances

Since what we smell can affect us physically, it is not surprising that we have used fragrances in healing since ancient times. The art of aromatherapy has in fact been practiced for thousands of years. The earliest record of its use was in China in 4,500 BCE. The Ancient Egyptians also used essential oils, both for therapeutic purposes and for embalming.

In Ancient Greece, the great physician Hippocrates (460–377 BCE), known as the "father of medicine," used aromatic herbs and spices to treat his patients, and later the Greek surgeon Galen (130–201 CE) used essential oils (see page 190) in his work. These essential oils, or aromatic liquids, were usually obtained from plants.

In medieval Europe, herbs were often used to help fight disease, and in Renaissance England, Queen Elizabeth I (1533–1603 CE) supported the use of aromatic herbs, spices, and oils.

Since then, a variety of European chemists have published studies on the therapeutic uses of essential oils, and today aromatherapy is becoming an increasingly popular way of treating ailments and maintaining good health.

Hippocrates used medicinal herbs to treat the sick.

The aromas of different herbs and flowers can have strong effects on our moods and well-being.

Herbal oils have been used therapeutically for thousands of years, and aromatherapy is now a widely used therapy.

Using the power of fragrances

You can use fragrances in your meditation in many ways. Incense, for example, can help to create the right atmosphere for your meditation. Choose incense sticks, smudge sticks, or burn incense on charcoal in an incense burner. You can also burn essential oils in an oil burner: just fill the reservoir with water, add a few drops of your chosen oil, and then light the candle underneath and it will fill your meditation space with your chosen fragrance. All of these are available from New Age or natural health shops.

Used in many religious ceremonies, incense can help to open the mind for meditation.

Burning an essential oil while you do a "Healing the body" meditation (see pages 170–171) is a very powerful way of using fragrances to heal the body and the mind. You could also add a few drops to your bath and perform a healing meditation while you soak.

The table opposite lists some of the main essential oils and their helpful qualities in relation to meditation. Bear in mind that these essential oils are very strong and some are not suitable for children, pregnant women, breastfeeding mothers, convalescents, or anyone suffering from a serious illness. If you are in any doubt, consult a qualified aromatherapist first.

Aromatherapy oils can create an atmosphere conducive to meditation or relaxation.

Many aromatic herbs, such as ylang ylang and bergamot, have medicinal properties.

Essential oils and their healing qualities

Essential oil	Action	Healing qualities
Bergamot	Uplifting, refreshing, calming, energizing, and revitalizing	Eases stress, restores appetite, and soothes anxiety and depression
Cypress	Purifying, soothing, and invigorating	Calms the nervous system and helps ease menopausal symptoms, hay fever, and stress
Geranium	Uplifting and balancing	Soothes premenstrual tension and depression, calms the nervous system, and lifts the spirits
Ginger	Warming, circulating, relaxing, and has anticatarrhal properties	Helps prevent and ease travel sickness and nausea, stimulates the immune system against colds, helps to clear catarrh, calms the digestive system, and improves circulation
Grapefruit	Relaxing, purifying, uplifting, and emotionally balancing	Helps to regulate the emotions, eases stress and anger, and helps treat colds and respiration problems
Juniper	Purifying, stimulating, uplifting, reassuring, and soothing	Helps to clear the mind and aid concentration, eases aches and pains, and soothes the mind and body
Lavender	Relaxing, soothing, cheering, balancing, cleansing, and harmonizing	Helps to ease high blood pressure, stress, and tension headaches, and is particularly soothing for women after childbirth
Lemon	Purifying, refreshing, and stimulating	Reduces mental exhaustion, eases stress, stimulates concentration, and improves circulation
Orange	Relaxing and soothing	Helps prevent travel sickness, aids digestion, and eases stress and tension headaches
Sandalwood	Purifying, relaxing, balancing, aphrodisiac, and decongestant	Calms the nervous system, helps to ease emotional problems, has a balancing effect on the mind, body, and spirit, and also calms the mind in preparation for meditation practice
Ylang ylang	Calming, uplifting, balancing, purifying, invigorating, and aphrodisiac	Helpful for sexual problems, prevents hyperventilation, soothes anxiety, helps regulate pulse, reduces panic attacks, and eases depression

Meditations for stressful situations

Sometimes, even with careful planning, life can become hectic or stressful. Traffic delays, unexpected calls, and unforeseen events can all play havoc with our daily lives. Problems may arise and may seem insurmountable. At times like these, when all you can do is watch your peace of mind go out the window, try these quick meditations.

Traveling meditation

This meditation is particularly good for relieving stress when you are running late. It can be performed anywhere: on a train, on a bus, in a traffic gridlock, but for safety's sake make sure you're not driving while you do it!

1. *Let the whole of your body go loose, relaxing any areas of tension, and take a couple of deep breaths.*
2. *Accept that you have now done all you can to make up the lost time. There is nothing more you can do to make you get there any faster.*
3. *Focus on your breathing, and visualize the anxiety or worry simply floating away with each exhalation. Don't follow it, just let it go.*
4. *Each time the anxiety tries to come back, gently silence it and bring your mind back to its inner calm and peace. If the chatter persists, try repeating the mantra "PEACE" with each exhalation.*

Visualization can transport your mind to the most tranquil of scenes in an instant.

Step at a time

This meditation provides quick relief if you feel overwhelmed by too many things to do. In the longer term, you should try to lighten your load (see page 138) and prioritize remaining tasks.

1 *Stop what you are doing and take a few seconds to relax yourself. Release the tension from your body and breathe deeply and naturally.*

2 *Accept that you can't do everything at once. You can only do one thing at a time. Decide to focus on just one task, and clear your mind of everything else. Whenever your mind tries to think of other things still to be done, gently bring it back to the task in hand.*

3 *Now focus on that one task with mindfulness (see page 146). Be aware of everything about it and use all your senses as much as possible: sight, smell, touch, and so on. Calmly watch yourself doing it until the job is done. Then move on and complete the next task.*

Seeing the bigger picture

This visualization is a good one to try if you find yourself in a particularly frustrating or stressful situation. It will help you to be aware of the bigger picture and put your problems into perspective. After a little practice you should be able to do the whole thing in just a few seconds.

1 *Take a few moments to stop and be aware of yourself. Then become aware of everything else around you.*

2 *As you do this, let your awareness expand so that you can feel everything happening within a couple of miles around you. Try to see everything: people traveling on buses, walking into buildings, or working in fields—wherever you are, let your mind become aware of it.*

3 *Gradually expand the picture that you see in your mind's eye so that you can take in the whole country. Imagine people going about their daily lives in the north and south, west and east, and in all the towns and cities.*

4 *Let your awareness expand further, until your country becomes a shape on the globe that is Earth. See the planet moving through space. Notice the tiny continents and seas on its surface. Be aware that you are there, but that you are so small that you have become invisible from this vantage point.*

5 *Whatever has been worrying you should now feel really small in comparison to this view of the planet. Try to keep that perspective as you zero back in on yourself: tell yourself that this situation is really very small and that you will be able to handle it.*

Expanding your awareness of the world can help you to put problems into perspective.

Bubble of protection

If ever you feel vulnerable, intimidated, or just in need of protection in some way, try this visualization. It will help you to distance yourself from the source of the worry and make you feel safe and protected.

1 *Shake out all the tension from your body, allow yourself to relax in whatever position you are in. Breathe naturally.*

2 *Imagine a bubble of blue-white light all around you. You are safe inside it. The bubble is charged with sparkling, protective energy. It moves with you, and although it is soft on the inside, on the outside it is strong and is shielding you from whatever is making you anxious. It is keeping whatever is worrying you at a distance.*

3 *While you are inside the bubble, focus on your breathing. Visualize the blue-white light flowing in and out of your pores as you inhale and exhale. The sparkling light is filling you with strength and energy.*

4 *Keep the bubble around you until the pressure is over and you feel comfortable enough to let it go.*

Consciously let go of tension in each area of your body to reach a truly relaxed state.

Boost your confidence

This visualization will help you to face difficult situations calmly, so if you need to soothe your nerves and boost your self-confidence, perhaps for a job interview or before speaking in public, this meditation is for you.

1 *Take a few moments to release all the tension from your body. Take a couple of deep breaths, then breathe naturally again.*

2 *Visualize yourself entering into the challenging situation with confidence. If it is a job interview or a public speech, for instance, see yourself walking in and exuding self-confidence. You are very relaxed and talking freely and confidently with the interviewer or the audience. The exchange between you is very positive, and the interviewer or audience looks enthusiastic when you are speaking. You answer all questions happily and with confidence. At the end, the interviewer or audience shows a lot of enthusiasm for what you have said and you feel happy that your performance has been so impressive.*

3 *Keep this image in your mind as long as possible. To reinforce the visualization, try repeating a positive affirmation, something like "I can handle this" or "I am supremely confident" (see page 148).*

Note

You can also do this meditation to help you get over exam nerves. Replace step 2 as follows:

Visualize yourself feeling very at ease about the exam and speaking or writing the answers very confidently. You are relaxed and happy, and speaking or writing smoothly and comfortably. At the end, see yourself feeling extremely pleased with what you have done and confident that you are going to pass.

When you are nervous, take a few minutes to visualize some new self-confidence.

Glossary

Adrenaline
A hormone that prepares the body for the "fight-or-flight" response. When it is released into the system by the adrenal gland, it has widespread effects on the muscles, circulation, and sugar metabolism. The heartbeat quickens, breathing becomes more rapid and shallow, and the metabolic rate increases.

Affirmation
A statement that you can repeat silently or out loud to yourself until the constant repetition becomes meaningless and you are aware only of the sound of the affirmation in your head. Repeating affirmations helps to still the mind, and can get messages through to the right side of the brain, which deals with feelings and intuition. When the affirmation reaches the right side of the brain and is transformed into feeling, it can have a great influence on the mind, body, and overall well-being.

Alpha state
This is when the brain emits slower electrical patterns, which are called "alpha" waves. In the alpha state we are less active and more receptive and open to our feelings. The alpha state is most likely to happen when we let ourselves live in the present moment rather than in the future or the past.

Aromatherapy
A system of healing based on treating ailments using essential plant oils. Methods include massage with essential oils, adding oils to bath water, or burning oils in a room.

Ayurveda
An Indian healing system that aims to restore health and balance to the body through herbal remedies, diet, breathing exercises, purification, yoga postures, and massage.

Beta state
This is when the brain emits faster electrical patterns, which are called "beta" waves. In this state we are able to rationalize, analyze, and think about the past and future. We are usually in a beta state when we are awake and in a busy, thinking state of mind.

Chakras
Energy centers in the body. These spinning wheels of spiritual energy keep our bodies and spirits in balance and store the invisible life force that Indian yogis call prana, the Chinese call ch'i, and the Japanese call ki.

Ch'i
The invisible life force that permeates everything; it surrounds everything and is within all things. Indian yogis call it prana and the Japanese call it ki.

Endorphins
Chemical compounds derived from a substance in the pituitary gland. They have pain-relieving properties and are responsible for sensations of pleasure. They are sometimes known as "happy chemicals."

Essential oils
These are aromatic liquids that are usually obtained by distilling or expressing them from parts of plants. They are very powerful and can be used for healing and to help create particular states of mind.

Kundalini
A dormant energy stored in the base chakra, which yogis aim to reactivate and send upward through the other chakras.

Mantra
A sound, word, or statement that you can repeat to yourself. The sound qualities of a mantra are important, and can resonate through the body to bring about a transformation of consciousness. Some people believe that mantras possess magical power.

Mindfulness
A state of mind where you are fully aware of everything in the present moment. It heightens sensitivity and enables us to feel things more intensely. It also helps us to be more aware and observant and perform tasks more efficiently.

Music therapy
A system of natural healing where patients are encouraged to listen to music to ease their pain and anxiety, and to promote recovery from a wide range of ailments.

Prana
The invisible universal life force energy that permeates everything. The Chinese call this energy ch'i and the Japanese call it ki.

Seasonal Affective Disorder Syndrome (SADS)
A disorder in which a person's mood is said to change according to the season of the year. During winter there is depression, slowing of the mind and body, and excessive eating and sleeping. With the arrival of spring the symptoms subside. Exposure to additional light during the day is believed to ease the symptoms. SADS is not yet a clinically recognized condition.

Sound therapy
A system of healing in which practitioners work with the voice or with electronic or musical instruments to generate sound waves that are believed to restore balance to the body and encourage healing.

Sushumna
A central channel in the body. The seven main chakras ascend up this channel and are linked to nerve centers along the spinal cord.

stress relief

Introduction

The definition of good health is a sense of well-being. But all too often we become caught up in a cycle of stress and strain that leaves us functioning below our best and feeling tired, anxious, and unhappy. This section offers practical advice to help overcome the pressures of modern life, maintain health, and regain vitality and peace of mind.

For long-term stress relief and optimum well-being you need periods of mental and physical relaxation throughout the day. Relaxation is a set of easily learned skills that will teach you how to combat the effects of stress and restore the balance between body and mind to enable healthy, happy living.

This section shows simple but effective ways of making relaxation an integral part of your everyday life. It opens with a description of the detrimental effects of too much strain on the body and mind. It will help you identify

Many people practice meditation techniques to achieve inner calm and improve their sense of well-being.

the traits that can undermine well-being so that you can make changes in your life for the better. Next it deals with physical and mental relaxation, and describes natural ways of restoring the balance between mind and body, using a variety of techniques taken from Eastern and Western traditions.

Finally, it looks at important lifestyle factors and environmental influences.

Reconnecting with the natural world is a particularly effective way of alleviating the pressures of modern living. A spectacular sunset can both rejuvenate and refresh the senses.

Many physical, mental, and emotional problems can be avoided if you put just a little effort into looking after yourself in a more caring way. This practical guide gives easy-to-follow advice for long-term calm and serenity, to help you unwind and enjoy life to the full.

Stress: the problem

The increasing demands of modern life put enormous pressure on the mind and body. Some stress is part of life and is not necessarily a bad thing: it is a normal response to danger, and positive stress provides the spur to achieve. But when stress is long-term it can affect you physically, emotionally, and spiritually, impacting on your well-being.

Causes of stress

There is an enormous spectrum of "stressors" (causes of stress)—from the relatively routine ring of the telephone to something life-threatening such as a car crash. Major life events, such as moving home, birth, marriage, divorce, or death; environmental factors, such as noise, flashing lights, overcrowding, pollution; lifestyle, including poor diet, and lack of sleep and exercise—these are just some of the things that can contribute to stress. Your own temperament, constitution, and previous experiences moderate the effects of stress but the more stressors there are, the less you are able to deal with them effectively.

The stages of adaptation

Stress has very definite physical effects but it sometimes takes years for you to notice this. In the 1950s an American doctor, Hans Selye, identified three stages of adaptation in the human response to long-term stress.

1. Alarm response

Exposure to stressors prompts an immediate biochemical reaction known as the "fight-or-flight" response. Stress hormones are released into the bloodstream, causing the following:

- increased heart rate and blood pressure
- raised blood-sugar and cholesterol levels
- faster breathing and perspiration
- increased muscle tension
- disruption of digestive processes
- suppression of the immune system
- emotional tension

Telephones ringing can amount to noise pollution and can, over time, cause a build-up of stress.

2. Adaptation

If the cause of stress is removed or dealt with, the body reverts to normal functioning, but if it continues, the body copes by adapting. Although you may feel as though everything has returned to normal, your body uses up energy stores and over time this affects your ability to function efficiently, resulting in fatigue, irritability, and lethargy.

3. Exhaustion

Long-term stress changes the balance of hormones in the body and leads to exhaustion. A suppressed immune system, slower metabolism, and slower rate of cell repair results in rapid aging, weight gain, and a greater risk of degenerative disease. Your body becomes run down, with recurring minor illnesses and psychological "burn-out." Eventually you may become seriously ill or suffer a breakdown.

But although stress may cause a variety of disorders, it is not in itself an illness. Stress is created by habitual responses to difficult situations and by an unhealthy lifestyle. It is a habit that you can break, if you are prepared to look carefully at your life and take control.

A balanced body

Your body's biochemical, structural, and psychological functions are delicately balanced to enable good physical and mental health, and an upset in any one area can lead to problems in others. Optimum health requires looking after all parts of the whole. A healthy body and a clear and active mind with a positive attitude will help you maintain this balance.

The body is an energy system that needs to keep balanced to function properly. Any kind of regular cardiovascular exercise—even walking—will keep the body in a healthy condition.

A strategy for relaxation

The key to relaxation is to be able to recognize when you are under too much pressure and then dedicate time to looking after yourself. Developing the ability to relax at will during times of intense pressure, as well as implementing long-term strategies for dealing with stress, will help you feel calmer and more in control of your life.

Benefits of relaxation

Relaxation can counter many of the effects of stress. Adrenaline levels decrease, reducing stress on the cardiovascular system and lowering blood pressure. Breathing becomes slower and more controlled. The muscles become less tense and digestive processes improve. The immune system becomes more active, making you less susceptible to illness.

Insomnia, coupled with constant tiredness, may be a sign that your immune system is under strain and that you need to change something in your life.

Recognizing stress

The symptoms of stress generally manifest in behavioral, emotional, and physical ways. If you regularly experience more than five of the following, you need to take action.

Behavioral:

- excessive drinking or smoking
- poor appetite or overeating
- avoiding others and an inability to enjoy company

Emotional:

- irritability, anger, and readiness to explode for no apparent reason
- difficulties in decision-making, concentration, or memory
- feelings of being overwhelmed and unable to cope
- depression
- tearfulness
- no sense of humor

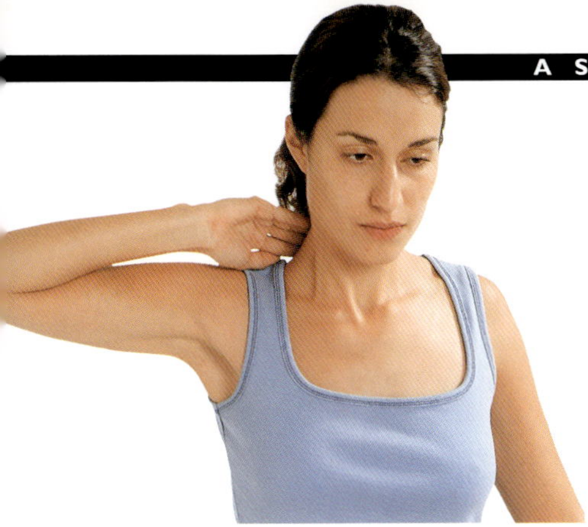

Back or neck ache are two of the many ways that stress manifests itself.

Physical:

- constant tiredness
- insomnia
- clumsiness
- muscular aches and pains including backache and headaches
- skin problems
- high blood pressure
- palpitations and panic attacks
- breathing problems including asthma, shallow breathing, and hyperventilation
- indigestion, heartburn, ulcers, nervous diarrhea, or constipation

You can't always avoid stress but being able to identify what causes it is the first step toward helping yourself cope better. In some cases you can take active steps to lead a calmer life—for example, if you find shopping stressful, why not order your groceries online instead?

Relaxation

Learn how to relax during times of great stress. Think of an activity that you associate with being calm, such as lying in the sun or having a warm bath. When you feel under pressure, think about your relaxation activity. Your mind will associate this with peace and you will soon start to feel relaxed.

On the record

Although you may recognize the symptoms of stress, it is sometimes difficult to pinpoint the cause. Keeping a record will help you to identify patterns of stress in your life.

1

Divide each page into sections, either an hourly breakdown, or for different times of the day (e.g., breakfast, morning, lunchtime, afternoon, evening).

2

Make a note of all your activities during the day and how you were feeling at the time.

3

Fill in your diary whenever a stress symptom occurs. If possible, make a note of what happened just before it occurred.

4

At the end of the week, evaluate the times when you felt stressed and when you felt relaxed.

	Monday	Tuesday	Wednesday	Thursday	Friday	Saturday	Sunday
Breakfast							
Morning							
Lunch							
Afternoon							
Evening							

PART 1: RELAXING YOUR BODY

Introduction

Efficient, controlled breathing and the ability to relax at will are vital in dealing effectively with stress. Simple breathing exercises and muscle relaxation techniques reduce the mental and physical effects of stress and enhance well-being. Touch and movement therapies benefit mind and body by increasing energy levels and engendering a sense of deep relaxation.

You can practice many different techniques originating from all over the world to enhance physical relaxation. You do not need to perform them all as part of your daily routine, but it is worth at least trying out as many as possible so that you can discover which are the most beneficial and comfortable for you. Some of these techniques normally depend on having a willing partner with you, but you can still reap the benefits of massage or reflexology by yourself.

Once you have found a range of relaxing exercises that suit you, it is important to develop a regular routine in the same way you would with any sport or exercise discipline. To see the true benefits you need to make it a part of your lifestyle rather than something that you do as a break from your routine. The small amount of time spent relaxing your body muscles and controlling your breathing each morning or evening will pay dividends over the rest of the day. Some people may find it more convenient to perform relaxing exercises in the evening, helping them unwind and preparing them for sleep. Should you do so, however, remember not to do any form of physical exercise straight after a meal or in the hours just before going to bed.

Relaxed, controlled breathing exercises before you go to work in the morning will put you in the right mood for a successful day.

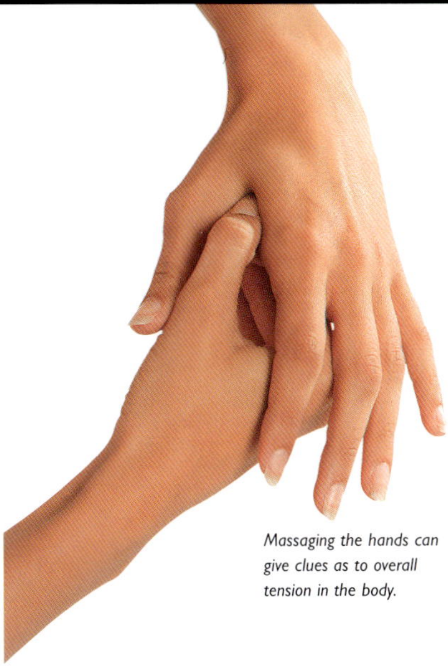

Massaging the hands can give clues as to overall tension in the body.

A space to relax

Just like any other form of physical exercise, your environment and clothing are as important as the routine you undertake. If at all possible, find a comfortable room that is without distractions—it will be far more difficult to relax if the television is on in the corner of the room. You should also be wearing loose-fitting clothing that allows you to move and breathe freely.

Although you should find that following a regular routine will provide you with a greater capacity to deal with stress in your day-to-day living, you will undoubtedly still be faced with unexpected crises at work or home. At such times you may find that taking a break to spend a few minutes working on your breathing or massaging yourself can put you in the right frame of mind to concentrate on finding a positive solution to the problem and so avoid being overwhelmed by the problem itself. Whichever routine you choose, it should improve your health and sense of well-being and help you deal with life's challenges more easily and with less stress.

This yoga position, a reversed namaste (Prayer pose) is good for stretching the shoulders and arm muscles and expanding the chest.

Breathing

Correct breathing is the key to calming mind and body. How you breathe reflects your health and how you feel about yourself. Your breathing becomes shallow and rapid when you are anxious, but slow and deep when you are at ease. Years of stress and poor lifestyle mean that rapid, shallow breathing is the norm for most of us.

Breathing is essential to life. As you breathe, oxygen is taken into the bloodstream and fuels the production of energy that enables your body to function. Breathing is an automatic, involuntary activity, but it can be consciously controlled. In times of acute stress, taking a minute to slow down and control your breathing will calm you instantly.

Correct, effective breathing should come from the deepest area of the lungs.

The effects of poor breathing

When stress levels rise, breathing tends to use only the top third of the lungs. There is a drop in levels of carbon dioxide, which is needed to maintain blood acidity, and harmful toxins are not breathed out. This has a direct detrimental effect on the nerves and muscles, and may result in tiredness, palpitations, and panic attacks. If you learn to breathe properly, these conditions can be alleviated and you will also benefit from a lower heart-rate, reduced blood pressure, and lower levels of stress hormones. So there are many benefits of learning to breathe correctly.

Breathing for health

Deeper breathing and a slower pulse are recognized signs of good health—the deeper the breath, the more body tissues can be oxygenated, and the stronger your heart is, the less often it needs to beat.

How to breathe

To improve your breathing you must first become aware of it. If you find your breathing is too fast or too shallow, the following exercise—known as abdominal breathing—will help you breathe more naturally. It uses the diaphragm (the sheet of muscle forming the top of the abdomen) to enable the lungs to inflate and deflate with minimal effort.

1

Sit in a comfortable position with your eyes open or closed. Place one hand on your chest and the other over your diaphragm just below the breastbone. Breathe in slowly through your nose, and try to breathe so that the hand on your chest remains relatively still.

2

Hold your breath for a few seconds, then breathe out slowly through your nose. Release as much air as possible.

3

Repeat for a few minutes until you feel calm.

Alternate nostril breathing

Blow your nose to clear the nasal passages. Place your forefinger and second finger on your forehead, with the thumb and third finger on either side of your nose. Close your right nostril, then inhale through your left. Close your left nostril, release and exhale through your right nostril. Continue to breathe in and out through alternate nostrils. This exercise helps you become aware of each breath, but stop if you feel dizzy.

Alternate nostril breathing can help you achieve mental balance and clarity.

Life force

Many Eastern philosophies believe that as well as containing oxygen, air also contains vital energy (known as prana in India, ch'i in China, and ki in Japan). By performing conscious breathing exercises you can accumulate this energy and revitalize both your mind and your body.

Reducing muscle tension

When your body and mind are under pressure, your muscles become constricted. Tight, cramped muscles restrict the body's blood supply, causing pain, fatigue, and tension. Over-tense muscles can dramatically affect your posture, movement, and body functioning. To relax, you must first locate the tension and try to release it.

Progressive muscle relaxation

This relaxation technique, which tenses and releases all the major muscle groups, will help you to slow down and let go of muscle tension. Choose a quiet time of day when you will not be disturbed.

1

Remove your shoes and loosen tight clothing. Lie on a mat on the floor or a firm bed, with a pillow under your head for support. Close your eyes and focus on breathing slowly, emphasizing the out-breath.

2

Tense the muscles in your right foot, hold for a few seconds then release. Tense and release the calf, then the thigh muscles. Repeat with the left foot and leg.

3

Tense and release the muscles in your right hand and arm, then the left.

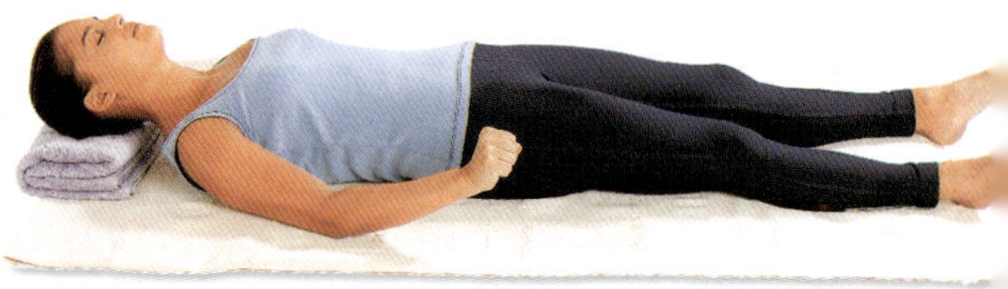

4

Tense and release each buttock, then the stomach muscles.

5

Lift your shoulders up to your ears, hold for a few seconds, then lower. Repeat three times. Rock your head gently from side to side.

6

Yawn, then pout. Frown, wrinkle your nose and let go. Raise your eyebrows, then relax your face muscles.

7

Focus on your breathing again. Wriggle your fingers and toes, bend your knees and gently roll on to your side, then get up slowly.

Alexander technique

This method of self-awareness, devised by an Australian actor, aims to improve balance, posture, and coordination so that the body can operate with minimum strain. By learning to stand and move correctly, you can alleviate muscular tension, and enable the body systems to function more efficiently.

The technique consists of three stages: releasing unwanted tension; learning new ways of moving, standing, or sitting; and learning new ways of reacting physically and mentally to various situations. It should be learned from a qualified teacher and practiced regularly.

Flotation and water therapy

Flotation tanks are sound-proofed tanks of warm water in which salts and minerals have been dissolved to enable the body to float effortlessly. This is a way of isolating body and mind from external stimuli in order to induce deep relaxation. During flotation the body and mind become profoundly relaxed and the brain releases endorphins, natural painkillers.

Hot water dilates blood vessels, reducing blood pressure. For a simple home remedy to relax stiff muscles, soak in a warm bath.

Massage

Using touch is a very effective way of becoming relaxed, and massage is one of the easiest and most reliable ways of relieving stress and relaxing painful muscles. This soothing therapy releases tension and reduces anxiety. There are numerous kinds of massage, many of which have been incorporated into various complementary therapies.

Physical effects of massage

Gentle massage stimulates sensory nerve endings in the skin, which transmit messages through the nervous system to the brain. The brain responds by releasing endorphins, natural painkillers that induce a feeling of well-being. Massage further aids relaxation by affecting the body systems that control blood pressure, heart rate, digestion, and breathing, resulting in increased health.

Massage can lower the amount of stress hormones circulating in the bloodstream.

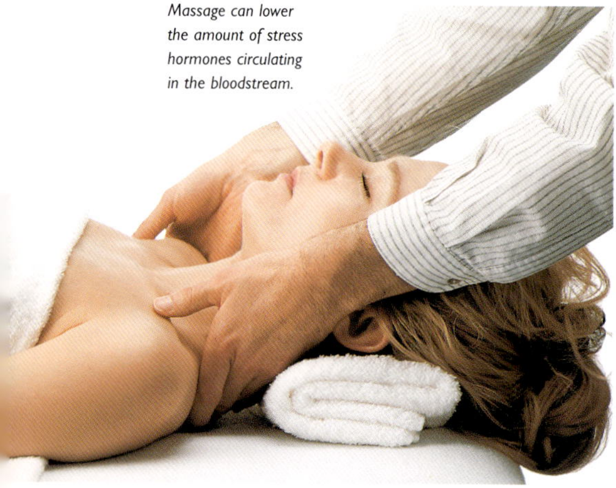

Neck and shoulder massage

Tense, aching muscles are usually felt in the neck and shoulders. When you are tired, your posture tends to slump, straining your neck and shoulder muscles. It is extremely relaxing to have someone massage your neck and shoulders, but you can easily massage yourself.

Receiving massage

Make sure the room is warm and comfortable, then undress and lie down. Your partner should warm his or her hands, then place a few drops of massage oil in the palms and knead the skin around your shoulder blades for a few minutes. Your partner can then place his or her hands between the tops of the shoulder blades and rotate the thumbs to massage lightly down the sides of the spine (not pressing on the bones) and along the shoulder blades. Your partner can finish the massage by squeezing the shoulder muscles to release deep-seated tension.

Self-massage

Shrug your shoulders and push them back as far as possible. Hold for five seconds, then release. Repeat five times. Put your hand at the top of your arm and knead the flesh firmly, moving slowly toward your neck. Repeat three times. Press your fingers into the back of your neck and move the fingertips in a circular motion toward the base of the skull. Repeat five times. Holding the back of your head, rotate your thumbs at the base of your skull.

Quick fixes for headaches

Smooth the tips of your fingers over your forehead, working from the center to the temples. Now place your palm on your forehead with your fingers pointing horizontally and gently move it up toward your hairline. Repeat with the other hand and continue until the tension ebbs away.

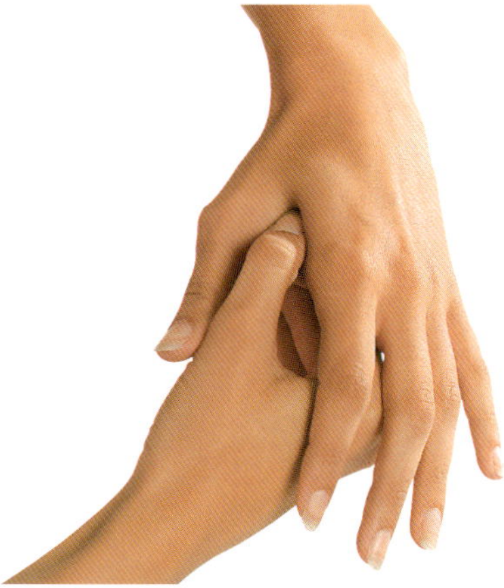

Regular hand massage can help relieve joint problems and arthritis.

Hand massage

Massage the web between your thumb and forefinger, using the opposite hand to press as close as possible to the point where the two bones meet. Continue for about a minute, then repeat on the other hand. This is a technique employed in acupressure, an ancient Chinese form of massage and healing.

Caution

Do not massage swellings, fractures, bruises, or infected skin. The stomach, legs, and feet should not be massaged in the first trimester of pregnancy. If you suffer from varicose veins, back pain, or thrombosis, seek professional medical advice before having any massage treatment.

Restoring vital energy

Every day we accumulate stress, which is stored in our minds as anxiety and in our bodies as tension. Many philosophies hold that tension blocks the flow of vital energy and prevents us from being rejuvenated. Therapies that unblock this tension have been devised to restore your body's state of equilibrium.

Yoga

Yoga has been practiced in India for thousands of years and is now popular around the world. There are many types of yoga but the form most common in the West is hatha yoga, which means balance of mind and body. This comprises body postures (asanas) and breathing techniques (pranayama) to prepare the body so that the mind can mediate without obstructions or obstacles.

Breathing correctly is the key to hatha yoga, and when done properly every movement is coordinated with the breath. Each asana is designed to stretch and strengthen the body, and is generally held for between 20 seconds and two minutes.

Everyone can practice yoga, regardless of fitness or age, but when learning it is advisable to attend classes held by a qualified teacher. Regular daily practice will increase energy and stamina, tone muscles, improve digestion and concentration, and help you relax and deal with life's daily stresses. See pages 68–129.

Natarajasana, or the Dancer position, helps strengthen the muscles in the legs, feet, and lower back, as well as improving balance.

Precautions

If you suffer from back pain, high blood pressure, or heart disease, or if you are pregnant, consult your doctor before starting a new exercise regime. When practicing yoga, certain postures such as headstands should be avoided during pregnancy or menstruation and others are not suitable if you have certain medical conditions—consult your yoga teacher first.

The physical benefits of the ancient Chinese practice of T'ai Chi Chuan include toned and strengthened muscles, more efficient internal organs, improved posture, and increased circulation.

T'ai Chi Chuan

This ancient Chinese martial art uses sequences of slow, graceful movements and breathing techniques to relax mind and body. T'ai Chi Chuan exercises aim to restore the balance of ch'i and enhance health and vitality.

Flow of *ch'i*

Ancient Chinese philosophy teaches the concept of yin and yang, opposite but complementary forces whose balance within the body is essential for well-being. The interaction of yin and yang gives rise to ch'i or qi, an invisible "life force" that flows around the body. The free circulation of ch'i is vital for good health: illness is thought to be caused by a blockage of ch'i.

Reflexology

Foot and hand massage have long been used to promote relaxation and improve health. The hands and feet are considered to be a mirror of the body and pressure on specific reflex points is thought to affect corresponding body parts. Reflexologists believe that granular deposits accumulate around reflex points, blocking energy flow, and the aim is to break down these deposits and improve the blood supply to flush away toxins.

Reflexology is generally performed on the feet by a trained practitioner and is deeply relaxing, but you can easily massage your hands at any time to relieve stress.

When pain, discomfort, or illness is found somewhere in the body, a good reflexologist can use reflexology maps of the feet to discover which part of the foot should be treated.

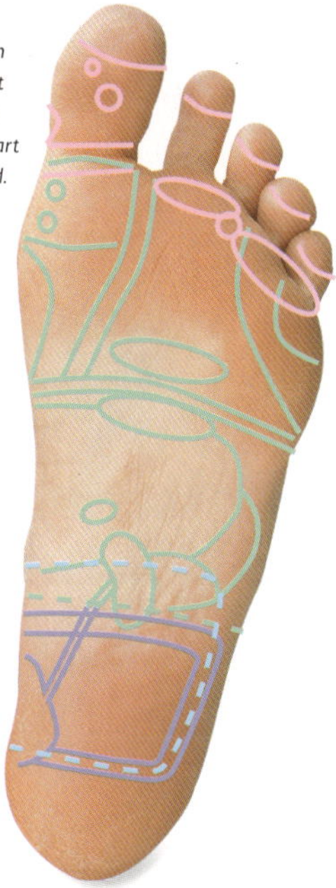

PART 2: RELAXING MIND AND SPIRIT

Introduction

Your thoughts, moods, emotions, and beliefs have a fundamental impact on your basic health, healing mechanisms, and immune system. To be truly healthy you need to look after your mind as well as your body. There are many different types of mind therapies designed for mental relaxation and to reverse the stress response. To a certain extent the type of person you are will determine how you react to a stressful event, but there are techniques you can learn to improve your self-image that will give you the ability to cope better with life's many challenges and difficulties.

The techniques described in this section, such as meditation and visualization, offer ways of relaxing your mind so that you can control its responses to stress, and also enable you to change the way you think about yourself and the challenges that you face.

Focus your senses on a favorite piece of music to find inner calm.

Know your mind

Relaxing your mind is the natural complement to relaxing your body, and to be able to deal with stress you need to master your ability to do both. For those who are not used to meditating and other forms of controlling their thoughts it may not feel natural at first but, as with any form of exercise, regular practice will soon lead to it becoming second nature.

Mental relaxation, like physical relaxation, requires a calm and comfortable environment to be effective, and you will find it far easier to separate your mind from your immediate surroundings if your senses are not being bombarded by the bustle of life around you. Indeed, in both meditation and visualization, many people find it easier if they have something relaxing to focus their senses on, whether it is peaceful music, images of a beautiful, calming scene, or a favorite aroma. These need not be physically present—even the memories of such sensations can help you to relax and take control of your mind.

As you become more experienced in controlling your mind's reactions, however, you may find that you are able to switch to a relaxed state despite the distractions around you, a situation that has obvious benefits for dealing with stressful situations.

Along with the need to relax your mind and control its responses to stress, the need to change the way you think about yourself and your life is important. Few people realize the destructive impact on their lives of thinking about what they haven't achieved, the unattainable goals they set themselves or even negative things that have not yet occurred. Learning to think about what you have achieved and setting realistic goals is a valuable way of avoiding generating unnecessary stress.

Mental relaxation is not based on purely internal factors, however, and relationships with other people can provide happiness and calm in your daily life and support in the most difficult of times. Developing and strengthening your relationships with family and friends is also vital to achieving inner calm.

Visualizing a favorite place can help you achieve a positive frame of mind in the most trying of times.

Meditation

Meditation is an effective way of focusing your mind to bring about relaxation, peace, and tranquillity. It will help you to gain a new perspective and enable you to stand back from your problems. Meditation is often practiced as a means of spiritual self-enlightenment, but it can also be used to relieve stress and promote relaxation.

What is meditation?

There are various types of meditation but they all focus on quietening the mind. The intention is to direct your concentration so that it is filled with peace and calm and cannot take off on its own and become stressed. When the mind is calm and focused in the present, it is neither reacting to memories nor worrying over the future, two major sources of chronic stress. Meditation techniques can be divided into two basic groups:

Meditation is a practical and effective way of dealing with stress.

1. Concentrative meditation

This focuses your attention on something specific, such as the intake of breath, or an image or a phrase, in order to still the mind and facilitate the emergence of a greater awareness and clarity.

2. Mindfulness meditation

Also known as vipassana, or "passive awareness," this describes a state of mind where you are aware of, but detached from, everything you are experiencing. Your attention is aware of sensations, feelings, images, thoughts, and sounds without thinking about them; you observe without making judgments. This means experiencing what happens in the here and now to gain a calmer, clearer, and non-reactive state of mind. If you use the analogy of a camera, it is like looking through a wide-angle lens—you experience more and your attention becomes broader.

Meditation and the brain

The brain is the body's computer, the center of all our thoughts, feelings, and sensory experiences, and the coordinator of all our bodily functions. The brain sends and receives messages via the spinal cord to all parts of the body. Brain cells communicate with each other by producing tiny electrical impulses. Meditation affects the electrical activity of the brain, causing the production of high-intensity alpha waves—brain waves associated with deep relaxation and mental alertness. These in turn help to undermine our habitual stressed responses to dangers and difficulties.

During alpha-wave states the part of the nervous system that governs automatic body functions—such as breathing, perspiration, salivation, digestion, and heart rate—predominates, reversing the "fight-or-flight" response to danger and stress.

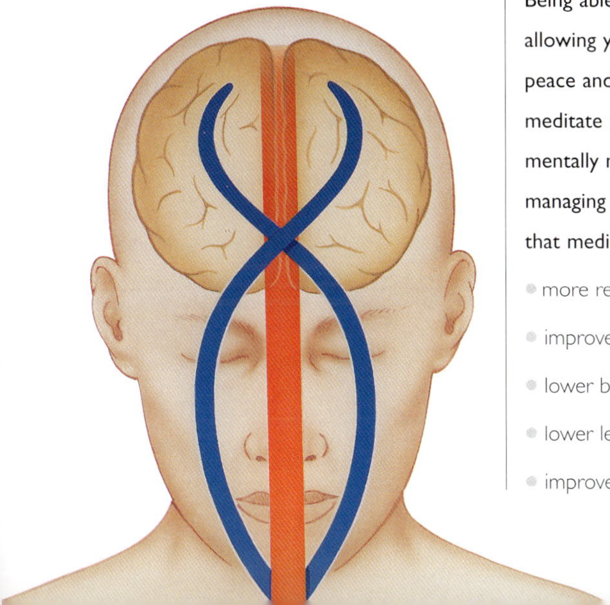

The brain produces four types of brain waves, which indicate our physical state: alpha (when we are deeply relaxed), beta (awake), delta (during a state of deep sleep), and theta (light sleep).

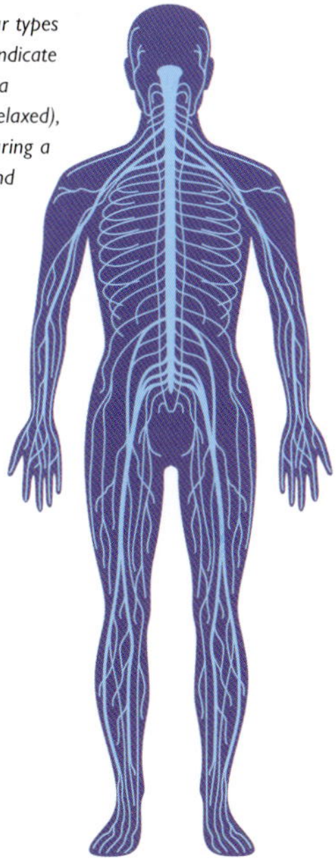

The benefits of meditation

Being able to control your mind instead of allowing your mind to control you will bring peace and harmony into your life. Those who meditate regularly are less anxious, calmer, mentally more alert, and more efficient in managing time and energy. Research suggests that meditation confers the following benefits:

- more relaxed body
- improved sleeping patterns
- lower blood pressure and reduced pulse rate
- lower levels of stress hormones in the blood
- improved circulation

How to meditate

It helps to consult a teacher who can show you how to achieve a meditative state but you can teach yourself if you are sufficiently disciplined. There is no "right" way to meditate but in order to do so successfully there are a few basic requirements to follow.

- a quiet place where you will not be disturbed
- regular practice, preferably for 15 minutes a day at the same time of day—meditation in the morning helps you to feel calm and centered for the rest of the day; meditation at night allows you to wind down
- an empty stomach
- a comfortable position (usually sitting to stop you from falling asleep)
- a focus for the mind to help you withdraw from your environment

Household items, such as a plant, candle, or picture, can provide a focus for object-centered meditation.

Focusing the mind

You may find it difficult to concentrate at first, but this will improve with practice. You may also feel sleepy to begin with but as you meditate for longer you will feel more alert. If you feel your attention wandering, just bring it back to the focus of meditation. People usually achieve a meditative state by one of the following methods:

Using an object such as a flower for meditation can help keep the mind concentrated and attention focused.

Object meditation

Concentrate on a particular object, feeling its presence and focusing on its texture, shape, and other qualities. A crystal, a candle flame, a flower, or a mandala (a picture with a focal point) are all suitable objects.

Chanting a mantra or phrase, such as the sacred "Om," can help you maintain concentration and meditate successfully.

Mantra meditation

A mantra is a word or phrase repeated continually, either silently or aloud. The Hindu "Om" is a sacred mantra that is widely used, though any word is suitable.

Touch

Rhythmically passing a rosary or worry beads through the fingers, or rubbing a piece of fabric, can induce a state of meditation.

Breath awareness

Focus on your breathing to achieve a state of meditation. Count "one" on each out-breath.

Active meditation

Rhythmic exercise such as T'ai Chi Chuan, swimming, or walking can focus the mind and are more energizing than sitting still.

Exercise: Quick and easy meditation

1

Sit comfortably with your spine straight. Look downward, but not focusing on anything.

2

Let your eyelids drop to a level that feels comfortable without closing your eyes completely.

3

Continue to look downward. You should notice that your breathing is slower and deeper.

4

Return your eyes to their normal focus after a couple of minutes. You should feel relaxed and calm.

Caution

Consult your doctor before starting meditation if you have a history of psychiatric disorders. Long-term meditation sometimes causes depression and withdrawal.

Visualization

Visualization, a technique that harnesses the imagination to deal with stress and illness, improve motivation, and change negative attitudes, is an important part of many relaxation therapies, and is used by athletes. Through imagining sights, sounds, tastes, or smells, you can use positive thinking to restore and maintain good health.

Self-help

Although you can consult a professional teacher to learn visualization, it is possible to learn the technique on your own. At first, you will probably need to practice for 15–20 minutes a day, either first thing in the morning or last thing at night, but as you become more skilled you should be able to do it for just a few minutes at a time as needed.

Choose a quiet, comfortable place where you won't be disturbed. Breathe slowly and try to relax your body. Then focus on your chosen image. It helps to repeat positive affirmations as you do this, such as "I feel relaxed" or "I am in control." You can perform this exercise in times of stress and it will help you gain control of a difficult or challenging situation.

Now visualize a calm, beautiful scene, real or imaginary, to help you relax. Suitable images include a peaceful garden, a beach, or a room. Try to envisage the sounds, smells, and sights of the scene and soak up the atmosphere until you feel truly relaxed.

Visualizing a calm, serene scene, such as a deserted sandy beach, is an effective way of using the imagination to help you relax and overcome stress and anxiety.

Fear of situations

Most people experience some degree of nerves or panic before important occasions, but visualization can help you feel more in control. For example, for several days before the event, anticipate dealing successfully with a job interview, or imagine the round of applause after public speaking, and the affirmation will take root in your subconscious.

Imagery can also be used to overcome stress. Think of an image that you associate with tension (such as a thunderstorm) and replace it with something calming (a rainbow).

Powerful, tense scenes—such as a thunderstorm—can be imagined and replaced with something calming, like a rainbow, to help induce inner calm.

Color visualization

Color can have a profound effect on your mood, vitality, and well-being. Yellows and reds are stimulating: blues and greens calming. Color therapists use different colors to improve your physical, emotional, and spiritual health, generally by shining colored lights onto your body. This exercise uses color visualization to calm the mind and help you relax.

1

Sit comfortably with your eyes closed.

2

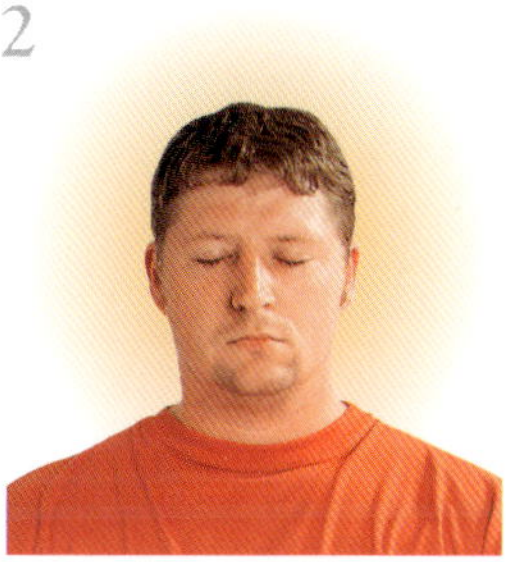

Imagine a ball of golden light just above your head. Visualize the ball of light slowly descending through your head until it fills your entire body. Imagine that this light is cleansing and healing your spirit.

3

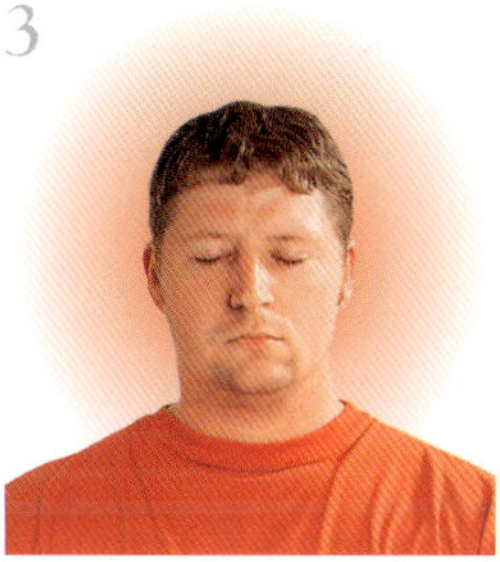

Repeat, visualizing a ball of red light. Continue slowly through the color spectrum—orange, yellow, green, blue, indigo and violet—until you feel completely relaxed.

The sound of crashing waves can be soothing, helping you to relieve stress and create inner calm.

Music and sounds

The therapeutic potential of music and sounds has long been recognized. Sound waves vibrate at different frequencies and have emotional and physical results, affecting your moods, heart rate, breathing, and even prompting the release of endorphins. Whether or not you can sing in tune, the very act of singing releases tension and encourages you to breathe deeply and rhythmically. Making or responding to music can connect you directly to your inner self, enabling you to express profound emotions. Soft, quiet music will calm you down, while loud music stirs the soul.

A relaxation tape

Making your own relaxation tape is much more effective than buying one off the shelf. Choose a gentle, relaxing piece of music, lasting for at least 10 minutes, that you associate with pleasant memories. Add some sounds of nature if you like (for example, birdsong, a breeze rustling through the trees, or sounds of the sea).

Choose a quiet room to relax in, sit or lie down, close your eyes and play the tape. Try to match the rhythm of your breathing to that of the music, and conjure up pleasant mental images as you do so. Listen to the tape once a day if possible, and soon you will be able to use the memory of this music to calm you down in times of stress.

Release healing endorphins by listening to your favorite music or sounds from nature.

Therapeutic touch

One of the surest ways of soothing stress is through touch. However, physical contact does not have to be sexual. Stroking a cat or giving someone a hug can be just as effective. For a quick relief from stress, sit quietly for a moment with your index finger touching the thumb of the same hand. Massage is another tried and tested way of relaxing and alleviating stress (see pages 206–207).

Sense of smell

Different aromas can lift your mood and make you feel much better about yourself. Smell molecules travel along the olfactory pathways and directly into the limbic system, which is the part of the brain that controls memories, instincts, and vital functions. For this reason, some smells are intensely evocative and can conjure up vivid scenes from nearly forgotten memories. Fragrant aromatherapy oils are used in a number of ways to aid relaxation (see pages 246–247).

You can also use the memory of scent and its powers of association to help you stay calm and relaxed during times of stress. Think about your favorite smells—a baby's skin, freshly ground coffee, oranges, frying bacon, sweetly scented flowers, new-mown grass—and you will instantly feel happier, more carefree, and more relaxed.

Aromatherapy oils and the scent of joss sticks can be relaxing to the mind and body.

Creative relaxation

Creative activities such as painting, drawing, and sculpting are excellent outlets for your emotions and can be deeply relaxing. Talent is not an issue—you do not need to produce a "good" work of art. The mere act of performing an activity that is creative rather than a chore is relaxing in itself. Let yourself become aware of the different textures and aromas of the art media you are using—whether paints, crayons, chalks, or clay—and enjoy the experience.

Visiting an art gallery can also be relaxing, particularly if you find a favorite picture or painting that has special associations for you. Go during a quiet time of day when you can sit and contemplate a piece without being disturbed.

More techniques for mind control

There are several other mind techniques you can be taught to reverse the body's stress response, including hypnotherapy, autogenic training, and biofeedback. Each of them will help you relax and take control of your life.

Hypnotherapy

A hypnotic trance is a state of consciousness similar to daydreaming, which can be used to change patterns of behavior and promote positive thinking. While you are in a hypnotic state, you are very relaxed and open to suggestions. One theory to explain this is that under hypnosis the conscious, rational part of the brain is bypassed (the left hemisphere) and the subconscious, non-analytical part (the right hemisphere) takes over. During hypnosis the practitioner may "feed" suggestions to your subconscious mind to overcome a specific problem, such as nicotine addiction or lack of confidence; or he or she might ask about past experiences to analyze current problems. A hypnotherapist can take you into a state of deep relaxation, which you may be able to recreate when faced with stressful situations.

Self-hypnosis

Most people can learn to hypnotize themselves. Find a place where you are unlikely to be disturbed and sit quietly or lie down. Relax and breathe slowly and deeply. Close your eyes and imagine yourself walking down a country lane, or descending a staircase, counting down from ten to zero as you go. Repeat positive affirmations to deal with your problem, or listen to a prerecorded tape of yourself. Bring yourself out of hypnosis by reversing the method with which you entered the hypnotic state.

To relax fully and go into a state of hypnosis, the mind has to envisage a quiet place, such as a country lane or a tranquil sky.

Caution

Hypnotherapy and autogenic training can be harmful to those who suffer from disorders such as severe depression, psychosis, or epilepsy. Always consult a qualified and reputable practitioner.

Autogenic training

Autogenic means "generated from within" and describes the way in which your mind can influence your body to train your autonomic nervous system—the part of the brain that governs automatic body functions—to become relaxed. Autogenic training (AT) consists of six silent mental exercises that enable you to switch off the body's stress response at will. With practice you should reach an altered state of consciousness known as "passive concentration," a state of awareness similar to meditation whereby you relax by not actively working to do so.

AT seems to work best when performed in a sequence and with set phrases, such as, "my right arm is heavy, my left arm is heavy, both of my arms are heavy." Each exercise is designed to relax different areas of the body. Once learned, the technique can be practiced at home. AT needs to be performed on a regular basis to maintain the technique and ensure its continued effectiveness.

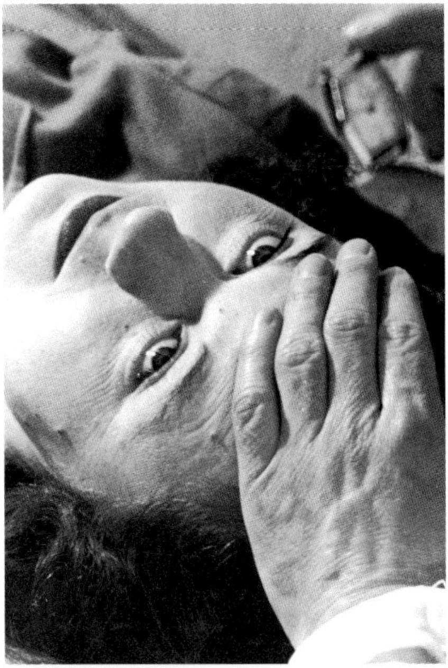

When in a state of hypnosis, the mind is very relaxed and open to suggestions, offering hypnotherapists the opportunity to replace negative thoughts and associations with positive ones.

Biofeedback

Biofeedback is a way of monitoring and controlling unconscious biological functions through electronic devices. It can also help you monitor your response to stress. Probes or electrodes are attached to your body and connected to electronic "biofeedback" instruments that monitor physical responses. While getting feedback you perform relaxation exercises to regulate body functions until you reach a state of relaxation.

A sense of self

How you feel about yourself is key to becoming relaxed and overcoming stress. Anything you can do to sustain a more positive frame of mind will be beneficial to your physical health. You need to be confident about who you are and what you want to achieve—this will help you to manage your life and relationships successfully.

Improving self-worth

It is all too easy to belittle your own abilities and achievements, and most of us regularly make negative statements about ourselves without even realizing it. But if you value yourself and your positive attributes, other people will value you as well.

Pioneered in the 1920s by French pharmacist Emile Coué, autosuggestion is a simple but effective technique that can change the way you think about yourself and the way you react to others. It consists of repeating simple, positive statements, made in the present tense, such as "Every day, in every way, I am getting better and better." Autosuggestion is most effective when you use preplanned and memorized phrases as a part of meditation or visualization.

Improve your self-worth by affirming your good characteristics and repeating positive statements to yourself.

Set yourself attainable life goals—write a plan or a series of steps to move toward them.

Setting goals

Change is inevitable and desirable, but can be deeply unnerving as it pushes us out into the unknown. When contemplating long-term, positive change, it will help you on your way to identify some short-term, attainable goals. First you need to think of goals you would like to achieve in different areas of your life—relationships, work, money matters, healthy lifestyle, for example—within a specific time frame; but these need to be realistic, and don't try to change too much at once. Write them down and think of at least three steps you can take to reach each one. Reward yourself after each step on the way. If a particular goal seems unattainable, perhaps you need to give yourself more steps to reach it, or maybe you are simply being unrealistic and need to modify what you are trying to achieve.

Going with the flow

In order to stay relaxed you have to accept that you only have control over your own actions. Fighting to control the world around you is exhausting and often unsuccessful. But if you accept that life is full of obstacles, they become easier to deal with.

Laughing it off

As well as being fun, laughing gives the heart and lungs a good workout, and research indicates that it also lowers blood pressure, relaxes muscles, reduces pain, reduces stress hormones, and boosts the immune system by increasing the production of disease-destroying cells. Laughter triggers the release of endorphins, the body's natural painkiller, and produces a general sense of well-being.

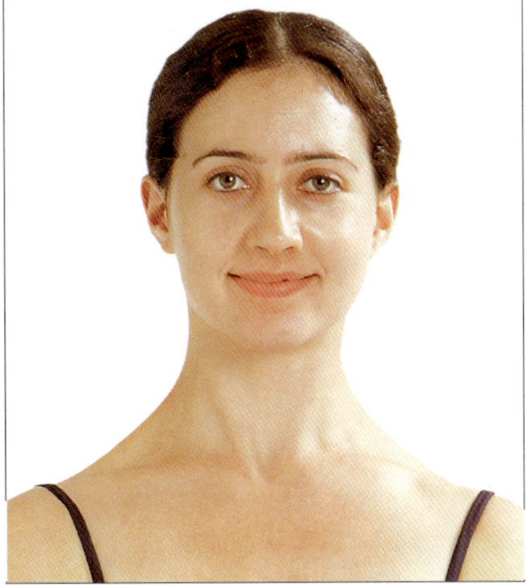

Living for the moment

Small children have a wonderful facility for enjoying the moment, because they are free of the heavy burden of the past and have not yet learned to fear the future. As adults we are so conditioned to think of a hundred things at once that we often find it difficult to break free and just "be" in the here and now. Many Eastern philosophies incorporate the idea of "mindfulness"—being acutely aware of the present by keeping the mind fully absorbed in the task you are performing.

Mindfulness is a technique that can be learned, although it takes practice to stop your attention from wandering. Next time you have to perform an unwelcome task (such as doing the ironing), instead of daydreaming, concentrate fully on the job in hand. Focus on the rhythmic movement of your chore. When you become fully involved in the moment, even the most mundane tasks can focus your mind, helping you to feel calm and centered.

Performing everyday tasks, such as washing up the dishes, can help you achieve mindfulness. Concentrate fully on the job in hand.

Positive commuting

Negative feelings sap your energy and set up a self-perpetuating cycle of disappointment, worry, and regret. Positive thinking gives you hope, and once set into motion you will feel better about many aspects of your life.

With practice you can change negative thoughts into positive ones. Think of an activity you find stressful—for example, commuting to work each day. Start by focusing on the downside (the wasted time, or the tiredness induced by a long journey). Tell these thoughts to go away. Consciously switch your negative thoughts to positive ones—think of using the time spent commuting to read, meditate, or listen to music.

With practice, it can become second nature to think of the positive things in life, rather than the negative.

Count your blessings

Competition and striving for material success cause much of the stress in our society, and it is all too easy to forget the truly important things in life. Take a few moments each day to think carefully about the good things you have. These can be anything—good relationships, special skills, good health, or happy children. Forget about competing for more things and feel at peace with yourself.

Freedom from fear

No one can be absolutely certain what lies ahead and often fear of what the future may hold prevents our enjoyment of the present. Instead of thinking about the "What ifs?" (What if I lose my job/become ill/can't pay my mortgage, for example), stop worrying and enjoy what you have at the moment. Visualization exercises, which enable you to create an image of the future as you want it to be, are particularly beneficial in helping you to look forward to the future, rather than dreading it, but again this should be something achievable and not just a fantasy. You may find it helps to dedicate a certain time of day for thinking about your worries. When the time is up, just stop thinking about them.

Relationships

Maintaining good relationships with family and friends gives you emotional support and makes you feel more positive, thus reducing stress levels and engendering calm. All relationships need to be worked at, so that everyone feels valued and loved.

Improving your relationships

Learn to listen to what others have to say and in return they will respond to you. Practice kindness, tolerance, forgiveness, and trust. Confide in your friends or family, and tell them how you are feeling.

Friends

For many people in the Western world, it is friends rather than family who provide emotional support, and just as we sometimes do with family members, we often take friends for granted. It is important to make time to show your appreciation for your friends, and to reflect upon the benefits they bring.

When spending time with your partner, burning aromatic candles can be a perfect way to create an intimate atmosphere.

Partners

Successful adult partnerships provide support, security, and fulfillment, and physical and emotional communication is essential for a stress-free relationship. To make the most of your partnership, it is vital to take time to be with each other. To promote intimacy in your relationship, try the following:

- Establish the mood by lighting candles and playing soft, relaxing music.
- Add aphrodisiac essential oils such as ylang ylang or jasmine to a massage oil, and give each other a sensual, soothing massage.
- Add essential oils to a warm bath, or burn in a vaporizer in the bedroom to give it a sensual scent.
- Take a relaxing bath together.
- Talk about the good things in your life, and plans for the future

Take time to enjoy your children; play with them, and their enthusiasm and vitality will rub off on you.

Discussion

Relationships are much more open and fulfilling if you are honest with each other about your problems and needs. But you still need to maintain a degree of tact and try to avoid hurtful statements and actions.

- Set aside a time for discussion, but reschedule if either of you is tired, stressed, or has had too much to drink.
- Think carefully about what you want to say beforehand—jot down a list of points you want to discuss.
- Try to be positive rather than focusing on the negative aspects of a situation.
- Don't hold your discussions in the bedroom, especially just before you are going to sleep, and avoid using a room where you would usually relax—you may even prefer to go for a walk, away from the home.
- Once you have reached an agreed conclusion, reaffirm your love for each other.

Children

Children are physically, emotionally, and financially draining. However, they are also an endless source of pleasure and unconditional love, and they grow up all too quickly.

Bereavement

The death of a loved one is a source of profound stress. Grief increases your susceptibility to illness and diminishes your ability to cope. Grieving is a process that passes through various stages, including shock, denial, anger, and finally acceptance. Expressing your emotions will prevent you from becoming overwhelmed by grief.

When grieving, don't bottle up your emotions—this will only prolong the pain and could lead to mental health problems.

PART 3: LIFESTYLE AND ENVIRONMENT

Introduction

Just a few simple adjustments to your lifestyle and environment can reap untold benefits for your general health and vitality. Making these changes is part of the process of taking more care of yourself. By organizing your work and leisure more effectively, you will feel on top of your problems and in control of your life.

While relaxing our minds teaches us to appreciate the present and not to worry unduly about the future, it does not mean that we should not think about the day ahead of us. It is common not to take stock of how we live in the short to medium term, yet spending a little time to plan the day or the week ahead can make a big difference to how healthy our lifestyle is, both physically and mentally. One of the most fundamental changes we can make to improve our well-being is to our diet; making a record of what you consume over a few days can be a real eye-opener and balancing your diet should be a priority. The changes may feel strange at first, but the benefits to your life should soon become apparent and the alterations will soon cease to seem like sacrifices.

The amount of exercise that people undertake in the developed world is far below what is considered a healthy level for an adult, yet it is surprising how easy it can be to incorporate an effective amount into your daily routine. As well as exercises that you can perform in the morning or early evening, most people will find it easy to incorporate more walking into their working day, for example.

With work being one of the most common causes of stress in our lives, it is not surprising that it is also one of the most fruitful areas for change, from the moment your alarm goes off in the morning to the time you return home in the evening. Paradoxically, planning short breaks at work and knowing how to switch off at the end of the day can lead to a more productive day in the long term. And if our homes are where we go to relax, it is sensible to make them as tranquil as possible, especially if you spend time at home during the day.

Our daily lives and the world around us may seem full of sources of stress, yet with planning, thought, and a positive outlook we can make every aspect and every situation a source of peace, pleasure, and tranquillity.

Try not to be a slave to a schedule—take the opportunity to slow down and enjoy the many things each day has to offer.

Change your lifestyle and do 10 minutes of stretching, yoga, or Pilates each morning—it will improve your health and fitness and give you more energy for the coming day.

Diet

"You are what you eat" is one of those irritating platitudes that happens to be true. Stuff yourself with junk food or drink too much alcohol and you will feel tired, bloated, and sluggish. Eat a well-balanced diet with plenty of fresh fruit and vegetables and you will feel much more alert and full of increased vitality and vigor.

A balanced diet

Eating the right balance of food can make a big difference to your health and vitality. Your body needs a diet that consists of about 50% carbohydrates, 30% fat, 15% protein, plenty of fiber, vitamins and minerals, and water.

Carbohydrates

These provide the body's basic source of energy. Simple carbohydrates, such as sugars, give instant energy but have no nutritional value. Complex carbohydrates, found in bread, pasta, rice, potatoes, cereals, and pulses, are better for you because they are slow-releasing.

The foods that contain complex carbohydrates also contain fiber, minerals, and essential vitamins.

Fats

These are essential for growth and healthy digestion, but too much fat can make you overweight and cause serious health problems.

Foods containing high amounts of fat and protein, such as milk, cheese, chocolate, and bacon, are best eaten in small quantities.

Protein

The body needs a daily supply of protein for cell growth, maintenance, and repair. Most Westerners get much more protein than they need, which usually becomes converted into fat.

Pulses, rice, and nuts are high in fiber, carbohydrate, and protein, and provide essential bulk for the diet.

Fiber

Dietary fiber, found in wholegrains, nuts, rice, pulses, and cereals, prevents constipation, lowers blood cholesterol, and helps protect against bowel disorders and diseases.

Vitamins and minerals

Although only needed in small amounts, these are essential for maintaining good health.

Foods for relaxation

Foods that contain calcium, magnesium and vitamin B6 are known to have a tranquilizing effect. Green leafy vegetables, milk and dairy products, apricots, bananas, nuts, and yeast extract are just some of the foods that will help you feel calmer. Meat, milk, and eggs contain tryptophan, an essential amino acid that turns into the important brain chemical serotonin, which enhances mood and regulates sleep.

What to eat

The healthiest diet is one that is high in fruit, vegetables, grains, and pulses, and low in animal and dairy products. Nutritional guidelines are based on the traditional eating habits of people who live around the Mediterranean, where there is a history of long life expectancy and low rates of heart disease.

- Complex carbohydrates should form half your daily diet.
- Eat at least five portions of fruit and vegetables a day, preferably organic.
- Try to consume low-fat dairy foods.
- Eat oily fish at least once a week.
- Limit your consumption of red meat and cheeses.
- Eat plenty of fiber-rich foods.
- Reduce your salt intake—use in cooking only.
- Limit your sugar intake—try not to use too much in tea and coffee.
- Eat fresh foods whenever possible and cut back on processed foods.
- Drink alcohol in moderation, and try to have at least two alcohol-free days a week.
- Drink enough fluids to keep your urine pale—at least four pints of water a day to flush out toxins. A glass of water every couple of hours will make you feel much more alert.
- Limit your consumption of tea, coffee, cola-type drinks, and chocolate.

When to eat

Optimum nutrition means eating the right foods at the right time, and good health depends on eating regular meals. Breakfast kick-starts the metabolism and boosts blood-sugar levels: if you miss it, you may feel tired and unable to concentrate. Lunch should be the biggest meal of the day because this is when the metabolism is at its most effective. Have a light supper at least two hours before you go to bed; it is hard for the body to digest a large meal at the end of the day.

How to eat

A leisurely meal is much more enjoyable than a snack on the run, and infinitely more relaxing. The next time you eat, sit down and savor each mouthful. Experience the different flavors and notice how they complement each other. If you are drinking a glass of wine, wait before swallowing and allow the complexities of taste to become apparent. As you chew, appreciate the different textures of food. If you take time to appreciate food, you are less likely to overeat and more likely to chew properly, which will benefit your digestion.

The problem with stimulants

Stimulants, such as tea, coffee, chocolate, and sugar, are chemicals that act on the body like rocket fuel, giving a quick burst of energy followed by a rapid burnout. They boost your energy levels by stimulating the adrenal glands, which sit on top of the kidneys and release hormones that give your body's cells an express delivery of glucose. You soon become caught in a vicious circle whereby you need more of the stimulant to get the same effect until you become dependent upon it. Stimulants also contain toxins, and your body has only a finite capacity to deal with these. As your body's chemistry becomes more exhausted, your body is in a constant state of red alert and you become prey to anxiety, fatigue, and mood swings.

After eight o'clock at night you should have no more than a light meal to ensure effective digestion.

Reducing dependencies on stimulants, such as coffee, tea, chocolate, and sugar, will make you feel much calmer and healthier.

Reducing stimulant dependence

Cutting down on stimulants is essential to helping you feel relaxed. Keep a diary for three days to identify which stimulants you rely on and be honest about just how much of each you are consuming. Try to identify at which point in the day you usually take them (as a reaction to a stressful situation, or as a pick-me-up, for example) and see if a pattern emerges. Try to replace these behavior patterns with healthier ones, such as eating a piece of fruit instead of a chocolate bar.

Cutting out stimulants completely is impossible for most people, but the way to cut down is to target one at a time and reduce your intake until it is no longer a daily necessity. You will probably feel groggy and get regular headaches for the first few days (particularly if you are addicted to coffee), but persevere and you will soon feel much better and healthier.

Nicotine and alcohol dependence are very hard habits to overcome, and may require professional counseling or group therapy.

Bowl of fruit

Buy a large fruit bowl and keep it well stocked with plenty of fresh, appetizing fruit, such as bananas, apples, plums, and oranges. Next time you want a snack, avoid the cookie jar and head for the fruit bowl instead.

The importance of exercise

One of the first things we neglect to do when stressed is to exercise. However, research has proven that exercise is a tremendous relaxation aid. Regular exercise frees your mind and your body: it can improve mood, increase self-esteem, reduce anxiety, promote sleep, reduce high blood pressure, and help weight loss.

How exercise helps you to relax

1. Exercise stimulates the appetite. Those who exercise regularly tend to eat better, and good nutrition helps your body to manage stress more effectively.

2. Exercise causes the release of the body's natural painkillers, endorphins, which reduce anxiety and leave you feeling relaxed and in a better mood.

3. Exercise releases adrenaline, which builds up in your body when you are stressed.

4. Muscular movement enables the body's systems to work more efficiently, removing toxins.

5. Physical activity makes you feel more confident about your body.

6. Exercise forces you to make time for yourself, distracting you from daily pressures, which will in turn reduce stress. Repetitive exercise such as walking, running or swimming is a golden opportunity for reflection, meditation, and mental relaxation.

7. Regular exercise will make you tired and help you sleep better (although strenuous exercise just before bedtime can stimulate the body too much).

8. Exercise promotes deep breathing, which is key to relaxation. And deep breathing will supply more oxygen to the brain, which improves mental stamina.

Practicing yoga is a great way of both improving your physical health and reducing stress.

Getting started

It is important to choose an activity you enjoy, because you are then much more likely to stick to it. Find an activity that suits your personality, and think of exercise as a joy and a means of relaxation rather than a chore. If you can keep to a regular program for at least six months, the chances are that you will continue for much longer. Consider your physical limitations and don't push your body too severely. Build up gradually, especially if you have not exercised for a while.

Improving general fitness

You don't have to give a lot of time, or join a gym, or spend lots of money to become fit. As little as 10 minutes a day of walking, dancing, gardening, swimming, or cycling can make a significant difference to your overall fitness levels, dramatically reduce stress, and make you feel more energetic, healthier, and happier.

You can choose forms of exercise that are easily incorporated into your daily life: walk or cycle to work if you can; walk up the stairs instead of taking the elevator; get off the bus to work one or two stops earlier and walk the remaining distance; regularly take the dog for a walk; take the children to the park on the weekend; or just put on some music and dance around the kitchen.

Caution

Consult a doctor before embarking on a vigorous program of exercise if your lifestyle is very sedentary, if you are pregnant, if you are over 45 years of age, if you have a history of high blood pressure, high cholesterol levels, heart or lung disease, or if you are a heavy smoker or considerably overweight.

Cycling is a great way to get plenty of fresh air and improve your cardiovascular fitness.

World of work

Most of us spend the majority of our day at work, and research shows that the hours we spend working are constantly increasing. You are unlikely to be able to change either the prevailing work ethic or your working environment, but you can keep hold of your priorities and devise strict routines to ensure you make the most of your time.

How to organize your day

If you're one of those people who, having rushed out the door in the morning, has to return because you have forgotten something, or if you are someone who spends much of your working day flapping about until you reach home in a state of exhaustion, you need to get organized and regain control.

Try out the following advice to take control of your day and reduce stress:

- Prepare as much as possible the night before—get your clothes ready, or lay the breakfast table, for example.
- Get up at least 10 minutes earlier than usual to give yourself the extra time to complete whatever it is that causes you to rush.
- Do not switch on the television because this will distract you and make you late.
- Do not answer the phone unless you think the call could be really important.
- Just before leaving the house, go over your mental checklist to reassure yourself you have everything you need.

Making a checklist is an effective way of organizing a busy day—you could even stick it to the refrigerator to make sure you haven't forgotten anything.

At work

Having a work routine helps you define your achievements and leave the stresses of work behind at the end of the day. Once a week, plan a weekly schedule. Then spend the first 15 minutes of each working day thinking about what you wish to achieve. It helps to make a list, but don't make it too long as this can be daunting and demotivating.

- Don't try to do too many things at once.
- Prioritize, and do the essential things first.
- Try to tackle at least one thing on your list that you really do not like doing—you will have a great sense of achievement when this task is completed.
- Leave a half-hour a day for the unexpected.
- Delegate as many tasks as possible—don't take on everything yourself.
- If you can't delegate, ask for help.
- Learn to say "no" politely, without feeling the need to justify yourself.
- Get a good diary and use it.
- Meetings should be to the point—always make it clear when they will end.
- If you are delayed, call and inform the person you are meeting; if you have to break an appointment, try to give as much notice as possible.
- Take time at the end of the day to review what you've done and to congratulate yourself on your achievements.

Telephone taming

- If you have to make a number of phone calls, group them together—it is much more efficient.
- Use an answering machine and switch off your mobile phone if you do not wish to be disturbed.
- If you work from home, invest in an extra line and don't answer the business one out of office hours.
- Do not answer the phone just before or during meals—if it is really important, the person will call back.

Don't let the telephone take over your life—answer calls only when it suits you, and make calls only when you have plenty of time.

Work space

A cluttered desk makes it more difficult to work effectively. Tidy your desk at the end of each day. Make use of in, out, and pending trays, and keep everything you need close to hand. Keep a supply of stationery and pens within easy reach of your desk, and dispose of those that no longer work.

Pause for thought

Most of us are governed by clocks, constantly under one deadline or another in order to become more efficient and productive. As slaves of time, we constantly rush to get things done, frequently making mistakes, instead of thinking about what we are trying to achieve. Taking a moment to stop and think gives you the opportunity to act with greater consciousness and react more appropriately to the situation. A pause also lets you say "no" and avoid committing yourself to too many things at once.

Take a break

It is universally recognized that to work for long hours without a regular break is damaging for your health and can on occasion be extremely dangerous. It's just like driving—you have to stop every couple of hours as your concentration and abilities begin to fail. Many office chairs are bad for the posture, and long hours spent staring at a computer screen can cause eyestrain, neck ache, and backache. Get up, stretch, and walk around at least once an hour. Take time off for lunch and eat away from your desk if possible. Remember that by law you are entitled to have regular breaks, and you will be much more productive if you take them.

At work, take time to enjoy a tasty, nutritious snack and recharge your batteries.

When to switch off

Don't fall into the trap of thinking that the longer you spend at work, the more you will get done when in fact the opposite is more likely. Working excessively long hours and taking work home is counterproductive. Keeping work and home separate, and being able to spend quality time with your family, is essential—if you spend your leisure time relaxing, you will return to work refreshed and be able to give it your full attention.

Instant calm at work

If you are being thrown into a state of panic by an approaching deadline, make a conscious effort to calm down. Instruct yourself to stop, then close your eyes and breathe slowly and deeply. Feel yourself becoming more relaxed; notice your heartbeat slowing down. Alternatively, follow the steps for quick and easy meditation on page 215.

Time off: vacations

A vacation is a chance to rest and recharge your batteries, but all too often it turns into another stressful event. Mental and physical preparation will make potential difficulties easier to deal with. Planning is the key to a successful vacation. First of all, choose a vacation that suits you and your family. Find out as much as you can about your destination before you go so that you know what your itinerary will be, and what to pack. A few days before, prepare yourself mentally by making an effort to slow down—maybe take an extra day off work to unwind.

Relaxing at home

Your home is your sanctuary. Your living environment has a tremendous impact on your sense of well-being. An untidy, cluttered home painted in dingy colors makes you feel stressed, while a bright, tidy home that reflects your character and family will create a happy, positive, and loving atmosphere where you can truly relax.

Light and space

Natural light is best for your eyes, so make the most of daylight and position desks near windows. A spacious, airy, and light environment is the most relaxing, but you can create space by keeping surfaces clear.

Turn down the volume

Noise can be incredibly stressful, even though you may not be aware of it. Only watch television if there's a program you really want to see, and turn it off at mealtimes. Soothe your soul by listening to music instead.

To create a serene atmosphere in your home, avoid harsh fluorescent lighting, and use soft light or candles in the evening.

Ten top tips for a tidy home

1. Remove your shoes at the door—it stops you bringing dirt into the house.
2. Do your least favorite household chore first.
3. Keep a waste-paper basket in each room.
4. The less you have, the easier it is to keep clean. Clear away clutter once a month and have a good sort out once a year. If you haven't used something in the last year, then you probably don't need it.
5. Keep work surfaces tidy.
6. Storage space is essential—invest in extra cupboards if you need them.
7. Encourage your children to tidy up after themselves.
8. To discourage random clutter, keep a "lost property box" in the living room.
9. Tidy up after a meal rather than leave the dishes until the morning.
10. Organize a rota so that all family members play their part.

Feng shui

Feng shui is the ancient Chinese art of arranging living and working spaces so that they are in harmony with the flow of ch'i, the universal life force (see page 209). Landscapes, buildings, and rooms are said to have their own flow of ch'i, and feng shui encourages blocked or diminished ch'i to move more freely in a certain area by altering its layout. A feng shui practitioner will make a detailed assessment of each room in your house and suggest changes, such as a new color scheme or repositioning of plants and furniture. To improve the feng shui in your home, clear up clutter and make sure there is plenty of space around furniture.

Encourage your children to help keep the house clean and tidy.

The world around you

Those who appreciate nature are generally happier, calmer people. Today, many people live in noisy, polluted, overcrowded cities where concrete predominates over greenery. But you don't have to live in the country to benefit from nature. Take a walk through the park or simply sit in the garden to relax and truly appreciate your surroundings.

The great outdoors

Ultimately, a relaxed state of being depends on you spending plenty of time outdoors. Light is recognized as essential for regulating the body's internal clock, which controls hormone production and sleep. Spend holidays in the mountains or at the shore to get maximum benefit from light and fresh air.

Plants pour oxygen into the environment while soaking up carbon dioxide and other toxins.

Park life

A walk in the park will help you to reconnect with the natural world. Visit the same park during each of the seasons so that you can appreciate nature's life cycle. Take time to notice the colors of the trees and flowers and the different smells. Breathe in deeply and inhale large amounts of fresh air.

Gardening

Gardening is a wonderfully relaxing activity because it releases physical tension, thus reducing the amount of circulating stress hormones in the body, while the act of cultivation in itself is soothing for the soul. Novice gardeners can nurture hardy, low-maintenance plants (see gardening books for inspiration and practical advice). If you don't have a garden, plant a window box instead.

Improve the oxygen levels in your home by keeping some pot plants.

Never judge a day by the weather

All too often we let the weather determine our mood: on a sunny day, a good mood; on a rainy day, gloom and introspection. Think positively about the different aspects of weather instead: the cool, crispness of snow, the rain that nurtures crops, or the fact that thunderstorms do literally clear the air.

A sense of time

Your body adheres to a natural sense of time without you even being aware of it. Ask yourself how often you really need to know what the time is.

Seasons

Air conditioning and modern central heating systems have removed much of the impact of the changing seasons, but if you can live in harmony with nature's cycle, you will appreciate life much more. Spring, traditionally the season of hope and renewal, is the time for starting afresh, clearing your life of clutter, and setting change in motion. Summer, associated with happiness and light, brings a sense of freedom and carefreeness. Fall, the season of fruition and abundance, is the time for reflecting upon what you have achieved and counting the year's blessings. Winter is a time of rest, retreat, and reflection on what has passed.

When you come home from work, and at weekends, take off your watch and remove yourself from time pressures.

Getting a good night's sleep

A good night's sleep is a period of profound rest that is essential for your physical and emotional well-being. Time spent sleeping is often the best way to recover from illness or cope with stress. When sleeping, your body will repair and regenerate itself, and your mind can resolve outstanding problems through dreams.

What is sleep?

Sleep is a naturally occurring state of unconsciousness, when the electrical activity of the brain is more rhythmical than when awake and reacts less to outside stimuli. There are two basic sleep states: deep sleep, known as non-REM (NREM) sleep, when the body repairs itself, interrupted by episodes of Rapid Eye Movement (REM) sleep, when most dreaming takes place.

Establishing a calming routine that helps you wind down and relax before bedtime will go a long way in helping you to get a good night's sleep.

How much sleep?

The amount of sleep necessary to be fully rested varies for each individual, and it decreases with age. Most adults get by on seven to eight hours' sleep, though some sleep experts claim we need more. The elderly can function on five or six hours a night.

Sleep problems

Sleep is one of the first things to suffer when you are stressed, and too little sleep will make you tired and irritable. A lack of sleep is itself a stress factor, and it is all too easy to become locked into a cycle of sleeplessness that is difficult to break. There are many different kinds of sleeplessness, including not being able to go to sleep, frequent waking, and waking too early in the morning.

Sleep enhancers

- Don't go to bed hungry, but avoid large meals before bedtime.
- Bananas, milky drinks, and wholemeal crackers are calming foods and ideal for eating before you go to sleep.
- Caffeine, alcohol, and nicotine all disturb sleep. Drink a cup of warm herbal tea before bedtime—chamomile is particularly effective.
- Exercise during the day will remove stress hormones from your body but avoid any form of exercise (apart from sex) at least three hours before bedtime.

Drink something calming and tasty before you sleep.

Establishing a routine

- Stop work at least an hour before bedtime to calm mental activity.
- A warm bath before bedtime will relax your muscles and soothe your body.
- Go to bed at the same time each night and get up at a regular time.
- Your bedroom needs to be a place for sleeping rather than an extension of your office or living room —keep it quiet and warm.
- If you really cannot sleep, get up and go into another room and read a book or watch something light on television until you feel sleepy.

The importance of dreams

We all have dreams, although we may not remember them when we wake up. Dreaming is thought to act as a psychological safety valve, allowing us to work through problems, emotions, and anxieties so we can start afresh each day.

Natural remedies for relaxation

Natural remedies are very effective in reducing the effects of stress and restoring the balance of body and mind. They are an enjoyable way of improving well-being and have been used around the world for thousands of years.

Aromatherapy

Essential oils distilled from plants, flowers, and resins can be used to promote good health and help you relax. Your sense of smell is directly linked to memories and mood (see page 219). Among other things, essential oils can be antidepressant, relieve pain and tension, ease headaches, act as a tonic, and help to ensure a good night's sleep.

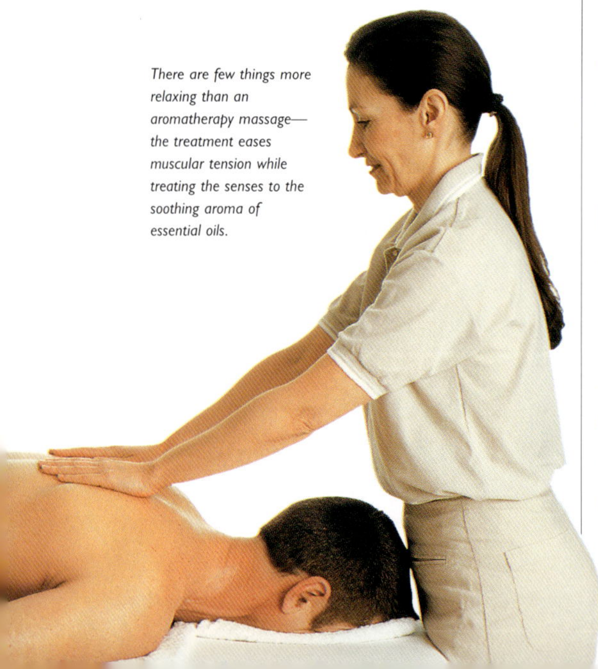

There are few things more relaxing than an aromatherapy massage—the treatment eases muscular tension while treating the senses to the soothing aroma of essential oils.

Oils can be inhaled, used in compresses to relieve pain, added to bathwater or massage oil, or used in a vaporizer.

Massage

An aromatherapy massage combines the relaxing properties of various oils with the benefits of touch. Dilute a few drops of two or three essential oils in a carrier oil such as sweet almond or apricot kernel oil; add a little jojoba oil for very dry skins. Blend six drops of essential oil with 3–4 tsp (15–20ml) of carrier oil to make enough for a full body massage.

Baths

Only add neat oils to bathwater if they are guaranteed to be non-irritants, such as Roman chamomile and lavender; otherwise, dilute in a carrier oil. Add five drops, then swirl the bathwater around to disperse the oils before stepping into the bath. Oils added to bathwater are inhaled and partly absorbed by the skin, bringing immediate physical benefits.

Ten relaxing essential oils

Bergamot (*Citrus bergamia*): soothing, uplifting, and good for tension and depression.

Chamomile (*Chamaemelum nobile*): calming; suitable for insomnia.

Jasmine (*Jasminum officinale*): a stimulant or a sedative, according to need; excellent antidepressant and aphrodisiac.

Juniper (*Juniperus communis*): good for fatigue and boosting self-esteem.

Lavender (*Lavandula angustifolia*): a very useful and popular oil, used for relaxing and as an antidepressant and painkiller.

Lemon balm (*Melissa officinalis*): long used to banish melancholy; balances the emotions.

Rosemary (*Rosmarinus officinalis*): refreshing and stimulating.

Sandalwood (*Santalum album*): used as an antidepressant and aphrodisiac.

Vetiver (*Vetiveria zizanioides*): balances the nervous system; good for insomnia.

Ylang ylang (*Cananga odorata*): calming; used as an aphrodisiac and good for panic attacks.

Cautions

- Always dilute oils before use (although lavender and tea tree can be used neat in first aid situations).
- Some oils are not safe to use in pregnancy.
- Seek professional advice before using essential oils if you have a long-standing medical condition such as heart disease, diabetes, or high blood pressure.
- Many oils are not suitable for small children, so check first.
- Some oils react adversely to sunlight.
- Do not use steam inhalations if you have a breathing disorder such as asthma.
- Never take oils internally, unless professionally prescribed.

Vaporization

Filling a room with an aroma of your choice is the easiest way to enjoy essential oils. Add a few drops to a saucer of water and place on a radiator, or in a burner.

Certain oils can improve mood and concentration, and are deeply relaxing.

Herbalism

Herbal remedies use plants to restore health and strengthen the body, enabling it to recover more easily. Many synthetic drugs, such as aspirin, are derived from plants, but herbalism uses the whole plant, believing that the complex mix of components creates a herbal "synergy" that is more effective than isolated constituents.

Using herbal remedies

Herbs are usually taken in the form of decoctions, infusions, and tinctures. They can also be made into ointments, massage oils, and creams to rub into the skin, and added to hot or cold compresses. Many preparations can be bought ready-made from health stores.

Decoctions

Tough plant material such as roots and bark are boiled in water to extract the active ingredients. The liquid is then strained and taken hot or cold. Boil down the liquid and add sugar to make a syrup.

Herbal remedies are a natural way of easing away the stresses of modern living. Remember not to exceed the recommended dose.

Infusions

An infusion is a herbal tea. Herbs are placed in a teapot, covered with boiling water, and left to steam for about 10 minutes. The liquid is drained into a cup and drunk hot or cold. It can be kept in the refrigerator for 24 hours and can be reheated.

Tinctures

Tinctures are made by steeping herbs in a mixture of alcohol and water. The alcohol acts as a preservative (the mixture can be kept for up to two years) and also extracts the medicinal constituents of the plant.

Caution

- Seek professional advice before taking herbal medicine if you are pregnant, or if you have a long-standing medical condition such as heart disease, diabetes, or high blood pressure.
- Consult a qualified herbalist before using herbal remedies if you are taking prescribed medication.

Popular herbs for relaxation

Chamomile (*Chamaemelum nobile*): promotes feelings of relaxation and settles digestion.

Echinacea (*Echinacea purpurea*): strengthens the immune system.

Ginkgo (*Ginkgo biloba*): improves blood flow and the activity of neurotransmitters in the brain; beneficial for sufferers of tinnitus.

Lavender (*Lavandula angustifolia*): lifts mood and relieves indigestion and headaches.

Lime flower (*Tilia cordata*): effective relaxant that reduces anxiety and restlessness.

St-John's-wort (*Hypericum perforatum*): a well-known antidepressant without side-effects.

Skullcap (*Scutellaria lateriflora*): a calming nerve tonic that reduces anxiety and restlessness.

Vervain (*Verbena officinalis*): sedative nerve tonic good for insomnia and for relieving tension and depression.

Flower remedies

Flower essences, made by infusing flower heads in water, then preserving the strained water in brandy, were developed in the 1920s by an English doctor and homeopath, Edward Bach. He believed that flowers possessed healing properties that could treat emotional illnesses. He thought that harmful emotions were the main cause of disease and identified seven states of mind—fear, uncertainty, lack of interest in present circumstances, loneliness, over-sensitivity, despondency, and over-concern for the welfare of others—which he subdivided into 38 negative feelings, each associated with a particular plant. Bach flower remedies aim to restore the harmony of mind and body necessary for good health. That flower remedies work is indisputable, although no one knows how: they do not work in any biochemical way, but therapists believe the remedies contain the energy, or imprint, of the plant and provide a stimulus to kick-start your own healing mechanism.

Glossary

Adrenaline
This is the hormone secreted by the adrenal glands that prepares the body for "fight-or-flight" and has widespread effects on circulation, the muscles, and the metabolic rate.

Amino acids
These are organic compounds found in proteins. Essential amino acids cannot be made by the body and must be obtained from food.

Autonomic nervous system
The part of the nervous system responsible for automatic body functions, such as breathing, perspiration, salivation, digestion, and heart rate. The sympathetic division activates the body's alarm response and prepares for action; the parasympathetic division is concerned with restoring and conserving bodily resources.

Cardiovascular system
The heart and blood vessels.

Central nervous system
The vast network of cells that carry information in the form of electrical impulses to and from all parts of the body to cause bodily activity.

Ch'i
The universal "life force" of Traditional Chinese Medicine (also known as ki); similar to prana in Ayurvedic medicine.

Cholesterol
A fat-like substance present in the blood and most tissues; high levels can damage blood vessel walls and lead to a thickening of the arteries. Excessively high levels of cholesterol can lead to heart problems.

Endorphin
A painkiller produced by the body.

Hormone
A substance produced in one part of the body that travels in the bloodstream to another organ or tissue, where it acts to modify structure or functions.

Hyperventilation
This is breathing at an abnormally rapid rate, which can lead to loss of consciousness as blood acidity falls dramatically.

Immune system
These are the organs responsible for immunity with the ability to resist infection.

Metabolism
Chemical processes that take place in the body, which enable continued growth and functioning of the whole system.

Neurotransmitter
A chemical that is released from nerve endings to transmit impulses between nerves, muscles, and glands.

Proteins
Essential constituents of the body that form its structural material and, as enzymes and hormones, regulate body functions.

Serotonin
A neurotransmitter whose levels in the brain have an important effect on mood.

Stimulant
Something that has an uplifting effect on the mind or body. Well-known stimulants include nicotine, alcohol, sugar, coffee, tea, and chocolate.

Useful addresses

Alexander technique

NASTAT
PO Box 806
Ansonia Station
New York
NY 10023-9998

Aromatherapy

National Association for Holistic Aromatherapy
836 Hanley Industrial Court
St. Louis
MO 63144

Herbalism

American Association of Naturopathic Physicians
8201 Greensboro Drive
Suite 300
McLean
VA 22102

American Botanical Council
PO Box 144345
Austin
TX 78714

Hypnotherapy

American Association of Professional Hypnotherapists
PO Box 29
Boones Mill
VA 24065

Massage

American Massage Therapy Association
820 Davis Street
Suite 100
Evanston
IL 60201

Meditation

Greater Washington DC
Association of Professionals Practicing the
Transcendental Meditation Program
4818 Montgomery Lane
Bethesda
MD 20814

American Buddhist Association
1151 West Leland Avenue
Chicago
IL 60640

Reflexology

Reflexology Association of America
4012 St. Rainbow Boulevard
Box K585
Las Vegas
NV
89103-2509

T'ai Chi

Universal T'ai Chi Chuan Association
Ben Lo
2901 Clement Street
San Francisco
CA 94121

Yoga

American Yoga Association
513 Orange Avenue
Sarasota
FL 34236

Index